ABU

CANCEL THIS BOOK

The Progressive Case Against Cancel Culture

DAN KOVALIK

HOT BOOKS

*This book is dedicated to Molly Rush, who is an inspiration
to so many of us striving for peace and justice in the world
and in our daily lives.*

Contents

Preface

As Vladimir Lenin once said, "There are decades where nothing happens; and there are weeks where decades happen." In 2020, we had many weeks where decades happened, and we are having such weeks now in 2021, as well. The events unfolding in our country and around the world are dizzying, and it is quite hard to make accurate assessments of these events as they roll by so quickly. This makes writing such a topical book as this quite difficult, but that is my task and I only hope that I am adequately up to it.

The event that truly gave me pause, just as this book was going to print, was the storming of the Capitol on January 6 by seemingly crazed Trump supporters. While some of these individuals seemed relatively harmless, if certainly misguided, others clearly set upon the Capitol building with ill and evil intent, including, quite possibly, the kidnapping and even killing of members of Congress and Vice President Pence. In the end, five people died in the process of this invasion, and much of the country and world were left shocked and horrified.

And just as horrifying as the actions of those who stormed the Capitol was the conduct of significant portions of the police and other law enforcement who seemed to stand down in the face of the assault and to permit it to take place. Many quite correctly pointed out the permissiveness with which police treated these invaders as contrasted with the heavy-handedness and violence police around the country treated Black Lives Matter (BLM) protesters, the vast majority of whom were peaceful, during the summer of 2020.

These events certainly put this book in a different light from when I wrote the lion's share of it before January 6, 2021, and other events will certainly transpire before and after publication that will do the same. For example, some may wonder why, after elements of the right wing exposed themselves as so extremely violent and even murderous, I have focused a book on the relatively more benign "cancel culture" of those on the left of the political spectrum; or why, after the effective incitement of these individuals with lies such as the bizarre QAnon conspiracy theory, I have written about liberals playing loose with facts and the truth and using "cancel culture" to perpetuate liberals' own myths.

My response is simple: because it matters, and because events such as those on January 6 do not give a free pass to liberals or leftists to cannibalize themselves through "cancellation" or to look down and shun huge swaths of the American people—most of whom are also horrified by the storming of the Capitol—whom they deem beneath them and even "deplorable," in the words of Hillary Clinton in referring to the working class in middle America.

Indeed, the liberal/left sermonizing, chest thumping, and display of outright hypocrisy after the Capitol invasion prove the point of this book. After the Capitol assault, we heard much moralizing about how terrible it was for people to attack this apparently sacred building that numerous pundits and politicians referred to as "the house of the people." All of a sudden, we were urged to care about historic landmarks when, in truth, liberal/left protesters spent a lot of the summer tearing down and vandalizing historic monuments. And the targets of this destruction, or "cancellation" if you will, were not just the scores of Confederate monuments nor ones of Christopher Columbus and his like, which I will assume for purposes of discussion were fair game, though others might disagree. For example, protesters took it upon themselves to topple, damage, or destroy statues of George Washington, Abraham Lincoln, Thomas Jefferson, Ulysses S. Grant, Teddy Roosevelt, Francis Scott Key, Philadelphia Mayor Frank Rizzo, Union Army Colonel and abolitionist Hans Christian Heg, as well as Madison's "Forward" statue and the statue of an elk in Portland.[1]

And of course, in Portland, protesters came out night after night for months to attack the federal court house.

The protesters had their reasons for targeting some of these monuments, some of them defensible while some not, but the point is that the message sent by this destruction was that nothing is sacred and that it is up to the whims of the protesters *du jour* to determine which monuments stand unscathed and which do not. And this message seemed accepted by at least some sectors of the US media, with NPR, for example, giving airtime on August 27, 2020, to Vicky Osterweil to publicize her book, *In Defense of Looting*.[2]

In this interview, which was quite favorable to Osterweil (though later revised after public criticism), she defended looting, which she defined as "an attack," in the context of a protest or demonstration, "on a business, a commercial space, maybe a government building—taking those things that would otherwise be commodified and controlled and sharing them for free." Osterweil claimed that such conduct "provides people with an imaginative sense of freedom and pleasure and helps them imagine a world that could be. And I think that's a part of it that doesn't really get talked about—that riots and looting are experienced as sort of joyous and liberatory."

Then, after January 6, 2021, we were urged to be horrified because people vandalized and caused damage to and looted the US Capitol building and various artifacts within. We were meant to care that one gentleman famously left the building, with a wide-eyed grin, with the lectern of Nancy Pelosi. But wasn't he just experiencing the joy and liberation that Osterweil believes he deserves? He certainly looked so from the photo.

And all of this is quite relevant to the heart of this book, which was inspired by the cancellation of longtime peace activist Molly Rush in Pittsburgh for a Facebook post that was critical of rioting and looting. This was condemned as "racist" in the context of the George Floyd protests, as it, in the view of the "cancellers," was seen as telling African Americans how to fight for their own liberation. I discuss this in detail below, but suffice it to say that Molly's criticism now seems almost prescient and would certainly be welcome as applied to the events of January 6.

Sadly, the hypocrisy does not end here. Thus, as some other commentators pointed out, the infamous "Viking guy" who invaded the Capitol on January 6, 2021, was videotaped on that day encouraging Venezuelans to follow his lead in overthrowing their "Communist" government to "take back their freedom."[3] Of course, in saying this, he was parroting the position of politicians and pundits, including Joe Biden and other Democrats, who are also calling for the overthrow of the Venezuelan government and who intend to help bring about this overthrow just as the US has done so many times throughout the world. Indeed, Joe Biden, now the liberals' champion of freedom and democracy, made it clear during his campaign that he would continue the US's coup efforts in countries such as Venezuela, just as his predecessor and former boss, Barack Obama, aided and abetted the military coup in Honduras in 2009.[4] Just so there was no doubt about this, Biden, even as he was denouncing what he and others termed a "coup attempt" at the Capitol, appointed Victoria Nuland as his Under Secretary for Political Affairs.[5] As some may recall, Ms. Nuland was "the driving force" behind Obama's 2014 coup in Ukraine, which brought to power a government, still in power, consisting quite substantially of neo-Nazis.

Of course, the mainstream media has all but ignored this incredible irony. However, this is not surprising, as the press has almost invariably been complicit in the US's coup attempts and wars abroad. And US liberals and even leftists, as I explain in detail below, have all but given up on opposing these policies, instead focusing much of their attention on the "culture wars," which include "cancel culture." As one notable example of this phenomenon, the trust fund liberal David Remnick of the *New Yorker* hosted a show just after the sacking of the Capitol in which he spent an hour bloviating against the crimes of the Capitol invaders.[6] Meanwhile, Remnick famously, and quite effectively, advocated for the invasion of Iraq in 2003—an invasion that has destroyed the lives of literally millions.[7] The violence such liberals have and continue to incite is, I would argue, many times more destructive than the violence we witnessed on January 6, though few are willing to admit this.

In addition, in the same breadth that liberals quite rightly condemned the QAnon conspiracy theory mongers for inciting the Capitol riot, they continued to peddle their own conspiracy theory that Russia and Vladimir Putin are behind nearly every evil in our society, including the Capitol riot itself. For example, former labor secretary for President Clinton, Robert Reich, tweeted out in reference to this riot, "Putin won . . ." For her part, Hillary Clinton, one of the founts of the Russia-gate conspiracy theory, claimed that Trump incited the riot on behalf of Putin. Such conspiracy theories, which help bring the US ever closer to a confrontation with Russia, are every bit as dangerous as the right-wing theories.

Finally, in the spirit of "cancel culture," many on the left of the political spectrum are excited about the new round of censorship being imposed by corporate giants such as Facebook and Twitter, which have now banned Donald Trump, and Google and Apple, which have kicked Parler off of their app platforms, making it nearly impossible to download that app.[8] All of a sudden, these corporate behemoths—the ones who have truly been engaged in the looting of America—are now the liberals' saviors, or so they may think.

Of course, as has always been the case, this type of censorship will be mostly turned against the left. Indeed, there is strong evidence that liberal social media accounts have been the much greater victims of censorship than right-leaning accounts.[9] This has always been the case. Thus, the landmark Supreme Court decision of *Schenck v. United States*, 249 U.S. 47 (1919)—the decision that established the legendary "clear and present danger" rule to justify limiting free speech—was issued in a case against a Socialist who was circulating flyers encouraging men to resist the draft to serve in World War I.

The ACLU, to its great credit, immediately warned of the "unchecked power" of the social media giants upon the suspension of Trump's accounts, arguing that "the decision to suspend Trump from social media could set a precedent for big tech companies to silence less privileged voices."[10] Of course this is true. But sadly, many on the left in this country have not learned this lesson and are calling for measures that will ultimately lead to their own suppression. Unfortunately, too many on the left, wielding the cudgel of "cancel culture," have decided that certain forms of censorship and speech and idea suppression are positive things that will advance social justice. I fear that those who take this view are in for a rude awakening.

 This is a time that calls for great soul-searching. And what most understand is that true soul-searching involves looking into one's own soul to find ways to advance and evolve morally and spiritually; it is not about peering into others' souls in an attempt to find them somehow lacking. Sadly, "cancel culture" is all about that latter, and it is a road that will not lead us into the light.

Introduction

The postmodern re-engineering of left-wing political theory has included the redefinition of "privilege" in a way that is separate from economics, a definition of "sex" that is separate from biology, and a definition of "violence" that does not involve actual violence. It's a language and a narrative that completely abandons the working class, while erroneously taking for granted our loyalty.[1]

—Edie Wyatt

Today, I woke up to an incredible sight—my once-liberal newspaper, the *Pittsburgh Post-Gazette*, with an editorial board endorsement of Donald Trump for president.[2] As the editorial noted, this was the paper's first endorsement of a Republican for president since the paper endorsed Richard Nixon in 1972. I myself have already voted by mail—for Joe Biden—but I found the editorial interesting for a few reasons relevant here.

The first thing that jumped out at me was this line: "the Biden-Harris ticket . . . will bow to the bullies and the woke who would tear down history rather than learning from history and building up the country."

Of course, this claim represents a significant distortion of reality. Thus, it is clear that the right has been doing much more to tear down this country than the liberal/left "woke."* In addition to selling off the

---

* The term "woke," according to Merriam-Webster's Dictionary, means "aware of and actively attentive to important facts and issues (especially issues of racial and social justice)." When used in this book, and oftentimes in public discourse, the

country to the super-rich and leaving the country's infrastructure to rot, it is the right that has been perpetrating the lion's share of political violence around the country, with one study tallying, for example, "21 victims killed in leftwing attacks since 2010, and 117 victims of right-wing attacks in that same period—nearly six times as much."[3] And, of course, as many have noted with great alarm, Donald Trump has openly encouraged right-wing violence while greatly exaggerating the violence of the left.

Meanwhile, in terms of violence over the summer of 2020, the worst of it was done against Black Lives Matter (BLM) protesters and not by them. Thus, according to the well-respected Armed Conflict Location and Event Data project (ACLED), of the eleven individuals killed in the course of the BLM protests, nine were BLM protest-ers themselves.[4] The ACLED also concluded that "the overwhelm-ing majority of the more than 9,000 Black Lives Matter demonstra-tions that took place across the US after the killing of George Floyd have been peaceful."

At the same time, as with most such hyperbolic claims, the editorial was pointing to a truth that I and many others have been witnessing for some time—i.e., that those on the ostensible left have been engaged in increasingly high-handed and bullying tactics, including, and indeed especially, against others on the left side of the political spectrum.

My concern, as a progressive and leftist, is not only that such tac-tics ruin individual lives quite unnecessarily, many times over a slip of the tongue or incorrect turn of phrase, but that they undermine the left movement and progressive causes, as well. Such tactics give excuses to such institutions as the *Post-Gazette* to make the endorse-ment of a right-wing demagogue like Trump, for example. They also take focus away from our quite justified demands for social, racial, and economic justice.

---

term refers to someone who is in fact *hyper*-aware of such issues, as well as issues of gender, and who therefore may tend to find violations of racial and gender norms even in the most innocent of circumstances, and who is quick to call people out for such perceived violations. Such calling out of others for allegedly violating such norms can rise to the level of "cancellation," which, again according to Merriam-Webster's, is the act of withdrawing support for someone, oftentimes but not always a public figure, usually as a consequence of "the person in question having expressed an objectionable opinion, or having conducted themselves in a way that is unacceptable . . ." The "cancellation" can take the form of public shaming, particularly on social media, but can also include the termination of the "offending" person's job or position.

In addition, the editorial's reference to those who "would tear down history" has some basis in fact. Here, the paper's editors refer to what many of us see as the left's obsessive concentration on purely symbolic struggle—for example, on removing statues (even of abolitionists) and of trying to cancel works of art and books that, though flawed in some ways, have tremendous historic and other value. These symbolic acts, while having some importance, take energy and effort away from the fight for things, such as healthcare and income support, that will actually help people, and that a greater proportion of people in this country would be willing to get behind. Such acts tend quite unnecessarily to alienate many people who might otherwise join the struggle for progressive reform.

SO TRUE

This brings us to the next issue. The other notable thing pointed out in the editorial is the following truth: that Trump has at least put "middle America" and "the Appalachian and hourly worker" "on the map again." As the editorial rightly asks, "Has Mr. Trump done enough for these struggling fellow citizens? No. But he recognized them. Maybe he was not articulate, but he recognized their pain." Sadly, it is these very people—otherwise known as the white working class—who have been largely forsaken by liberals who openly look down on those from "middle America" and Appalachia as ignorant rubes.

These people are the "deplorables" that Hillary Clinton referred to in her 2016 campaign, much to the detriment of her presidential bid and to the Democratic Party. But Clinton was certainly not alone in making public her disdain for these people who once saw the Democratic Party as fighting for their interests.

One of the more bizarre expressions of this contempt that I have seen is this tweet by self-described feminist Marcie Bianco: "If you say 'working class' your white supremacy is showing THE END." This statement, which I believe is emblematic of the sentiments of many liberals, exhibits a stunning measure of ignorance. The first thing that comes to my mind when I hear this is the fact that Martin Luther King, Jr. was killed in Memphis, Tennessee, where he had gone specifically to support a strike by sanitation workers there. As historian Peter Dreier explains, "King went to Memphis to support African American garbage workers, who were on strike to protest unsafe conditions, abusive white supervisors and low wages—and to gain recognition for their union. Their picket signs relayed a simple but profound message: 'I Am A Man.'"[5]

Dreier, who believes King to be one of America's greatest working-class heroes, emphasizes, "let's remember that King was committed to building bridges between the civil rights and labor movements." As Dreier notes, King addressed the AFL-CIO Convention in 1961 and explained the connection between the rights of African Americans and the struggle of labor (a.k.a., the "working class") in the following words:

> Our needs are identical with labor's needs: decent wages, fair working conditions, livable housing, old-age security, health and welfare measures, conditions in which families can grow, have education for their children, and respect in the community. That is why Negroes support labor's demands and fight laws which curb labor. That is why the labor-hater and labor-baiter is virtually always a twin-headed creature spewing anti-Negro epithets from one mouth and anti-labor propaganda from the other mouth.[6]

In short, King would be shocked to hear that the mere mention of the term *working class* was somehow a sign of white supremacy. Indeed, given King's assertion that antilabor sentiments come from the very same two-headed monster as racist sentiments, he might go so far as to say that it is the likes of Ms. Bianco who are showing their white supremacy by deriding the working class.

Black Marxists such as W.E.B. Du Bois, considered quite possibly the greatest American intellectual of the 20th century, would also be quite surprised, and indeed appalled, to hear such a thing spoken. Thus, while Du Bois's view of class and race was complex and nuanced, and while he believed that, as a consequence of slavery and racism, there were two distinct working classes—one white and one Black—he held out hope that the two could come together, in order to defeat capitalism and create a more just and equitable social order.[7]

Du Bois and like thinkers would be quite dismayed to see the whole of the working class—Black and white—simply written off in such a way.

But I doubt Ms. Bianco and her ilk have ever heard of MLK's support of labor. I also doubt that they have ever heard of W.E.B. Du Bois, much less read any of his works. Sadly, such ignorance is quite acceptable among today's "woke," who seem to know and care little for history and facts. Maybe these "woke" should heed Du Bois's warning that "Either America will destroy ignorance or ignorance will destroy the United States."

Meanwhile, Trump seized upon the abandonment of the working class in middle America to win the 2016 election. While his appeal may have been cynical and not in earnest, it cannot be overlooked or underestimated.

Much to the shame of Clinton and nearly the entire liberal elite and rank and file, there was little honest self-reflection on Clinton's failures to connect with working-class voters. Instead, Clinton and her liberal base blamed their own shortcomings on the perceived moral and intellectual inferiority of the white working class. They also blamed their failings on a tried-and-true enemy—Russia—and vilified those who dared challenge them (such as Bernie Sanders and Tulsi Gabbard) as tools of Russia. By their "cancellation" of the millions of people making up the white working class, and of progressives such as Sanders and Gabbard, the liberal/left has defeated itself and undermined the cause of building a better country and a better world.

This blame-Russia game also revealed something else: that liberals are as capable of generating and clinging to fake news as the right wing is. In a similar vein, as I will discuss below, liberals have also shown themselves as willing to deny science and facts as much as the right in order to advance their own political goals. In the process, the very idea of and belief in truth and the real world have been fatally undermined—a quite dangerous situation, especially in the middle of a global pandemic.

It is time for an honest reflection on such matters—reflection that has been made difficult to impossible because of the tendency of too many people on the ostensible left—believing themselves to be smarter than everyone else, to be "woke" when everyone else is apparently asleep—to attack others in quite inflammatory terms for just being willing to ask questions. It is my hope that this book contributes to this much-needed reflection.

CHAPTER ONE

Importance of Speaking Freely

Loneliness does not come from having no people about one, but from being unable to communicate the things that seem important to oneself, or from holding certain views which others find inadmissible.

—Carl Jung

When I was in law school at Columbia University, I had the good fortune of learning from a professor named john a. powell, an African American and a lawyer, at that time, for the American Civil Liberties Union (ACLU). The class he taught was about balancing free speech rights under the First Amendment with the rights to equality embodied in the Fourteenth Amendment and the civil rights statutes that followed—sets of rights that powell argues are of great and equal value, though sometimes very hard to reconcile when they find themselves in competition, such as in the case of offensive, discriminatory speech.[1] The tension arises from such speech, of course, because, though the individual has the right to free expression, such expression may infringe on others' rights, and particularly on others' rights to be included and to participate equally in the institution or forum in which the speech is being made. It is this right of participation that, powell argues, should be protected in resolving this tension.

As Professor powell has argued:

There is reason to believe or construct a notion of harm that is similar in both contexts and that is not so broad that it destroys free speech or equality. Not all harms are to be avoided, but only a limited class of harms. I have identified the central harm that is to be avoided as the harm to participation and membership and, as a corollary, the harm to communicative self-respect and autonomy. There are other harms, such as offense, that will not rise to this level. I have argued that the harm which undermines, distorts, or destroys the ability to participate in critical institutions and locations is of the first order and should be cognizable in and regulated by our jurisprudence. . . .

Free speech and equality should be promoted by this approach, in part, because they support, and are necessary for participation. When there is a sharp conflict between free speech and equality, I would try to resolve the tension in a way that protects the right of participation.[2]

In short, speech that offends, but does not interfere with another's right of participation, should not be banned or otherwise suppressed. Rather, such speech, as I took from Professor powell's class, should be met with speech; with argument and dialogue, as a means to advance both free speech and hopefully equality, as well. Such dialogue is especially important, and especially possible, when the speaker is at least well-intentioned, though possibly ill-informed or mistaken about proper semantics. Professor powell, who comes from a place of deep compassion, argues that such people should be treated with understanding and empathy, rather than with judgment and derision.

In a recent talk he gave in a symposium titled "Belonging in Practice: How to be an Antiracist," Professor powell specifically addressed the question about "cancel culture" in the following way:

> And just one thing that I want. . . . The ability to make mistakes, to be held in love. And I think the culture that we're in right now, we oftentimes think it's better to call someone out than to call them in. And we actually score points, especially on Twitter and Facebook. And so we make it very dangerous to say something. Because even

if we are trying, often times there's a community that's like waiting for you to make a slip. And there's a gotcha. And I'm not saying we give people a pass. But if people are working, work with them. So that's one thing, how do we actually create a space where we're gonna hold each other accountable but we're gonna hold each other, we're gonna love each other, we're gonna care about each other. You belong in this community and part of the thing, you will make mistakes but you also will grow.

Similarly, at the very same symposium, Ibram X. Kendi, who was described by the event organizers as "one of America's leading anti-racist voices and the author of *How to Be an Antiracist*," stated, "those who are constantly growing and striving to be a better form of themselves are constantly recognizing and admitting their mistakes, and constantly seeking to be better for them. And so, I think that we should take the pressure off of our backs to essentially be perfect. But we should simultaneously do that for other people. And so, an anti-racist doesn't just recognize that they're gonna make mistakes. They're gonna allow other people to make mistakes."

If the goal of activism is to win people over to a cause in order to organize protest and to win reforms and change, it is the softer approach—rather than an approach of finger wagging, shaming, and cancelling—that is more effective. There is indeed empirical evidence for this.

For example, a 2020 study of 700 interactions between liberal campaign activists and potential voters demonstrated that "the practice of having non-judgmental, in-depth conversations with voters about their experiences and struggles was 102 times more effective" in actually convincing these voters than brief, "drive-by" interactions.[3] And the former, more empathetic approach was effective in communities often ignored, if not vilified, by liberals and the left. As one individual who participated in this study explains:

These results are transformative and tell us a different story about rural America. For so long, people in rural and small towns have been neglected and cast out because no one took the time to listen to them, . . . But we did, and we've found that compassion and empathy, rather than division and hatred, can lead us to a multiracial democracy that works for all of us.

Another incredible example of the power of persuasion through empathy and compassion is the story of Daryl Davis, an African American who, beginning in the 1980s and continuing for the next 30 years, befriended members of the KKK in order to convince them to leave the organization and to see people of color in a different way.[4] Ultimately, Mr. Davis convinced 200 Klan members to give up their robes. Many would consider such an effort as naive, impossible, and not worth it and would cancel such Klan members instead. Indeed, it is my perception that many on the left get a thrill from canceling and physically confronting such people—people who often come to their racist beliefs through ignorance—resulting in racists simply doubling down on their bigotry.

That the "unwashed masses" of the hinterlands can be reached was proven again over the summer of 2020 when we saw people coming out to march in support of Black lives in such largely white towns as Lexington, Kentucky; College Station, Texas; Des Moines, Iowa; and Omaha, Nebraska.[5]

Even Hazard, Kentucky—remember *The Dukes of Hazard*?—had a BLM protest in which hundreds of people participated.[6] Speaking of *The Dukes of Hazard*, I have to point out a fascinating fact from my own life. When I was attending high school in the mid-80s at a Catholic school in Cincinnati, Moeller High School, one of the African American students, Hiawatha Francisco, who happened to be our school's star running back, used to drive a perfect replica of "The General Lee," which the Duke boys drove on the show. This bright orange Dodge Charger, complete with a Confederate flag on the top, played "Dixie" when Hiawatha honked the horn, just as in the show. We thought nothing of this then, except that we all thought it was so cool. I imagine that Hiawatha would be expelled today for insisting on driving that to school.

Meanwhile, even Ammon Bundy, the antigovernment activist who led the 41-day armed takeover of the Malheur National Wildlife

Refuge in Idaho in 2016, was won over to the cause of Black Lives Matter and the demand to "defund the police."[7]

In short, it turns out that the "deplorables"—the term Hillary Clinton used to describe and cancel the white working-class people of middle America's small and rural towns—are not so deplorable.

I have had my own experience with these alleged "deplorables" during my 26-year tenure as an attorney for the United Steelworkers union (USW). My first boss there was the legendary Bernie Kleiman, who served the union as general counsel for decades. Bernie was a fascinating individual. As a Jew growing up in northern Indiana, he was often the victim of anti-Semitic bullying. This made him quite empathetic to others, such as Black Americans, who were similarly treated. As a young man, Bernie single-handedly desegregated the local businesses of his northern Indiana town.

What he discovered is that the white business owners there were not, as individuals, opposed to serving Blacks in their establishments. Rather, they did not want to have a competitive disadvantage with other businesses by doing so. Bernie came up with the solution. He went to each store owner and asked him to sign a pledge saying that he would open his business to Blacks if every other store owner signed on to the agreement. Bernie was able to get all the store owners to agree to this, and the color line was thereby broken. This was the first of Bernie's many collective bargaining experiences, and it showed how a little creativity can be used to deal with thorny issues such as racist business practices.

For much of my tenure at the USW, I was assigned to District 8, the union's Appalachian district that included West Virginia, Kentucky, Virginia, and Maryland. I cannot tell you how many times local union guys from this district came to my office, dressed in Harley Davidson t-shirts, many of which included an American flag, and liberally tattooed with eagles and other patriotic images.

Upon first sight, and upon first hearing their Appalachian twang, many would assume these individuals to be ignorant, bigoted rubes. However, I almost invariably found them to be intelligent, progressive, and tolerant people. Indeed, it was my observation, and that of the other union staff I worked with, that industrial unionization and activity—which requires workers of all races, genders, and backgrounds to work together in common cause—inevitably made workers less racist and sexist.

The USW as an institution was founded in the 1930s as an industrial union dedicated to organizing all workers in the steel industry, regardless of race and ethnicity. This represented a huge move forward at the time from the old craft unions that had organized only skilled labor—a form of organization that inevitably privileged white workers given that Black workers had been excluded from skilled jobs due to racism, and the craft unions worked in ways to guarantee that this racial exclusion continued. In organizing workers on an industrial basis, the USW and like unions helped to raise the standard of living for all workers, both white and Black.

Someone who understood the importance of the union struggle to the cause of African Americans was the great jurist Thurgood Marshall, who argued the case for the plaintiffs before the Supreme Court in the case of *Brown v. Board of Education* (1954). The Supreme Court, agreeing with Marshall, ruled that the racist "separate but equal" education system in the Jim Crow South did not comport with the requirements of the US Constitution. Marshall had spent years patiently and methodically teeing up this case, which ultimately led to the dismantling of legal segregation in the US.

Marshall became the first African American Supreme Court Justice. And, when he had the chance to rule on an important labor case—that of *Letter Carriers v. Austin* 418 U.S. 268 (1975)—he did so seemingly with great delight. Thus, in ruling that a union's use of the word *scab*—a term used to describe a worker who refuses to join a union or who crosses a union picket line—was protected by the First Amendment, he quoted with approval the following piece on this subject by Jack London:

The Scab
   After God had finished the rattlesnake, the toad, and the vampire, He had some awful substance left with which He made a scab.

A scab is a two-legged animal with a corkscrew soul, a water brain, a combination backbone of jelly and glue. Where others have hearts, he carries a tumor of rotten principles.

When a scab comes down the street, men turn their backs and Angels weep in Heaven, and the Devil shuts the gates of hell to keep him out.

No man (or woman) has a right to scab so long as there is a pool of water to drown his carcass in, or a rope long enough to hang his body with. Judas was a gentleman compared with a scab. For betraying his Master, he had character enough to hang himself. A scab has not.

Esau sold his birthright for a mess of pottage. Judas sold his Savior for thirty pieces of silver. Benedict Arnold sold his country for a promise of a commission in the British Army. *The scab sells his birthright, country, his wife, his children and his fellowmen for an unfulfilled promise from his employer.*

"Esau was a traitor to himself; Judas was a traitor to his God; Benedict Arnold was a traitor to his country; a SCAB is a traitor to his God, his country, his family and his class."

Scabs were considered so awful at one point in the not-so-distant past that James Earl Jones, playing Few Clothes in the legendary *Matewan*—the 1987 movie by John Sayles about the real-life struggle of Appalachian, Black, and Italian immigrant mineworkers who come together to try to build a union, only to be massacred—exclaims during one tense scene, "I've been called n*****, and I can't help that's the way white folks is, but I ain't never been called no scab!"

While the USW did not always live up to its principle as a nonracist union, it did contribute in many ways to making the industrial shop, and the society at large, more inclusive. For example, the USW contributed to the defense fund of civil rights activists in the 1950s and 1960s. In addition, the USW fought for affirmative action in hiring, going all the way to the Supreme Court to defend its agreement with steel companies to engage in just such hiring. The USW was ultimately successful in this case, known as *United Steelworkers of America v. Weber*, 443 U.S. 193 (1979)—a landmark case in which the

Court held that such affirmative action is consistent with Title VII of the Civil Rights Act, which prohibits discrimination in employment.

Carl Frankel, an older colleague of mine in the USW Legal Department, was quite proud of his work on this case that upheld the USW's attempt to rectify the historic discrimination in the industrial sector, which had for so long kept Blacks out of the mills entirely, and later relegated them to the dirtiest and most dangerous jobs when they finally began to be hired. An excellent resource on the struggle of Black workers for equality, dignity, and better jobs in the steel mills is *Struggles in Steels*—a documentary by fellow Pittsburgher Tony Buba.

The affirmative action policies upheld in the *Weber* case opened up opportunities for Black workers never seen before in this country and helped lift many Blacks out of poverty and into the middle class. The tragedy, though, is that these policies were put in place not too long before the huge steel mill shutdowns in the early 1980s, causing the job losses of tens of thousands of steelworkers. And, because Black workers had been the last ones hired, they were the first ones fired when the mills went down. This is important to note because, in the current discussion about racism and Black lives, it is often forgotten or ignored how the deindustrialization of America has disproportionately hurt Black Americans, and how it has helped lead to and solidify the great inequalities between whites and Blacks in US economic life. That is, deindustrialization and the loss of good manufacturing jobs are not just white working-class issues, as we are often led to believe, in the prevailing political discourse.

Many of the local union leaders I encountered from District 8 warned that the USW's failure to support the 2016 nomination campaign of Bernie Sanders and the ultimate defeat of Sanders—a candidate hugely liked by their membership—would result in their membership voting for Donald Trump, which is indeed what happened. That is, they knew that their members would support a progressive candidate like Sanders because of his policy positions, such as Medicare for All, but not Hillary Clinton, whom they viewed as a liberal elitist who looked down on them and whose husband, Bill Clinton, negotiated many of the free trade agreements that led to the mass flushing of good, union, industrial jobs out of the United

States. And, just in case there was any misunderstanding about how she felt about working-class voters, Hillary Clinton made her feelings abundantly clear when she decided not to even step foot in the battleground state of Wisconsin—a state that had a long tradition of progressive worker and farmer activism but that the Democrats have increasingly turned their backs on.

There is more than anecdotal evidence that a significant number of working-class voters who would have voted for Bernie Sanders in 2016 ended up voting for Trump when the choice was between him and Hillary Clinton. Thus, polls showed that about 12 percent of Bernie supporters in 2016 ended up voting for Donald Trump—enough to possibly have made the difference in this hotly-contested election.[8] And this group of voters was disproportionately white and older— that is, they were largely the "deplorables" that Clinton and her ilk openly despise. It seems to me, at least, that these voters are eminently reachable by progressives and worth wooing instead of disparaging.

I am not the first to raise such points. Probably the most articulate proponent of the view that the white working class has not abandoned liberalism or the Democratic Party, but that they have in fact been the ones abandoned and left behind, is Thomas Frank. In such books as *What's Wrong with Kansas* and *Listen Liberal,* Frank sets out the thesis that the reason the white working class has drifted toward the Republican Party is that the Democratic Party, which historically claimed to and in fact did substantially represent its interests, stopped offering anything of substance, particularly on pressing economic issues, certainly by the time Bill Clinton became president. Indeed, Clinton, while running as the defender of the working class in 1992, simply turned around once elected and began to offshore working-class jobs en masse, while he cut social programs that could have softened the blow. And the Democrats have largely continued such policies ever since.

Frank argues that the Democratic Party has for decades simply taken the working-class vote for granted while not bothering to give anything in return. Seeing no party that represents their economic interests, white workers started to cast votes based upon social and cultural issues—the infamous issues of "God, Gays, and Guns."

Bernie Sanders has recently echoed such a view, stating, "I think it is fair to say that in many ways the Democratic Party has become a party of the coastal elites, folks who have a lot of money, upper-middle-class people who are good people, who believe in social justice in many respects. . . . But I think for many, many years the Democratic Party has not paid the kind of attention to working-class needs that they should've."[9]

In the 2017 afterword of his book *Listen Liberal,*[10] Frank explains the rise of Donald Trump in a way that is compelling, and this rise, according to Frank, was not due to the fact that the white working class is racist and bigoted. Rather, white working-class voters were attracted to a candidate, who albeit a billionaire himself, talked directly to ordinary, working class voters without the condescension of the Democrats and Hillary Clinton, and he offered policies (if not in earnest) to alleviate their economic woes after years of neoliberalism and betrayal. As Frank explains:

> Donald Trump was a bigot, yes, and this was inexcusable, but he also talked about trade: the destructive free trade deals our leaders have made, the many companies that have moved their production facilities to other lands, the phone calls he would make to those companies' CEOs in order to threaten them with steep tariffs unless they move back to the US.[11]

As Frank notes, the most concrete example of Trump's direct appeal to working-class issues was his threats against Carrier air conditioning if they carried out their announcement, caught on video, to shut down its plant in Indiana and move the jobs to Mexico—a move made easy by the North American Free Trade Agreement (NAFTA), which Bill Clinton had negotiated and which Hillary Clinton helped lobby for as First Lady.

I vividly remember this because I was working for the United Steelworkers at the time, and this Carrier plant happened to be a Steelworker-represented facility. I thought at the time that Trump's open support for these workers put the USW—which had aggressively opposed NAFTA and like trade agreements but was now endorsing

Hillary Clinton—in a difficult bind, and that the rank and file of the USW, about 500,000 workers spread out around a number of battle-ground states, would end up flocking to Trump despite their union's endorsement of Clinton. And in fact, this scenario was played out in the 2016 election.

I also remember how Trump, shortly after he was elected but before he was inaugurated, negotiated with Carrier to save at least a portion of the jobs at this facility.

Could anyone blame these Carrier workers—some who were Black, by the way—for voting for Trump in these circumstances, especially when the Democrats were largely responsible for the job losses such workers were suffering and when the Democrats now had nothing to say about this tragedy? Did this make them racist and "deplorable"?

I certainly don't think so. Indeed, quoted by Frank, Tom Lewandowski, then president of the Northeast Indiana Central Council in Fort Wayne, Indiana, tried to explain to anyone who would listen that the workers his Council represented weren't racist. Rather, they were disillusioned by a political establishment that had betrayed them and now saw a politician who was finally singing their tune. As Lewandowski stated:

> When Trump talks about trade, we think about the Clinton Administration, first with NAFTA and then with PNTR China, and here in Northeast Indiana, we hemorrhaged jobs . . . And here's Trump talking about trade, in a ham-handed way, but at least he's representing emotionally. We've had all the political establishment standing behind every free trade deal, and we endorsed some of these people, and then we've had to fight them to get them to rep-resent us.[12]

In 2016, Trump was also openly campaigning against the new trade agreement that President Obama had just signed, the Trans-Pacific Partnership (TPP)—another agreement that manufacturing unions opposed and fully expected would lead to only more unemployment for industrial workers in the US. Trump promised he would kill this deal in the interest of protecting jobs—another way in which he made himself attractive to working-class voters.

The point of all this is that we need to stop writing off such workers as racist, bigoted and somehow beyond redemption, even when they think and speak in ways that may not meet the ever-evolving and changing norms of the "woke." In the end, if we can't talk to the Tom Lewandowskis of the world and listen to their very real concerns, we are turning our backs on our natural allies in the fight for a more just, equitable, and prosperous society.

CHAPTER TWO

Cancellation of a Peace Activist

Left politics are inaccessible to most people because people on the left make people feel dumb for not knowing something and then make them feel even dumber when they finally do realize because they'll be like "you're just realizing this?"
—Claire Halacy, Twitter (October 4, 2020)

When I announced to my family that I was going to write this book, my oldest son, Joe, smiled and said, "Well, be careful. The surest way to be cancelled is to write something critical of cancel culture." As I explained to him, "I am certainly well aware of this fact, but I none-theless feel compelled to tackle this issue." Similarly, in talking to a good friend of mine in the UK about writing this book, I said, well, Arundhati Roy once said, "The duty of a writer is to be hated." "If that is the measure of a good writer," I quipped, "I think I will easily manage that with this book."

This is not a book I ever intended on writing. I did not want to wade into these treacherous waters that I knew may consume me. But now, the prevailing "cancel culture" has come too close to home, consuming a person and an organization which I hold too dear. And so, I must tell this story.

Before I get to that story, however, I must point out that there is another reason I feel compelled to write this book—because I believe in the words and ideas I am writing, and I am not being true to myself if I do not articulate them. The main problem with "cancel culture" as I see it is that it suppresses speech and coerces people into staying silent about things they believe and that others believe too, but about which they are afraid to speak. I do not believe this is a situation that is desirable—either for the individual, or for society—and the only way to challenge this is to speak up. So that is what I am doing, even if I am censured as a result. I do believe that many will agree with at least most of what I write here, even if they will not say so publicly, and even if they have to shamefully carry my book around with a brown paper wrapping as if it were pornography. I will undoubtedly hear from such people, even if anonymously, and this will give me some comfort.

In any case, on to my story.

This concerns the Thomas Merton Center (TMC) of Pittsburgh, PA—a peace and justice organization of nearly 50 years—and one of its founders, Molly Rush. Molly, now 85 years old, is a courageous activist whom I have known and worked with for almost 30 years. At the same time, she is quite unassuming and lives a simple and humble life. Indeed, if you did not know better, you might mistake her for a Catholic nun.

Molly was one of the Plowshares 8, a group of individuals including the legendary Berrigan brothers, who entered a hydrogen bomb manufacturing facility in King of Prussia, Pennsylvania, in 1980. They proceeded to pound with a hammer on an intercontinental ballistic missile delivery system to protest the arms race between the US and the USSR. Molly, who was married and had young children at the time and who left to engage in this high-stakes act of civil disobedience without prior notice to her family, spent 11 weeks in jail for this action but risked a potential life sentence. She has dedicated her life to nonviolent civil disobedience, in the interest of peace and justice, ever since.

This is how Molly is, and I believe quite accurately, described in the book *Hammer of Justice*, which details the Plowshares 8 action:

She is one of the many ordinary people who made an individual decision, took individual action, and bore, individually, the consequences. Her action was something her government called illegal: she disobeyed laws protecting property. She thought she acted legally, in obedience not only to spiritual but also to international legal requirements. Because what she did was colorful and unusual, she became something of a hero, a singularity that dismays her, because she thinks such regard sets her—falsely—apart and above. And Molly is above all things a connecter, a linker, a practitioner of what Riane Eisler calls the "partnership model." Eisler's *The Chalise and the Blade* defines the partnership mode as an egalitarian, goddess-centered, social-welfare-minded, non-violent model of social organization, rooted in prehistory and often resurgent.

Fast-forward to 2020. Molly, a naive user of Facebook, saw a meme that, on the spur of the moment, she decided to repost. The meme contained a photo of Martin Luther King, Jr. and stated: "Looted nothing, Burned nothing, Attacked no one, Changed the World." I had seen the meme myself and liked it initially and almost reposted it myself, again, almost as a matter of reflex. I soon was relieved that I had not.

Quickly, comments to Molly's post came forward, many criticizing this repost as insensitive in the context of the present moment, with others claiming it rose to the level of "racist." In response, Molly took down the post and issued a public apology on Facebook, stating, "I apologize for the hasty post about Dr. King. I've learned a lot. Thank you, friends."[1] She also met personally with the board of the TMC, with which she is no longer officially associated but with which she still does political work, and she apologized to them.

It should be noted that not all the activists who were made aware of Molly's Facebook post saw it as "racist." Most notably, a longtime member and former board member of the TMC, Rick Adams, an African American, stated quite directly in an email: "As a former 'looter' April 5th 1968—Molly said nothing that was racist or offensive and those zealots can K. M. A." "K.M.A." of course standing for "Kiss My Ass."

Still, there were others who were initially offended by Molly's post but who happily accepted her Facebook apology. One such individual was Celeste Taylor, an African American activist, who wrote:

> I'm blessed to know many elders in the Peace and Justice arena in Pittsburgh. Molly Rush is one of them but so is Alma Fox who is still with us too. She is a mentor of mine. I thought of her before I shared this with you and as I also shared with the Pittsburgh Friends Meeting. This is not an attempt to have the last word but in hopes of continuing progress. I'm 64 now! This is in response to a Friend who rejoices in Molly's apology. I said I'm glad that happened. There is still much work to be done. I noticed that there were few Black people that acknowledged her apology. I was one of the few. Also, many Black people are never given the benefit of the doubt and their apologies are met with silence, defensiveness, long harboring resentments or pandering to smooth things over without much more progress. This is my personal experience and observations without speaking for all Black people.[2]

Still, as Celeste Taylor's comment alluded to, Molly's apologies were apparently not enough for many. Indeed, the more she apologized, the more people piled on with claims of racism. Some individuals even went so far as to send Molly's repost to journalists via Twitter to see if they could have her nationally called out as a racist.

When Molly's adult children and grandchildren attempted to defend her, moreover, they were called "white trash." As Felicity Ansonia, a local lawyer and activist, wrote in a Facebook comment: "oh and you missed her white granddaughters with Black kids who (1) was the original sharer of the first meme, but she actually apologized. The other came in angry and accusatory. Typical Pittsburgh white trash."[3] This is a rather curious comment with the mention of one of Molly's granddaughters "with Black kids." Is the fact that she was with Black children part of the indictment against her? It seems so, but it is not clear how.

Maybe this comment came from the same fount as the recent, notorious cancellation of a white man, Thomas Wrocklage, for bouncing a Black child (the child of a "dear friend" whom he was watching) on his knee while on a Zoom call of the NYC Community Education Council—an act that was somehow viewed as a display of white supremacy. As one of the cancelers asserted emotionally, "It *hurts* people when they see a white man bouncing a brown baby on their lap and they don't know the context! That is harmful. It makes people cry! It makes people log out of our meetings."[4] While the Black parent of the child in question said that she had no idea what those claiming offense—none of them Black, by the way—were even talking about, and that she was grateful for Mr. Wrocklage's help with her child, this did not allay the attacks.

Meanwhile, Ms. Ansonia, who kept screen shots of Molly's posts for posterity, presumably so people would be able to hate her in perpetuity, then called for the TMC to cancel her. Thus, she wrote a post on the TMC Facebook wall, stating: "Still no accountability or actual apology from Molly. Again, I am waiting for the Thomas Merton Center to issue a public statement condemning Molly's original post as well as her responses, severing all ties with Molly, and committing to anti-racism training for their board members and staff with paid Black consultants."[5]

There is much to parse here, but the one thing that stands out is that, at the time of these events, Molly was neither a TMC Board member nor staff person, and she had not been so for some time. But somehow, her Facebook post had now gone viral—in the sense of an illness—and had infected the TMC by loose association. Now, everyone associated with the TMC had to be collectively punished and reeducated by consultants from the burgeoning and profitable diversity training industry. It should be noted, by the way, that this industry is horribly ineffective.

As *Market Watch* explains, "[i]n terms of reducing bias and promoting equal opportunity, diversity training has 'failed spectacularly,' according to the expert assessment of sociologists Frank Dobbin and Alexandra Kalev. When Dobbin and Kalev evaluated the impact of diversity training at more than 800 companies over three decades, they found that the positive effects are short-lived and that compulsory training generates resistance and resentment."[6] Indeed, this study showed that diversity training tends to enforce racial stereotypes and to lower sympathy toward poor whites. Of course, the lowering of sympathy for poor whites may be seen as a real achievement for these diversity trainers and for the "woke" movement in general.

In any case, these trainings tend to make people more bigoted. This should not be too surprising, for, as the study found, these trainings' practice of "emphasizing cultural differences across racial groups can lead to an increased belief in fundamental biological differences among races. This means that well-intentioned efforts to celebrate diversity may in fact reinforce racial stereotyping." In addition, few people respond well to being told, as these trainings do, that they are racist even though they didn't know it, and that they somehow benefit from "white supremacy" even though they may be struggling just to make ends meet, and even though they may be making less in a month than the training consultant makes in a day. Who knew that publicly judging and exposing people in front of their peers would cause resentment?

In addition to making people more racist and resentful, these trainings also chill open discussion—just as "cancel culture" itself does. Again, the aforementioned article explains, "[w]ith its emphasis on dos and don'ts, diversity training tends to be little more than a form of etiquette. It spells out rules that are just as rigid as those that govern the placement of salad forks and soup spoons. The fear of saying 'the wrong thing' often leads to unproductive, highly scripted conversations." But it's all good, because employers can have the benefit of virtue signaling by pretending to do something for racial and gender equality—when in reality they are doing nothing or even doing harm—and the consultants themselves can cash in. Thus, as the article relates, "[t]he main beneficiaries of the forthcoming explosion in diversity programming will be the swelling ranks of 'diversity and inclusion' consultants who stand to make a pretty penny. A one-day training session for around 50 people costs anywhere between $2,000 and $6,000. Robin DiAngelo, the best-selling author of *White Fragility*, charges up to $15,000 per event." This is capitalism at its worst.

Answering the call to cancel Molly Rush, the TMC Board issued a public statement officially denouncing Molly. Without even saying what Molly had posted, or noting that she had already apologized, the TMC Board stated:

> We apologize for the harm recently caused by TMC co-founder Molly Rush posting a racist meme on Facebook, while recognizing that our overall problems of institutionalized white supremacy are larger than just one person or event. While Molly no longer sits on our TMC Board, we feel a responsibility to address this because of her long history with TMC and ongoing influence over the center. We ask that Molly publicly apologize in a way that acknowledges the harm people experienced and what she learned. We cannot work with Molly until she demonstrates both accountability to the people she has harmed and a commitment to continuous learning about how her behavior embodies white supremacy culture and impacts the people around her.
>
> The real impact of actions matters more than our intent. The previous good works of people or organization do not exempt anyone from taking accountability when their actions hurt others and failing to do this tarnishes whatever legacy we may value.
>
> We affirm our previous organizational position that white people should not tell Black people how to work towards their own liberation, or how to protest, organize, mourn, or celebrate. This perpetuates white supremacy itself, undermines movements for racial justice, and wastes people's time.
>
> We ask that white people connected with TMC, and especially people who've historically held strong influence through social capital or major donations, to step back and open space to center Black people, people of color, and marginalized people. Our mission and values require us to direct our resources to support people most impacted by interwoven injustices. We understand the problems of institutionalized white supremacy culture as more than an intergenerational misunderstanding or interpersonal conflict, but instead as a deep flaw that has always existed in social justice movements in the so-called united states.

We are working on a timeline and action steps for continuously addressing white supremacy culture within our organization and membership.[7]

This statement was emailed to all TMC members and also posted on Facebook. A number of people, including myself, posted comments in support of Molly, while others continued to pile on. For defending Molly, I was schooled by one individual on Facebook who told me how I had to be more "empathetic," as if my defense of Molly were motivated by anything but empathy.

At the time of this writing, the TMC continues to shun Molly and to refuse to work with her. In short, Molly Rush was effectively "cancelled," and she was left emotionally devastated, having seen her life's work discarded because of one Facebook post.

Let me just say here that my own personal position, at least at the outset of the protests, was that they were unequivocally a good thing, and that the violence accompanying the protests was indeed justified and possibly necessary. As I posted on Facebook on May 28, 2020:

My brief thoughts on the events in Minneapolis:

I am frankly surprised that it took this long for people to manifest the type of anger we saw unleashed last night.

We are living in a nation that is relentlessly cruel and unjust. Our rulers have exploited the chaos of the pandemic to enrich themselves while throwing crumbs to the rest of us. After two and a half months of lockdown, Congress has deigned to send individual workers a mere $1200, while sending billions to corporations and the banks. $1200!!! And many haven't even received that. This is an insult, and everyone knows it and feels it to their core.

Meanwhile, the police state has tightened its grip over society, and especially over black and brown members of our communities. And still, our nation wages wars abroad without pause.

The message is clear: our government has money for the super-rich, for the police and for war, but not for the vast majority of people.

Instead of protective gear, our brave medical personnel get wasteful military flyovers that cost $60,000 an hour. And now, the government is trying to rush people back to work and to their deaths even as we reach the grim body count of 100,000 due to the virus. And again, it is black and brown people who are disproportionately dying.

And what do we have to look forward to in addition to a second wave of COVID-19? A broken-down election process in November which will give us the choice between a racist psychopath and an old man riddled with dementia. Take your pick, for this, apparently, is the best our "democracy" has to offer.

This is sick. There is no other way to describe the state of affairs of this nation—a nation which claims to be the paragon of virtue in the world. Such a claim would be hilarious if the truth weren't so downright tragic and infuriating.

And so, people are finally venting their righteous rage on police stations and Target stores. Our rulers have no one to blame for this but themselves, and soon we will be coming for them. The Revolution is long overdue.[8]

My feelings about the protests changed as the weeks went on for a number of reasons, including the fact that they seemed to go on seemingly aimlessly, with frustratingly vague and limited demands that did not include many of the issues I mentioned in my Facebook screed and that I thought would have had mass appeal. Moreover, the violence that accompanied some of the protests seemed increasingly misdirected against small, and sometimes minority-owned, businesses, which I believe did not deserve to be attacked, especially during a pandemic. But in any case, as my post demonstrates, I am not, as Molly Rush, committed to nonviolence in all cases. Still, I respect Molly and her very principled stance against violence, and I certainly do not believe she should have been attacked for taking a position that she had for her entire life and career.

The "cancellation" of Molly Rush, moreover, went well beyond her as an individual. Thus, while the TMC Board and staff had rallied against Molly, a number of those who joined in commenting in opposition to Molly and who ostensibly supported the TMC missive stated that it might be better after all if the TMC disbanded itself. That is, there were some who would rather see a 50-year-old peace and justice organization dissolved, and the TMC staff who issued a statement against Molly on the unemployment line, just so long as Molly Rush, an octogenarian peace activist, was taught a lesson.

What is clear to me is that there is no amount of apologizing Molly could do for her impulsive reposting of a meme that, if fairly read, was critical of rioting and looting by Black and white individuals alike—and therefore NOT racist—to successfully defend herself and her reputation. It is important to note, indeed, that in Pittsburgh, the most publicized act of vandalism that took place during the BLM protests at the time of Molly's post (the firebombing of a police car) had been carried out by a young white man from a suburb of Pittsburgh.[9] In New York City, in the meantime, seven rich, privileged, and white youths were arrested for violently rioting there.[10]

Meanwhile, the *New York Times* ran a story in October 2020 about how mostly white "insurrectionary anarchists" had been doing a lot of the rioting and burning over the summer as an intentional political tactic of "asymmetric warfare," and how they did so much to the chagrin of some Black leaders who believed that they were hijacking and undermining the goals of promoting racial justice. This story focused on the journalistic work of Jeremey Quinn, who had studied this phenomenon throughout the US over the four most active months of the protests. As the *Times* explained:

> Mr. Quinn began studying footage of looting from around the country and saw the same Black outfits and, in some cases, the same masks. He decided to go to a protest dressed like that himself, to figure out what was really going on. He expected to find white supremacists who wanted to help re-elect President Trump by stoking fear of Black people. What he discovered instead were true believers in "insurrectionary anarchism."[11]

As the *Times* continued, "[w]hile talking heads on television routinely described it as a spontaneous eruption of anger at racial injustice, it was strategically planned, facilitated and advertised on social media by anarchists who believed that their actions advanced the cause of racial justice. In some cities, they were a fringe element, quickly expelled by peaceful organizers. But in Washington, Portland and Seattle they have attracted a 'cult-like energy' . . ."

These same "talking heads on television" and other media outlets were the very same who spoke incessantly about "mostly-peaceful protests" even while real damage was being done to businesses, many minority-owned, and the economy during a pandemic that was already destroying people's livelihoods. One of the more hilarious headlines came from the BBC, which led one of its stories about the BLM demonstrations with the patently implausible claim: "27 police officers injured during largely peaceful anti-racism protests in London."[12] British native George Orwell would have had a field day with that one.

Meanwhile, it was not just businesses burned to the ground. As the *Times* highlighted, "Migizi, a Native American nonprofit in Minneapolis, raised more than $1 million to buy and renovate a place where Native American teenagers could learn about their culture— only to watch it go up in flames, alongside dozens of others, including a police station. It can take years to build a building—and only one night to burn it down."

For his part, journalist Michael Tracey traveled throughout the US to assess the damage done by rioting. He found that it was indeed small, minority-owned businesses that bore the brunt of the rioting. He gave the examples of a coffee shop in Fort Wayne, IN, that suffered property damage from "white kids with skateboards" who smashed its windows; and an Arab-owned grocery store in Atlantic City that also suffered broken windows from "a rioter wielding a baseball bat."

Similar fates, we are told by Tracey, were met in Minneapolis by a low-income housing unit under construction, a Somali-owned grocery store, a Lao American community center, a Black-owned hair salon, an Ethiopian-owned auto repair business, a Mexican restaurant, and an Ecuadorian restaurant; in Green Bay, by a small tobacco and convenience store; and in Olympia, WA, by an independent music store.

Again, it was Tracey's observation that such damage was, for the most part, inflicted in the course of "'riots' motivated by consciously insurrectionist ideology—consisting of arson attacks and other actions intended to maximize chaos—[and] appear to have largely instigated by left-wing activist whites."

And still, I remember many white progressives arguing glibly that property damage was not a big deal—nothing compared to the damage and looting done by the capitalists (an assertion I certainly agree with, but sadly it was not the capitalists' property that, for the most part, was being damaged during the demonstrations)—and that the damage wrought was a necessity, if regrettable one, in the war against racism. I'm not sure that the Native Americans and Laotians who lost their centers in Minneapolis, or the minority business owners in that city and others, were so easily able to shrug their shoulders about their losses. And the indifference of white progressives to this loss might itself be seen as a manifestation of racism and white supremacy, but few dared to call it out as such.

One of the great theorists of revolutionary thought and practice was Vladimir Lenin, the leader of the 1917 Russia Revolution and the founder of the Soviet Union. Back in 1902, Lenin was already writing against the violent tactics of those revolutionaries in Russia who believed, as the "insurrectionary anarchists" of today, that "the politics of the deed," which Lenin simply referred to as "terrorism," would inspire the masses to rise up and overthrow the state. As Lenin explained back then in his essay "Revolutionary Adventurism,"[13] in which he criticized the assassination of a government minister by Socialist Revolutionaries:

> Although everyone knows and sees perfectly well that this act was in no way connected with the masses and, moreover, could not have been by reason of the very way in which it was carried out—that the persons who committed this terrorist act neither counted on nor hoped for any definite action or support on the part of the masses. In their naïveté, the Socialist-Revolutionaries do not realize that their predilection for terrorism is causally most intimately linked with the fact that, from the very outset, they have always

kept, and still keep, aloof from the working-class movement, without even attempting to become a party of the revolutionary class which is waging its class struggle. Over-ardent protestations very often lead one to doubt and suspect the worth of whatever it is that requires such strong seasoning. Do not these protestations weary them?—I often think of these words, when I read assurances by the Socialist-Revolutionaries: "by terrorism we are not relegating work among the masses into the background." After all, these assurances come from the very people who have already drifted away from the Social-Democratic labor movement, which really rouses the masses; they come from people who are continuing to drift away from this movement, clutching at fragments of any kind of theory.

Of course, these words are well applied to the young, white anarchists of today who do not even make a pretense of being connected to the working-class masses, and who even seem to despise them. Another piece by Lenin, "Left-wing Communism, An Infantile Disorder," would also seem to apply well to these anarchists.

As Lenin saw back then, the violent acts against people and property by people hoping to incite mass uprisings tend only to turn off and alienate the masses from the struggle. And remember, Lenin was talking about an act that at least seemed logically intended to elicit such an uprising—the assassination of a hated government minister. Even more off-putting are the violent attacks by today's anarchists against small businesses and even community centers. It should also be said, and anyone who knows anything about Soviet history would know, that Lenin and his comrades were not big fans of anarchists generally, to put it quite mildly. Nor am I, and I believe the events of the summer of 2020 demonstrate why they don't represent a constructive left alternative.

Indeed, I must confess that I did not truly understand the following famous words, now 100 years old, of W. B. Yeats until I witnessed some of the nonsense carried out by white anarchists during the summer of 2020: "Things fall apart; the centre cannot hold; Mere anarchy is loosed upon the world; . . . The best lack all conviction, while the worst are full of passionate intensity."

The chutzpah demonstrated by white protesters considering themselves more revolutionary than thou seemed to have no bounds. And it is worthy to note that, throughout the summer of 2020 and throughout the country, it was mostly white people who were doing the protesting. Thus, according to a July *PR News Wire* article, "[a] substantial majority of the protesters were white, in the cities where the data was gathered, with the highest percentage in Minneapolis (85%), followed by Los Angeles (78%), and Atlanta and New York (both at 76%). A total of 18% of the protesters were African American in Atlanta, 11% in Minneapolis, 13% in New York and 3% in Los Angeles. Those numbers remained steady during the nighttime hours. Hispanic and Asian American participation was less than 10% in all four cities."[14] The relatively small number of African Americans participating in the BLM protests seems significant. While we are constantly told by the mainstream press that the summer of 2020 was one of "racial reckoning," the level of participation of African Americans in the protests makes me wonder to what extent this was true. As commentators on the left-wing *Jacobin Show* commented, the makeup of the protests convinced them that, whatever these protests were, they were not "The Civil Rights Movement 2.0."[15]

This reality really came home to me when I saw scenes in Chicago with the mostly African American residents of Englewood organizing to keep the mostly white BLM protesters out of their neighborhood for fear that the protesters would antagonize the local police and tear up the neighborhood.[16]

Incredibly, a number of white protesters in other cities had the audacity to tell longtime Black activists how they thought things should be done. As the *Times* explained[17], white protesters dared to assault Black leaders whom they deemed too conciliatory:

> In Portland, Jo Ann Hardesty, an activist turned city councilor, has pushed for the creation of a pilot program of unarmed street responders to handle mental illness and homelessness, a practical step to help protect populations that experience violence at the hands of police. Yet Ms. Hardesty is shouted down at protests by

anarchists who want to abolish the police, not merely reform or defund them.

"As a Black woman who has been working on this for 30 years, to have young white activists who have just discovered that Black lives matter yelling at me that I'm not doing enough for Black people—it's kind of ironic, is what it is," Ms. Hardesty told me.

In Seattle, Andrè Taylor, a Black man who lost his brother to police violence in 2016, helped change state law that made it nearly impossible to prosecute officers for killing civilians. But he has been branded a "pig cop" by young anarchists because his nonprofit organization receives funds from the city, and because he cooperates with the police.

Moreover, as far back as July 2020, the NAACP was complaining that the original message of the protests in Portland—that is, of protecting Black Lives—had been "diluted" by some protestors who seemed to have their own agenda.[18] The NAACP specifically singled out "actions made by mostly white anarchists" that were taking away from the Black Lives message. As one news source reported: "After midnight a new type of 'protestor' has been descending on downtown, intent on breaking things and damaging BLM's credibility with the public, Antjuan Tolbert, Portland NAACP board secretary, pointed out. Unrest is not an endorsement of anarchy. These protests are demanding changes to the state, not its abolition."[19] And yet, the type of protests the NAACP criticized continued for months after this by some white protestors who thought they knew better.

Similar sentiments were uttered at the beginning of September 2020, after white anarchists attempted to set fire to the Portland mayor's 16-story apartment building, which happened to house other families, and to a nearby health clinic.[20] Portland Black Lives Matter organizer Seneca Cayson expressed frustration by these events and expressed the feeling that "more and more . . . the Black Lives Matter protests have been taken over by political sides taking shots at each other, and that Black people and the movement for social justice are suffering for it."[21] A resident in the mayor's apartment building echoed such thoughts, saying that while he supported Black Lives Matter,

"I think, sadly, this no longer has anything to do with Black Lives Matter and that's the tragedy of this. I think that message has been co-opted by people with a totally different agenda."

And indeed, George Floyd's own family members publicly denounced the violence that accompanied some of the protests around the country.[22]

Again, it is deemed heresy in the "woke" left to even discuss the episodes of white protestor condescension toward Black leaders or their hijacking of the message of the BLM protests, even while we are constantly told that we must "listen to Black leaders." The truth is that it is largely white "woke" activists who are determining which Black voices we are to listen to and follow. Indeed, there is a huge irony in all this as we see certain Black voices drowned out and ignored—and in fact cancelled—when they fail to express the "acceptable" narrative of the world. An example of this is the case of left-wing journalist Lee Fang, who, in an article published in *The Intercept* during the summer of 2020, quoted an African American resident of East Oakland, CA, named Maximum Fr, who stated, "I always question, why does a Black life matter only when a white man takes it? . . . Like, if a white man takes my life tonight, it's going to be national news, but if a Black man takes my life, it might not even be spoken of. . . . It's stuff just like that that I just want in the mix."[23] Fang was immediately attacked by a fellow *Intercept* journalist, Akela Lacey, who accused Fang on Twitter of being a "racist" for including this quote in his article, for the quote touched on an issue now verboten in public discourse, just as Maximum Fr complained. As Matt Taibbi relates, Lacey's "tweet received tens of thousands of likes and responses along the lines of, 'Lee Fang has been like this for years, but the current moment only makes his anti-Blackness more glaring,' and 'Lee Fang spouting racist bullshit it must be a day ending in day.' A significant number of Fang's coworkers, nearly all white, as well as reporters from other major news organizations like the *New York Times* and MSNBC and political activists (one former Elizabeth Warren staffer tweeted, 'Get him!'), issued likes and messages of support for the notion that Fang was a racist. Though he had support within the organization, no one among his coworkers was willing to say anything in his defense publicly."[24]

Again, the attempt to cancel Fang was as much about trying to silence Maximum Fr and other African Americans who feel the same way he does—and of course these are less privileged African Americans who live in poorer neighborhoods with higher crime rates—and this is all being done in the name of "wokeness" and "social justice." There is something very wrong about this.

In the end, the high-handed tactics of the "insurrectionary anarchists" largely backfired over time, with support for BLM falling, and with, for example, a majority of voters in Oregon (whose city of Portland was the epicenter of their unrestrained tactics) eventually saying by early September 2020 that the protests were violent, counterproductive, and should actually be suppressed by the police.[25]

So much for the chief call of the BLM movement to "defund the police"—a concept that had little support amongst the American population to begin with and that received even less support as the protests raged on. As a study from the Cato Institute from June 4 showed, while the majority of Americans of all races support police and prison reform, few of any race support defunding the police or removing police from their communities.[26] According to the study, "few people support calls to abolish or defund the police: 9 in 10 black, white and Hispanic Americans oppose reducing the number of police officers in their community—and a third say their community needs more officers. . . . And a Yahoo/Yougov survey found that only 16 percent of Americans favor cutting funding for police departments, including 12 percent of whites, 33 percent of blacks, and 17 percent of Hispanics."

Moreover, the same study revealed that "[w]hile Americans support (57 percent) the general purpose behind the protests in response to the death of George Floyd. They do not like protests that turn violent and lead to rioting. And the Yahoo/YouGov poll found that 51 percent felt the Minneapolis protests were mostly violent riots, not peaceful. This may be why a Morning Consult poll found that 71 percent of Americans support sending in the national guard to address the protests."

The main point here is that Molly Rush's post could have been seen as directed toward such white individuals as much as anyone else, and therefore as anything but racist. What's more, her post could have been the catalyst for an honest, full-throated discussion and debate about protest tactics and strategies—a discussion that was sorely needed at the outset of the protests and as they continued on into the summer. Instead, her relatively innocuous post was seized upon as an occasion to cancel a lifelong peace activist.

Meanwhile, others were similarly canceled for taking the "wrong" position on peaceful versus violent protesting. Thus, as *New York Magazine* related, a liberal data analyst named David Shor was fired and then kicked off a progressive listserv after simply tweeting out a copy of a study, carried out by a Black professor at Princeton, Omar Wasow, that purported to show that peaceful protests are more effective at winning over public support than violent protests.[27] As in the case of Molly, this was followed by "a cruel attempt to destroy the professional reputation of Shor" by painting him publicly as a racist.

One of the responses to Shor's tweet and its aftermath is almost textbook in such circumstances, and thus worth quoting:

> I'd like to be heard. I have been following along with these posts all day and I'm exhausted. I was working and wanted to offer my thoughts now that my day has died down. I've been in progressive spaces since 2006, and it didn't take long for me to understand that in our spaces, racism isn't always loud. It isn't always brash or demanding, spewing racial slurs with a foaming tongue. Sometimes it's quiet; steeped in seemingly innocuous data and facts. Racism can wrap itself in the trappings of credible logic and I swear it can make sense. But when you see how data can and has been used to oppress, undermine and devalue movements, it's impossible not to offer a critical eye.

Others claimed, in quite typical fashion, that Shor's tweet had made them feel "unsafe," though they did not say how, and frankly this is hard to believe given that he seemed to be advocating for nonviolence. And when some defended Shor's tweet by mentioning that the author of the study he had tweeted was indeed Black, this defense was also met with allegations of racism. Molly faced the same allegations when she tried to mention that a well-respected African American activist had expressed the view that she was not offended by Molly's FB post.

In the end, Molly Rush and David Shor may well have been right about the efficacy of peaceful versus violent protesting, especially insofar as the violent protesting is directed at the very people the protests purport to be supporting.

Thus, as the summer is becoming fall in 2020, it appears that the public support for the BLM protests is softening, in part due to the violence that has accompanied some of them. As *USA Today* reported on August 31, 2020, in an article titled "Rioting is beginning to turn people off to BLM and protests while Biden has no solution,"[28] "[n]et approval for the Black Lives Matter movement peaked back on June 3 and has fallen sharply since. This was just over a week after George Floyd was killed in Minneapolis, when riots had begun to sweep major cities. Among whites, net approval is already negative and headed downward. And . . . white Independents have shown a dramatic falloff in BLM support, going from a net 24 percent in early June to net 3 percent now, which is lower than before Floyd was killed. Of course, BLM is not synonymous with rioting, but this trend may show the extent to which the issues have been conflated in the public mind."

And in Pittsburgh itself, the local BLM protest movement was undermined greatly by an act of ill-conceived aggression by some of the most prominent BLM leaders associated with a group called "I Can't Breathe—Pittsburgh." Thus, in early of September 2020, some of these folks, in the process of leading what they called "Civil Saturdays"—weekly protests begun shortly after the death of George Floyd—decided to confront some white patrons who were eating brunch at a local eating establishment.

In an incident that resulted in a viral video that received millions of views, international media attention, and a condemnatory tweet by President Trump, some of the organizers berated the patrons, yelling, "Fuck white people."[29] One of the protestors then ran over to a table, grabbed a full glass of beer off it, and quickly downed it, as the stunned patrons looked on in disbelief. Still another protester smashed a glass on the ground. While the individuals involved in this incident claimed they were somehow provoked by the patrons, and while that might have been true, there is no video evidence of this. In any case, the confrontation with the restaurant patrons was a huge, tactical blunder.

Meanwhile, the same individuals proceeded to march down the street on the same occasion to a local McDonald's, where they were videotaped causing a loud scene with a bullhorn and physically confronting the Black manager of the restaurant.[30]

Great damage was done to the movement by these events, as the BLM organizers themselves seemed to recognize. For, without any explanation, they announced that the week following these incidents would see the last "Civil Saturdays" demonstration. They were true to their word on this.

I should note that I attended four of these "Civil Saturdays" demonstrations before they were unceremoniously canceled, and I did so as a full participant with my family—not as a journalist or passive observer. While I hesitate to say this, I was pretty quickly turned off by some of what I witnessed even before the strange incidents described above. To cut to the quick, I did not find these Saturday demonstrations to be particularly "civil."

Thus, I was troubled by how the leaders—the very ones involved in the confrontation of the restaurant patrons and McDonald's manager—hectored and bullied the white protestors. This seemed all the more strange given that the vast majority of protesters were white, and that there indeed would have been no protest of any note without them. Nonetheless, the leaders seemed utterly contemptuous of them.

For example, on a hot, blistering day of upward of 90 degrees and humid, the leaders yelled at several of us for sitting down at one point, saying something to the effect that "if you are sitting down and you are white, you should get up and do the work." I've never ever been at a protest, and I've been to many in my life, where fellow protesters were yelled at for sitting down. And, by the way, I protested in Harlem in the 1990s after the savage beating of Rodney King in L.A. by police, and there was no such treatment of white protesters then. I remember marching then arm in arm with a buff African American man whose bicep was bigger than my thigh, and I felt quite welcome and indeed content. What I am reporting here now seems to be a quite new thing.

The protest leaders at the Civil Saturday marches, meanwhile, were also aggressive in making sure that everyone was holding up their fist at certain times or at holding up their hands. And at one point they demanded that all the white protesters chant after them about our experiences as white people, or at least what they assumed to be our experiences. This quasi-religious rite was quite off-putting to some of us, like myself, who had left the Church long ago out of a disdain for such rituals. In addition, I simply did not have some of the experiences that we were being demanded to say we did. For example, while we were being told to declare, "I did not discuss racism as a child," this was not true. Actually, I had, quite a lot, and it's not clear to me, in any case, why it mattered whether I had or not.

I am not alone in the view that the BLM protests, at least the ones I witnessed, were indeed more religious in nature than they were political. They seemed more about white protesters going to somehow purify themselves than about achieving any particular political ends, and that's quite possibly why they didn't really achieve any such ends. As John McWhorter, linguistics professor at Columbia University and an African American, wrote back in 2017:

> The Antiracism religion, then, has clergy, creed, and also even a conception of Original Sin. Note the current idea that the enlightened white person is to, I assume regularly (ritually?), "acknowledge" that they possess White Privilege. Classes, seminars, teach-ins are devoted to making whites understand the need for this. Nominally, this acknowledgment of White Privilege is couched as a prelude to activism, but in practice, the acknowledgment itself is treated as the main meal, as I have noted in this space. A typical presentation getting around lately is 11 Things White People Need to Realize About Race, where the purpose of the "acknowledgment" is couched as "moving the conversation forward." A little vague, no? More conversation? About what? Why not actually say that the purpose is policy and legislation?

> Because this isn't what is actually on the Antiracists' mind. The call for people to soberly "acknowledge" their White Privilege as a self-standing, totemic act is based on the same justification as acknowledging one's fundamental sinfulness is as a Christian. One is born marked by original sin; to be white is to be born with the stain of unearned privilege.[31]

As explained by McWhorter—an individual who is of course reviled by the "woke" for being a heretic and apostate—the acknowledgment of "white privilege" is the "main meal" and activism a secondary goal. And even the activism, it appears, is mostly a religious rite—consisting, again, of acknowledging sin and engaging in penance.

As Molly Rush found out the hard way, the other aspect of the "woke" religion, again as any religion, is that one is not permitted to ask too many questions—blind adherence, after all, is the rule. As McWhorter notes, "It is inherent to a religion that one is to accept certain suspensions of disbelief. Certain questions are not to be asked, or if asked, only politely—and the answer one gets, despite being somewhat half-cocked, is to be accepted as doing the job. . . . One is not to question, and people can be quite explicit about that. For example, in the 'Conversation' about race that we are so often told we need to have, the tacit idea is that black people will express their grievances and whites will agree—again, no questions, or at least not real ones."

Another recent cancellation that underscores this particular religious aspect of the current "cancel culture" movement involved a white high school principal in Vermont who was fired for publicly raising questions on social media about the BLM protests.[32] Thus, Tiffany Riley was fired after posting the following on her personal Facebook page: "Black Lives Matter, but I DO NOT agree with the coercive measures taken to get this point across; some of which are falsified in an attempt to prove a point. . . . I do not think people should be made to feel they have to choose black race over human race. While I understand the urgency to feel compelled to advocate for black lives, what about our fellow law enforcement? What about all others who advocate for and demand equity for all?"

The school board's justification for the discharge of Ms. Riley was as follows: "The June 10 [2020] Facebook post is readily susceptible to being construed to suggest racist themes, . . . While there is no evidence that Employee personally holds racist beliefs, that is irrelevant to the point that the content of the post contains messaging reasonably susceptible to being construed as espousing racist views." Ms. Riley was ultimately fired, even though she recited the obligatory "Black Lives Matter," simply because she had some questions about the tactics of the (mostly white) BLM protests, some of their demands, and because she wondered aloud whether other lives mattered as well in the current climate. Aren't these the very types of questions that educators should be asking and encouraging their students to ask? To me, the obvious answer is yes. Indeed, we might even call this a teaching moment, but again, because she did not accept every tenet and rite of the prevailing religion, Ms. Riley had to go. Trying to use her doubts, publicly expressed, as an occasion to have a wider discussion of these important issues posed too great a risk to the authority of the self-appointed high priests, apparently. And my guess is that Ms. Riley, waiting on the unemployment line, is still not quite sure what she had done to lose her job and quite possibly her career.

Another key part of this religion, as any religion, is dividing the world into the "saved" and the "damned," for what good, after all, is it to be "saved" unless there are others destined for Hell? That would be no fun at all.

And that is where "cancel culture" fits into all of this—it is the practice of condemning and shunning—as they do to the fallen-away in the Amish community—of the "sinners."

And of course, the "damned" are not, as I believe them to be, the Jeff Bezoses or Waltons of the world—that is, the capitalists who make billions by exploiting their workers, both white and Black—but poor, uneducated white people. Again, as Professor McWhorter writes, "[k]ey to being an Antiracist is a sense that there is always a flock of unconverted heathen 'out there,' as it is often put about the whites who were so widely feared as possibly keeping Barack Obama from being elected (twice) [or those who voted for Trump]. One is blessed with, as it were, the Good News in being someone who 'gets it,' complete with the Acknowledging."

Given this, it is not surprising that it was never clear to me what we were really protesting for or against in the Civil Saturday demonstrations. And this lack of purpose and direction played out in some of the tactics.

For instance, on one occasion when we were marching in downtown Pittsburgh, the leaders kept directing the chant of "white bodies protect Black bodies." That particular call did not bother me at first. I understand how sometimes this might be necessary. What I did find strange was that there were no police or counterprotesters in sight. So it wasn't clear from what or whom white bodies were to protect Black bodies. But then, after quite a long time of marching, maybe two hours throughout the whole of downtown, the march came to the end of the permitted area, near the onramp to the Fort Pitt Bridge—the bridge connecting downtown to the southern suburbs and the airport.

At this point, police marched out en masse from vans parked on the perimeter of the permitted area. These were very scary folks, indeed. The police, who were physically huge, made a line between the protesters and the bridge and stood shoulder to shoulder with long wooden batons drawn. And they seemed quite ready and willing to use them on our heads. White protesters were encouraged to come to the fore to physically face the police, which many, including my two young adult sons, dutifully did. Meanwhile, the Black leaders of the protest would go up to the police, some of whom themselves were Black, and yell obscenities at them.

I wasn't exactly sure what was supposed to be accomplished by all this. Were we protesting not being able to go beyond the permit area? I just don't know. Meanwhile, this lasted a long time, and I feared for my two young adult boys who were up in front of the police. I was not eager for any of us to be beaten down by the cops, especially in furtherance of a goal that seemed ellusive to me. It seemed that we were being led into a confrontation for its own sake, and that did bother me. Ultimately, the showdown ended without incident, but I was not happy. I felt that the protest leaders were cavalier with the safety and physical integrity of the rank and file, and that gave me an uneasy feeling.

It also bothered me that those who questioned what the protest leaders were doing were publicly called out for "not listening to Black voices." Indeed, when someone questioned one of the leaders about the seemingly senseless confrontation with the police, we were all told that only Black voices would be heard during the protest given that "the system was already rigged in favor of white people." I am all good with listening to Black voices and following Black leaders, but I had some real questions about these particular voices and leaders, and events soon showed that I should have been.

Moreover, there are a lot of whites living in abject poverty and squalor in this country who would be surprised to hear that the system is rigged in their favor. For just one example, the UN Human Rights Council recently reported that in West Virginia—a state that is over 93 percent white and that is a mere one-hour drive from Pittsburgh—and in Alabama as well, there are huge areas where people are forced to live without running water or sewage.[33] As the UN HRC reports, "[i]n Alabama and West Virginia, a high proportion of the population is not served by public sewerage and water supply services. Contrary to the assumption in most developed countries that such services should be extended by the government systematically and eventually comprehensively to all areas, neither state was able to provide figures as to the magnitude of the challenge or details of any planned government response."[34] The system is clearly not working for those people, and there is little prospect that it ever will be.

And the system is not working for many white people in this country. Again, the UN HRC has something interesting to say about this: "[i]n imagining the poor, racist stereotypes are usually not far beneath the surface. The poor are overwhelmingly assumed to be people of color, whether African Americans or Hispanic 'immigrants.' The reality is that there are 8 million more poor Whites than there are poor Blacks. The face of poverty in America is not only Black or Hispanic, but also White, Asian, and many other backgrounds."

All of these poor, their differences in ethnicity, race, or skin tone notwithstanding, have more in common with one another than they have differences. It seems to me that trying to find this common ground as a means to organize for improvements in the economy in ways that will benefit all of those struggling to survive in this country is the way to go to effectively bring about meaningful social change. Effectively writing off millions of poor by pretending the system is somehow rigged in their favor because of their skin color—in other words, applying the "racial stereotypes" about poverty referred to by the HRC—undermines such a goal.

Let me be clear: I was not offended personally, or as an individual, by any of this, but I was offended as an activist. I wondered how long people would keep going to demonstrations only to be yelled at and berated, and specifically for being white, and being led into dangerous situations for no discernable reason. One would have to be a masochist to keep coming to these events.

While many of my comrades used to quote Emma Goldman, who famously said, "If I can't dance, I don't want to be part of your revolution," the new revolution would now forbid such frivolous displays of happiness.

I think *Rolling Stone* writer Matt Taibbi said it best when he described these protests as "the all-stick, no carrot revolution." Of course, there did seem to be plenty of masochists at the protests, with a number of protesters, including some of my friends, cheering as they were yelled at essentially for being white. Indeed, some of my white friends carried signs telling "white people" to "do the work" to fight racism and sexism and transphobia, etc.

The funny thing is that there were hardly ever any onlookers witnessing the protests—that is, these signs were only seen by the protesters themselves, and I think it can be fairly said that they were already doing some work anyway by protesting. I guess there will always be people who will respond to the stick, who will voluntarily wear a hair shirt as penance for sins they didn't even know till recently they had committed, but for how long?

I believed then, as I believe now, that this is not a way to build a mass, ongoing movement. And while the BLM protests over the summer were undeniably "mass"—possibly the biggest ever in US history, we have been told—they have not been able to keep up their steam or public support. Indeed, I feel that these protests, while showing great promise at first, represented a huge lost opportunity, and I am saddened by that.

In short, Molly's advice about peaceful protests went unheeded with adverse consequences. But again, the fact that folks may have been factually correct about such matters will never save them from being canceled. Indeed, that they are right probably intensifies the desire amongst some to cancel them, for as J. K. Rowling—an individual who has suffered many attempts to cancel her—wrote in her sixth *Harry Potter* installment, "People find it far easier to forgive others for being wrong than for being right."

J.K. Rowling is an apt reference here, for people have tried to cancel her for her allegedly being "transphobic" because, amongst other things, she has taken umbrage (forgive the pun) at women being called things like "menstruators," "people with cervixes," or, as the Harvard Medical Postgraduate and Continuing Education program recently referred to women in a tweet, "birthing people."[35] The attempts to cancel Rowling, who was sexually abused as a child, have included threats of rape and death.[36] Rowling and others like her believe that women are being erased in today's public discourse, and I think they have a point. In truth, I don't think it is a coincidence that Molly Rush is a woman "of a certain age," as they say. Women often complain of disappearing in the eyes of others as they get older. As one article on this subject explains, "Even the beautiful and talented 53-year-old actress Kristin Scott Thomas has spoken about her experience of 'vanishing' as a middle-aged woman. 'When you're walking down the street, you get bumped into,' she said. 'People slam doors in your face—they just don't notice you.'"[37]

I believe that some of the persecution of women like J. K. Rowling and Molly Rush is just old-fashioned sexism and ageism dressed up as "wokeness." Take, for example, the pejorative "Karen" term that is applied only to middle-aged and older white women. There is no other analogous slur like this that is acceptable in polite circles, but it is acceptably applied to this demographic because older women are, and always have been, fair game for derision. I saw one post, at least it was an honest one, that said, "You should be lucky we call you 'Karen,'

and not what we want to call you—'cunt.'" Of course, that is what the
"Karen" term is meant to signify, and I think that is quite troubling,
to say the least.

The other thing that concerns me is that the goal of "canceling," it
seems to me, is not to educate or to advance the cause of social justice,
but to punish and ostracize; it is not a means to an end, it is the end.
Another well-publicized incident illustrates this reality well.

In the *New York Times* article titled "A Racial Slur, A Viral Video
and a Reckoning," we learn of how the life of a high school senior,
Mimi Groves, was horribly impacted by a short, three-second video
she made four years before when she was a freshman of barely 16
years of age.[38] In the video, which she made after receiving her driver's
permit, she told a friend on snapchat, "I can drive," followed by the
N-word. The video was seen by some other students at the time, we
are told, but it "did not cause much of a stir," and Ms. Groves apologized to a Black friend about the video sometime after she made it.

Then, in the spring of 2020, a fellow student named Jimmy
Galligan was given the video by a friend and decided to lie in wait to
use it against Ms. Groves. As Mr. Galligan, pictured in the article in
front of his very nice home, told the *Times*, "'I wanted to get her where
she would understand the severity of that word,' Mr. Galligan, 18,
whose mother is Black and father is white, said of the classmate who
uttered the slur, Mimi Groves. He tucked the video away, deciding to
post it publicly when the time was right." He decided the time was
right in June of 2020, when Ms. Groves, in response to the BLM protests at the time, "in a public Instagram post, urged people to 'protest,
donate, sign a petition, rally, do something' in support of the Black
Lives Matter movement." That is, Mr. Galligan decided that the time
was right to punish and shame Ms. Groves for something she did four
years before, when Ms. Groves had come out in support of Black lives.
So Mr. Galligan posted the video, which quickly went viral.

As the *Times* explained, "[b]y that June evening, about a week after
Mr. Floyd's killing, teenagers across the country had begun leveraging
social media to call out their peers for racist behavior. Some students
set up anonymous pages on Instagram devoted to holding classmates

accountable, including in Loudoun County," where Mr. Galligan and Ms. Groves lived and attended school.

The upshot was that Ms. Groves was publicly humiliated, threatened with physical violence, thrown off the cheerleading squad, and forced to withdraw her application to the University of Tennessee upon the University's threat to retract its acceptance of her otherwise. As her mother claimed, this incident "'vaporized' 12 years of her daughter's hard work." As for Mr. Galligan, the *Times* tells us, he has no regrets. The *Times* indeed ended the story with this quote from Mr. Galligan: "'I'm going to remind myself, you started something,' he said with satisfaction. 'You taught someone a lesson.'"

There is much to be said about this episode. In my own view, what Mr. Galligan did was simply cruelty dressed up as social justice, as many of these cancellations are. When he talked about waiting "to get her where she would understand the severity of that word," he meant that he waited to release the old video when she was at her most vulnerable and when he could do the most damage to her. He did not bother to talk to her first, to see if possibly she was a different person than the one who had originally made the video; whether, for example, she already came to understand the severity of the word, which, by the way, Mr. Galligan explained to the *Times* was regularly bandied about at his mother's family reunions. He had no idea whether Ms. Groves really needed a lesson to be taught, and clearly this did not matter to him. And he certainly did not offer her any chance at redemption before or after lowering the boom. Neither did the high school or the University of Tennessee.

In the end, Mr. Galligan just hurt this person as much as he could and went on his way with apparently no care in the world. This was not some civil rights crusade, but rather, a scene out of *Lord of the Flies*. But Mr. Galligan could, of course, be forgiven somewhat for not really understanding this because many others were doing the very same thing at the time and saw other institutions respond to them as if they were true whistleblowers. For his part, Mr. Galligan was even rewarded with a story in our paper of record, the *New York Times*. And while I believe he came out rather poorly in the story, mostly by his own admissions, I am certain others have given him a pat on the back for his now-well-publicized actions.

At a time when our nation's youths are being warned against bullying others, they are at the same time being rewarded for bullying in such instances. I shudder to think of what type of adults they will become.

I have heard a number of people refer to such cancellations as the new McCarthyism, and I believe there is some truth to this. Still, one commentator on Facebook, in response to the claim that the attacks on Molly Rush were McCarthyite in nature, stated that this was not so because no one was demanding to "incarcerate" Molly. In other words, those of us concerned about the well-being of Molly should be mollified because those wanting to punish her were not going so far as to have her put her in jail. Possibly, an old-fashioned tar and feathering, or dragging her through the street naked, would do. Meanwhile, the claim that the absence of incarceration somehow meant that the attack upon Molly was not McCarthyite in nature showed an amazing lack of knowledge about the McCarthy period and the tactics used to destroy undesirables during that time.

Thus, while incarceration, and the threat thereof, were used against those accused of communist ties or leanings, the main tools used against such individuals were the same being used today to "cancel" people—public humiliation and job/career loss.

A great example of this McCarthyite harassment was that meted out to one of my heroes, Paul Robeson. I actually attended Columbia University School of Law, in part, because Robeson had graduated from there. Unable to find a job in law because of the color of his skin, Robeson, the son of a slave, became a singer after discovering that, without any training, he had an amazing baritone voice. Robeson traveled around the world delighting audiences with his singing. It is worth mentioning here that one of Robeson's most famous performances was in Wales to (white) Welsh miners. As the publication *Wales Online* explains,

> Despite his many achievements, one of the causes closest to Robeson's heart was the plight of the south Wales miners—and his

connection with Wales is still remembered and commemorated to this day.

The son of a Presbyterian minister born into slavery, Robeson saw parallels between his experiences of living as a black man in the USA during the Jim Crow era and the Welsh miners who faced extreme hardship during the years of the general strike.

It was a relationship which would endure and as much as Robeson contributed to the miners' cause and made a massive impact on Wales, he was inspired by Wales and the country helped to mould his political outlook and determination to strive for equality on a global scale.

In a speech made to a reception in Wales given in his honour in 1958, Robeson told the audience "You have shaped my life—I have learned a lot from you."[39]

In other words, Robeson had an incredible rapport with these members of the white working class. He loved them, and they loved him back. Such connections are indeed possible in this world.

In addition to being a singer, Robeson was a social activist and a Communist and was greatly impressed by how he was treated in the Soviet Union and, frankly, just about everywhere else outside the US. As a means to silence Robeson, literally, the US State Department, during the McCarthy period, revoked his passport, making it impossible for him to travel and making it quite difficult for him to earn a living given that he did so much international performing. While Robeson was creative and resourceful, singing to audiences in Canada just on the other side of the border and to an audience in the UK over the telephone, his career and livelihood were greatly damaged, and he struggled with depression until the end of his days. As one article notes, "he died a recluse at the age of 77 after suffering from ill health caused by his treatment at the hands of the CIA who viewed his pro-Communist sympathies as a threat."[40]

A key point, as I indicated in my own post on Facebook, and as a group letter to the TMC Board stated, Molly is not an enemy of the TMC, of social justice, or of the cause of racial equality. And yet, she is being treated as such.

If the self-proclaimed "left" cannot distinguish between the Mollys of the world and real white supremacists or between statues of Confederate generals on the one hand and those of Lincoln, General Ulysses S. Grant, and Walt Whitman on the other, then that is not a "left" I wish to be a part of. It is also not a "left" that will succeed in creating significant social change.

Cornel West himself expressed such a view in an interview with the *Guardian* newspaper:

> From race matters to Black Lives Matter: "A beautiful new moment in the struggle for Black freedom." But even there West sees pitfalls and offers advice. There must be clear objectives, he says. It must be "a profoundly human affair that is always multi-racial, multinational, multigender, multi-sexual orientation." Crucially, it must prioritize those who need it most. "The focus must be on empowering the least of these, to use the biblical term—the poor and working class. When you are overthrowing monuments, that is not empowering poor people. It becomes a symbolic gesture."
>
> That strategy, he says, requires deep thought. "Lincoln was a white supremacist for most of his life but, I mean, my God, he grew. He was a force for good. What happens is you begin to alienate certain members of a larger community that you are trying to speak to."[41]

Amen!

This makes me think that these "leftists" who engage in such "cancellation" do not want real social change. Instead, they wish, at best, to settle scores, to advance their own careers and their own reputations, and to enjoy the schadenfreude of persecuting old progressives. A Latina* friend of mine, and National Lawyers Guild lawyer,

---

* You will note that I do not use the "woke" term "Latinx" here or elsewhere, for I reject it as an elitist, and frankly imperialist, term invented by academics and not at all embraced by the Latino community itself. As John McWhorter, an African American professor of linguistics at Columbia, argues in his December 2019 *Atlantic* article titled "Why *Latinx* Can't Catch On," the term "Latinx," invented in 2014, has been accepted by only around 2 percent of Latinos. And this is because, McWhorter argues, unlike the term "African American," which was immediately embraced by Black Americans when publicly announced by activist Jesse Jackson in 1988 as the term Black Americans prefer to be called, "Latinx" was not created in response to any need or demand of the Latino community. Rather, it has been imposed from above by intellectual elites. Moreover, as is quite obvious to the passive observer, and as argued by McWhorter, this term does violence to the otherwise lyrical Spanish Romance language spoken by millions of Latinos and Latinas

Natasha Lycia Ora Bannan, expressed this observation well when she wrote, quite bravely, on Facebook:

> If you think being woke means a call-out culture or hyper policing the language and beliefs of people you think should know what a new generation thinks being "woke" is, then clearly you are far removed from the arduous and real work of organizing. A culture that is so quick to dispose of people and cancel them out based on whether they use certain words or gestures is not only disconnected from every other culture but disconnected from inter-generational organizing as well. Its dismissive of those who come from distinct cultures with other forms of knowledge. Its dismissive of our elders (who are already deemed disposable by this culture). That kind of culture actually just replicates capitalism and patriarchy with punishment, rigidity and competition.
>
> It is easy to dispose of people you think don't have the political orientation or language you do (which you surely learned along the way also), but that will not get you far if what you're looking for is transformation, not righteousness.†

But again, I believe that it is a mistake to believe that those engage in the cancellation of relatively innocent people want actual "transformation." Indeed, there is actual evidence that there are much baser motivations behind cancellation.

Thus, a study of 511 very diverse Americans showed that those who could be described as Politically Correct Authoritarians (PCAs)— that is, who were committed to meting out punishment to others that they viewed to be less than "woke" on racial and gender issues—share the very same "Triad" of pathologies that authoritarian right-wing

---

around the world. It is a word that hardly rolls off the tongue after all. Meanwhile, it is Latinos themselves who insisted decades ago upon being called "Latinos" and "Latinas" instead of "Hispanics." But, of course, intellectuals do not care what the people want; they will simply tell the people what they must do. In this case, Latinos are simply not listening or complying, and good for them.

† Shortly after writing this, and just before publication of this book, Ms. Bannan herself came under attempts to "cancel" her by people claiming that she was not in fact Latina as she claimed to be. Apparently, while Ms. Bannan was raised by two successive Latino stepfathers and was immersed in the Latin culture and language as a result, her blood parents were both of European, including Italian, descent. I will allow the reader to decide if these circumstances allow Ms. Bannan to claim to be of Latin heritage. What I will say is that I do question why we are meant to accept that men can become women just by saying so, though one's sex is determined on a chromosomal level, even while one is not permitted to self-identify in regard to race or ethnicity, which are social constructs.

individuals possess.[42] These pathologies are "Machiavellianism, narcissism, and psychopathy." As one commentator concluded about this study: "Whereas the dominant strain of cultural leftism once was primarily characterized by a spirit of compassion, it increasingly has come to be dominated by intolerant scolds who seem more eager to shame heretics than to do actual good in the world. Studies like this one should serve as a wake-up call: Given the strident manner with which progressives denounce bigotry, it surely should trouble them to know that, where underlying personalities are concerned, priests and heretics look very much alike."[43]

What's more, it would seem, the authoritarian "left" and authoritarian right, in addition to sharing the same psychological traits, possess a symbiotic relationship with each other. They feed off each other, with the one hardly able to exist without the other. And so one will witness pitched battles between these two forces, with little to nothing to be gained by either side except the physical routing of the other. The varying political values of these two forces seem hardly relevant in the struggle. In the process of these battles, social justice appears at best an afterthought of the authoritarian "left" and is certainly not advanced.

In addition, I fear that there are least some who engage in such tactics in order to intentionally sew discord and division, and to undermine the movement. And there is some evidence of this, as well. Thus, a number of news outlets, most notably *VICE*, have reported on right-wing "accelerationists" (again, mostly young, white males) infiltrating BLM protests with the specific intent to promote a violent race war that, they believe, will lead to the collapse of the government.[44]

Indeed, as I write this, the news just broke that Ivan Harrison Hunter, a member of the right-wing Boogaloo Bois, traveled from Boerne, TX, to Minneapolis in the early days of the George Floyd protests with the intention of stoking violence, and he did just that by instigating the attack upon the Third Precinct police station.[45] According to federal investigators, he coordinated his attack with other members of the Boogaloo Bois—a group that has explicitly called for a civil war in the US.

As some commentators like Michael Tracey have quipped,[46] however, the "race war" being provoked has so far played out as one largely between young white anarchists and young white right-wingers. This strange spectacle underscores the absurdity of the tactics of both sides of this struggle—tactics that, it should be emphasized, are identical.

The type of infiltration discussed above is an age-old tactic of those, including law enforcement agencies, who wish to undermine legitimate protest movements. Indeed, there is an old term for such individuals—*agents provocateurs*.

The FBI, for example, is famous for urging on people to carry out violence, even terrorist violence, in order to undermine various movements, such as those for environmental protection, racial justice, and economic equality.[47] Indeed, as an article in *The Intercept* explains, "sting operations and the use of informants and agents provocateurs have become a staple of FBI operations in part because the courts have been 'unwilling to find that their actions meet the legal definition of entrapment.'"[48] *The Intercept* article, citing an expert on FBI tactics, continues: "The FBI has embraced this flawed theory of radicalization, that it's the ideas that are a problem, not the violence. . . . [T]hey have embraced a very aggressive sting operation protocol, no longer targeting people who are engaged in violence or illegal acts, but rather finding people who have ideas they don't like, and then encouraging them to commit violent acts, and provide weapons to them to accomplish those acts, only to then arrest them."

This is why there is a maxim in the protest movement that whoever says they can get you guns is probably a cop, so beware! I was told this when I first started protesting over 30 years ago. In an article detailing tales of what appear to be various right-wing groups and law enforcement personnel attempting to stir up violence during the BLM protests, author David Rosen echoes this sentiment, stating, "[a]gents provocateurs, outside agitators and police infiltrators play an important role in how law enforcement offices—be they federal or local—turn legitimate protests into civil disturbances, often involving 'terrorist' acts. So, be suspicious of those who express the most 'radical' actions at a demonstration or popular mobilization as it might be a calculated action to delegitimize the protest."[49]

This is all to say that there are many reasons to question violence, rioting, and looting in the course of a protest movement that one supports. To cancel someone for doing just this seems shortsighted and counterproductive at the very least. And I profoundly question the judgment, and even the intentions, of those who would do so.

One last note on the question of violence during the protests over the summer of 2020. What also concerns me about this, and it is connected to the practice of "canceling" as well, is that such violence is destructive, rather than constructive, creative, and generative. It has always been my view that social justice movements must engage in work to create the society and world that we are fighting for even as we protest against the current order. I am obviously not alone in this view.

Indeed, there have been former leaders of the Black Panther Party (BPP)—an organization that ran food kitchens, free clinics, and day-care centers in their communities—who have been critical of the BLM movement for failing to do just this type of work. For example, former BPP leader Elaine Brown was the subject of an article over the summer of 2020 in which she was quoted as saying that she was critical of the BLM movement because she had no idea what BLM did beyond simply protesting.[50] She explained that "[t]hey will protest but they will not rise up in an organized fashion, with an agenda, to create revolutionary change," as the BPP did. As the article continued, "Brown described the Party as a '24-hour' job, that included armed members patrolling neighborhoods, monitoring and fighting back against police brutality, and implementing social programs within Black neighborhoods. As chairwoman from 1974-1977, Brown assisted in the Black Panther's well known 'survival programs' like the Free Breakfast for Children and health care programs."

Especially in the midst of a pandemic and a catastrophic economic recession, if not depression, it seemed that it would have made sense for what passed as a social justice movement to focus more on building something up than in tearing down things (such as statues and the more than odd small business). Why should people have to risk being "canceled" for saying this; for raising questions that the protests seemed to demand? Because, I believe, the movement as currently

constituted knows how to destroy (people and things) and not to create, and that is the problem.

In the end, and I'm sure I'll be accused of virtue signaling[‡] here,
I decided to spend my energy during the pandemic bringing food to
those in dire need of it. This seemed much more constructive and
productive than continuing to go to protests that really didn't seem
aimed at helping anyone.

---

‡ "Virtue Signaling" is a pejorative term, according to the Cambridge Dictionary, for someone's attempting "to show other people that you are a good person, for example by expressing opinions that will be acceptable to them, especially on social media."

CHAPTER THREE

Taking Out the "White Trash"

Honestly, it ain't just Blacks. It's yellow, it's brown, it's red. It's anyone who ain't got cash, poor whites that they call trash. While we're busy fighting about race, religion and other things, the joke's on us. The reality is no lives matter, except those of the wealthy, to the ones in power.

—Ice-T

As I mentioned above, in the midst of the cancellation of Molly Rush, the term "white trash" was thrown out by Molly's detractors to describe some of her children. That this term was used is quite telling, for it says more about the individuals using it than those being targeted by it. As a few commentators have noted, there seems to be a consensus among the "tolerant" and "inclusive" liberal sector of the US that looking down upon and even making fun of those deemed to be "white trash" is one form of discrimination that is allowed, if not encouraged. Again, these are the "deplorables" whom Hillary Clinton and the establishment of the Democratic Party have shunned, much to their detriment, but there is little pushback on this by the Democratic rank and file.

Writing for a small Marxist publication, River Page explains[1] that the term "white trash" "is pejorative, and . . . carries with it connotations of immorality, immodesty, and sloth. The existence of a

permanent white underclass is often unacknowledged in this country, although we all implicitly understand that one exists. One need
not look any farther than classic films like *Deliverance* and *The Texas
Chainsaw Massacre* to see how the specter of the poor rural white
haunts the American mind. In politics, we see that working-class
whites—especially those from the South—are the primary recipients
of liberal derision."

Page explains why this is so:

> The term "liberal," in the popular imagination, has become synon-
> ymous with upper-middle-class white urbanites, a stereotype borne
> out by statistics. They are a well-educated cohort—widely-read
> enough to understand the problems with society and capitalism but
> too insecure in their position to do anything that might challenge
> the system that has brought them relative benefit. . . .
>
> They hate the white trash because of the insecurity of their class
> position. At any time, they can look into the eyes of some poor hon-
> key in the trailer park and see themselves looking back. It frightens
> them, and that fear turns to anger. But they can still pity the poor
> Black person because they know they will never be one.
>
> The origins of their derision toward the poor is not new. Calling
> themselves "progressives" then, as some do now, the petit bour-
> geois were at the forefront of the eugenics movement, sterilizing
> poor whites, particularly in the South, whom they viewed as merely
> the perpetually poor descendants of the British underclass: street
> urchins, criminals, prostitutes, and drunks.

Page makes approving reference to Nancy Isenberg's book *White
Trash: The 400-Year Untold History of Class in America*, which explains
that US elites have a long history of viewing the white underclass
with derision, as a caste of people who are indeed not fully white and
who will always be condemned to poverty—a poverty that they have
earned by their moral turpitude and that they therefore deserve.

Of course, the flip side of this is that those amongst us who are
prosperous are so because of our moral superiority. We therefore

deserve our wealth, security, and material comforts. This is, of course, a comforting thought for those who have.

As Page, I believe quite correctly, explains, it is because the liberals (by definition well-off) do not want to bear any cost in their righteousness that they have decided to show their virtue by focusing almost entirely on issues that will not burden their wallets, such as flying a rainbow flag to show support for LGBT rights or putting up a "Black Lives Matter" sign in their yard. And the fact that "white trash" by and large do not do such things, and do not apparently understand the importance of doing them, demonstrates their moral and intellectual inferiority, and thus their deserving to be canceled.

Thomas Frank, in an article in the French paper *Le Monde Diplomatique*,[2] recently expounded on the phenomenon of "cancel culture" and how it is interlinked with these condescending feelings of self-proclaimed liberals in this country. As Frank explains, the middle class (once known as the "working class") resents the "liberal elite" in return, only fueling support for Trump and other right-wing extremists:

> Why do Americans despise liberals? The answer is in our face, all the time. Liberal leaders may have given up talking about the middle class, but they have become absolutely adamant about their own goodness; about their contempt for their less refined inferiors. The liberalism of scolding is the result, and it is everywhere in Covidtime, playing constantly on a social media outlet near you. As I write this there is a video making the rounds in which a throng of protesters for Black Lives Matter (a cause I happen to believe in) corner a woman eating at a sidewalk café; they shriek at her, demanding she raise her fist in conformity with them. Watching it, one starts to understand what living in the McCarthy era must have felt like.
>
> Similar but larger episodes—society-wide paroxysms of accusation and denunciation—seem to sweep over social media every single day. Three acquaintances of mine—all of them well to the left of liberal—have seen their reputations attacked in episodes of

this kind, and in each of them the judicial process by which they were declared guilty was outrageously unfair, more like a political show trial than a judicious weighing of arguments. I would hazard a guess that millions of other Americans know of similar stories.

That liberalism has become a politics of upper-class bullying and of character assassination is an impression that daily becomes more and more difficult to avoid. To say that people regard this form of politics with hate and fear would be a vast understatement. Panic, confusion, accusation, shrieking denunciation: that is the world into which we are descending, and plenty of Americans don't blame Trump for it. They blame liberals. They blame the rich. Reader, they blame you.

I believe Frank is right on the money here, and his mention of the intensification of the liberal drama of finger-pointing during "Covidtime," as Frank refers to life during the pandemic, is well-taken. Thus, since the pandemic began back in March 2020, the Internet, as well as videos from out-of-work movie personalities, have been filled with self-satisfied scolding about the need to "stay home" in order to keep everyone safe. And those who complain that they may need to go to work or to try to run a small business, all in the interest of trying to eke out a living, have been portrayed as selfish if not as would-be killers. Moreover, those who contract COVID-19 in the so-called "red states" deserve it because they have not done what they have been told to prevent the spread and contraction of the virus. There was indeed a study that was well-circulated around social media that argued that those who tended not to follow lockdown measures tended to be psychopaths.[3]

Again, a lot of this is about class and social position—those of us who have the luxury of having a desk job that we can do comfortably from home in a bathrobe and slippers are the ones moralizing about the imperative of staying home, even while this is not a real a choice for many—the many who have patronizingly been called "essential workers," when in fact they are treated more like "expendable workers."

As a report focusing on Pittsburgh and examining this class divide and its impact on how people have been handling the pandemic explains: "[w]hile both high-income and low-income people are moving around far less than usual, cellphone tracking data from the marketing intelligence company Cuebiq shows that during the pandemic, people in the lowest-income areas are traveling about seven times more than people in the highest-income areas in the Pittsburgh region."[4] As this report explains, similar discrepancies between income levels have been seen in other cities, such as New York and Boston. And, while the data do not show why this is, "amid social distancing, many experts and community leaders believe it may be because residents in low-income areas are traveling for food, to assist family and to get to jobs that can't be done remotely." And, of course, this stands to reason.

Thus, low-income workers cannot afford to have food delivered to them. Indeed, they may have to go to food banks or other food distribution events where they may wait in long lines just to get food to put on their table. And as for working, the report relates, "[a]n analysis of federal labor data found that people in higher-paying jobs are more likely to be able to work from home, while the vast majority of low-paying jobs—including many now considered essential—require workers to be there in person, such as transportation and retail jobs." Not surprisingly, "low-income residents are disproportionately people of color."

The report, quoting Barbara Johnson, senior director of race and gender equity at the YWCA Greater Pittsburgh, "many essential workers are in a tough spot. 'They have to go to those jobs, whether they want to or not. They don't have a choice,' she said. 'They're putting their health at a greater risk because they're working in places where they're exposed.'" However, I'm sure these workers are comforted by the BLM signs lining the big houses they ride past on their way to their jobs—jobs in which they get to serve these people in the big houses, possibly by delivering delicacies from Whole Foods or Grubhub to their door.

Following is a very illuminating post about this reality confronting working-class Americans during the pandemic, from a longtime African American activist in Pittsburgh who wishes to remain anonymous:

> My family's experience is helping me to understand why COVID is spreading so rapidly. As many of you know, due to raising many nieces and nephews (due to a sister dying of cancer in 2006 and another sister having severe mental illness), I now have a lot of millenial and generation Z young adult children. Several of them currently have part-time jobs in places like Target and Whole Foods while they are either in college or pursuing entrepreneurial goals.
>
> What I have learned about these two companies is that they say one thing in their public corporate policies about how they treat their workers, but the real experience for their employees is very different.
>
> While they do tell everybody to wear PPE, social distancing is a farce. These places take clearly ineffective measures to promote it.
>
> Then there is their real (not public relations) approach to employee exposure to COVID. First, if an employee turns positive, they will just say that person will be out sick for a week or two. The co-workers, themselves, often confirm that that worker has COVID by calling them. Then they discourage people from getting tested and do not help them find out where to get tested for free or offer to pay for it, even if they suspect exposure. Next, they tell employees that if they self-quarantine for the recommended 14 days in response to exposure to COVID they will have to let them go. So nobody quarantines, even though at one store where one of my kids worked, every single day, at least one employee was testing positive for COVID. In fact, I suspect these big corporations are behind the CDC considering to decrease the recommendation for quarantine from 14 to 7 days though there is no scientific basis for making such a change.
>
> This is what you get for letting greedy corporations determine public policy, no concern for human lives. As for the corporate policies, they're all a sham to make the corporations look good sand hide the inhumane way they treat their workers.

In the above, we see illustrated the fact that the burden of this pandemic has fallen on working people, disproportionately people of color, and it is the rich and powerful, such as corporations, who have guaranteed that this is so and who have profited from this situation.

This fact was highlighted also by the awful treatment of workers in the meat factories throughout the US who were forced to work as "essential workers" without proper protections and who suffered greatly from COVID-19 as a result. As Bernie Sanders tweeted, in voicing his opposition to Republican proposals to condition a new stimulus program on a blanket immunity for corporations: "[w]hile the owner of Tyson Foods became $600 million richer during the pandemic, 11,000 of his workers got COVID-19 because they were forced back to work in unsafe and unhealthy plants as managers placed bets on how many would get sick. We must end this disgusting corporate greed."[5]

One of the best descriptions of this reality was from Daniel Hermes on Facebook:

> I have noticed, on airplanes in the past six months, that they always make an announcement, soon after takeoff, about no longer being able to serve meals on the plane, due to Covid19. Then a little while later, they serve a meal to all the people at the front of the plane.
>
> I kid you not.
>
> I have watched this probably 20 times, this year—and I have come to see it as a microcosm of what is happening all over the world.
>
> The poor people are being told all the things they are no longer allowed to do—"for their safety". . . while the rich are still allowed to do basically everything.
>
> The small businesses are all being strangled into Bankruptcy and Oblivion—while the large businesses are being dubbed "Essential," and watching more and more funds funneled into their accounts.
>
> To pretend that there is no classism going on here, is to have one's head in the sand.[6]

One could add to this that not only are those in first class able to do as they desire, but when anyone in coach complains, those in first class have the prerogative to vilify those complaining as selfishly courting the death of themselves and others.

In my view, the ire people have had about the handling of the pandemic should have been directed upward toward the profiteers in first class and beyond rather than toward working people. Just acknowledging that people of color were especially impacted by COVID-19 and attributing this to the specter of a vague "systematic racism" rather than to the struggles and exploitation of the working class, as was so often done, is not, in my view, very helpful. Indeed, I believe this obscures more than it illuminates.

Even more concerning is the utter shutdown of debate about the necessity and utility of the pandemic lockdowns that, no one denies, have ravaged the economy, caused the loss of millions of jobs, many likely permanently, and condemned millions worldwide to poverty and starvation. Indeed, the UN estimates that more people will die from the hunger resulting from the lockdowns than from COVID-19 itself.[7] In addition, the lockdowns, according to the CDC, have led to a steep increase in depression, drug and alcohol use, and even suicide.[8] The lockdowns have also caused people to forgo, either voluntarily or not, much-needed healthcare for life-threatening, but non-COVID-19, illnesses, such as cancer, strokes, and heart disease.[9]

In short, the lockdowns have themselves exacted a huge cost in terms of life, well-being, and happiness, and they will exact a much greater cost as tens of millions in this country are poised to be evicted from their homes[10]—the homes they were supposed to stay locked down in. And yet, there has not been open and honest debate about the relative cost and benefits of the lockdowns, with people being accused of being selfish and cruel—of wanting to kill their grandparents, for example—for even raising this issue.

One of the few leftist publications to question all this is *Dissident Voice*, which opined:

> Now, recent polls suggest that half of Americans reject the idea of more lockdowns. That's a lot of people. Yet very few of those

people speak up, or post opinions on social media. And this is an interesting phenomenon. There is an enormous fear of being called "conspiracy theorist" or "anti vaxxer" or "Covid truther," etc. There is a tacit assault on the truth itself embedded in this stigmatizing. A pathologization of the search for truth. And this seems something that has arisen out of the culture of social media.

One understands that if the law says wear a mask or be fined, then people will wear the mask. But there is no law (yet) in expressing a dissenting opinion. . . . Of course, major social media platforms like Twitter and Facebook are perilously close to outright censorship now. One is labeled dangerous if one questions the narrative on the pandemic. Simply pointing out that the fatality rate is extremely low despite all the lurid headlines is cause for censorship on Facebook. Stating facts has become, quite literally, dangerous.[11]

I myself have witnessed such "canceling" of people, including good friends, on social media simply because they asked honest questions about the measures being taken to handle the pandemic. This, despite the fact that many quite reputable people have themselves questioned whether the lockdowns were necessary or even effective in combating COVID-19.

For example, the World Health Organization (WHO) has cautioned about the use of lockdowns, with the WHO's Special Envoy on COVID-19, Dr. David Nabarro, stating, "The only time we believe a lockdown is justified is to buy you time to reorganize, regroup, rebalance your resources; protect your health workers who are exhausted, . . . But by and large, we'd rather not do it."[12] And, given that hundreds of hospitals, even during the height of the COVID-19 pandemic, had so few patients that they were forced to lay off staff, with some even closing their doors permanently,[13] lockdowns would certainly be contraindicated by this advice.

The *Wall Street Journal* explains that, five months into the pandemic, many experts indeed question whether the lockdowns made sense after all. As the *WSJ* explains:

The evidence suggests lockdowns were an overly blunt and econom-ically costly tool. They are politically difficult to keep in place for long enough to stamp out the virus. The evidence also points to alternative strategies that could slow the spread of the epidemic at much less cost. As cases flare up throughout the US, some experts are urging policy makers to pursue these more targeted restrictions and interventions rather than another crippling round of lockdowns.[14]

And indeed, as the BBC reported in October 2020, 6,000 health experts signed a letter urging governments not to engage in further lockdowns, urging that steps be taken to protect the vulnerable while healthy people be permitted to live their lives.[15] While the BBC also indicated that other health experts questioned this advice, the point is that there is reasonable disagreement on this subject—certainly wor-thy of discussion instead of vilification or cancellation. And yet, as far as I could tell, little such discussion was had or even permitted, except on penalty of being vilified as a death monger.

The other tragic impact of the lockdowns has been the historic setback to women's gains in the workplace. Amanda Taub explained this well in a *New York Times* article titled "Pandemic Will 'Take Our Women 10 Years Back' in the Workplace."[16] As Taub explains:

> As if working mothers did not have enough to worry about, experts are now sounding the alarm that progress toward gender equal-ity may be the latest in a long list of casualties of the coronavirus pandemic.
>
> Substantial research has shown that most professional gender gaps are in fact motherhood gaps: women without children are much closer to parity with men when it comes to salaries and pro-motions, but mothers pay a large career penalty.
>
> Women tend to take on more of the burdens of caring for chil-dren and the family. To go to work, they need someone to help with that care. But fathers have been slow to change their behavior. *And without subsidies, private childcare can be prohibitively expensive* [emphasis added].

Workplaces already tend to penalize women who choose to work fewer hours or need more flexibility, and that, too, is proving to be exacerbated in the pandemic.

While Taub blames the pandemic itself for this setback to women, she at least alludes to the true cause—the lockdowns (in particular, the shutdown of schools) combined with the total lack of childcare subsidies and/or government-provided childcare, which many other governments in the world provide.

Of course, the biggest problem with all of the finger-pointing about whether people were properly social distancing and mask wearing is that this places all of the burden on fighting and enduring the pandemic on the individual, when in fact it should have been placed on society as a whole and on the government. Thus, while the government should have made it much easier for everyone to socially distance by making sure that everyone had COVID-19 tests, proper protective equipment, soap, toilet paper, and hand sanitizer, and while it should have been demanded to do so, this was barely discussed and certainly never demanded.

As longtime leftist journalist Jeffrey St. Claire wrote on a Facebook post, imagine a country (and there are some in the world, by the way) in which such things were mailed or brought to your door every week. That would have been a big help, as would have been an adequate basic income, and free healthcare and daycare.

What also would have helped is a national program of testing and tracing, mask wearing, and social distance guidelines implemented and enforced in all 50 states as if we were an actual nation. Apparently, such a program had been developed but then was scrapped by the White House when, at least at the outset of the pandemic, it looked like it was "blue" states that were getting hit hardest by COVID-19.[17] And so, for political gain, a life-saving program was never rolled out. It is hard to see this as anything short of willful murder.

In short, individuals should not have been left to their own devices to navigate a historic pandemic, and they should not have been condemned when they made the "wrong" choices. And yet, they have been, and that is why our country has done worse than any other in handling it.

Sadly, few in this country, and few who took to the streets in the summer of 2020, raised such issues and such demands, and this was possibly the biggest failing of the ostensible left in the US.

One of the notable exceptions to this came from mostly "deplorable" members of the working class who, in April 2020, protested General Electric to be able to make ventilators for use by people stricken with COVID-19—a demand necessitated by the failure of the "free market" and the government to guarantee the provision of such equipment. As *USA Today* explained, "GE workers staged a series of protests . . . demanding that they be able to make critically needed ventilators to help patients stricken with COVID-19. Workers demonstrated at factories in Schenectady, New York, Dallas, and Salem, Virginia, as well as the company's aviation facility in Lynn, Massachusetts."[18]

In addition, in the early weeks of the pandemic and continuing throughout 2020, there were strikes by workers at places like Amazon, Whole Foods, Walmart, Target, Instacart, and Trader Joe's over the compromising safety conditions they were being placed in by their employers.[19] These protests, with specific demands for better safety equipment, sick leave policies, and hazard pay, were multiracial and pointed the finger at the right targets—the wealthy corporations, which were only getting richer during the pandemic—and had clear objectives that could save lives.

Moreover, if done on a large scale, such strikes throughout the country would have struck fear in corporate America and could have led to real and concrete social change, including, but not limited to, much more health and income support for workers during the pandemic. The BLM protests, on the other hand, were not feared by corporate America one bit, as demonstrated by the fact that nearly every major corporation vocally expressed support for these protests and even gave huge donations to efforts purporting to advance racial justice. As *New York Magazine* explained in June 2020, "our nation's top consumer-facing firms have been 'woke' for a while now. But over the past three weeks of anti-racist protest, our brands have taken their allyship to the next level. Now, McDonald's is cutting checks to the

Urban League, Jeff Bezos is castigating white-supremacist Amazon customers over Instagram, and the Walton family is on the cusp of rebranding as the vanguard of the Third Reconstruction."[20] In short, while the "woke" revolution will not be televised (actually it is, quite a bit), it will receive corporate sponsorship.

Of course, such corporations did all this, the same article noted, even while, in practice, breaking unions and contributing to racial inequities in our society. And they did so for the cynical purpose of building their consumer base among the type of young, urban professionals who aspire to being "woke." But again, in this postmodern world, it is appearances that matter beyond all else.

Sadly, the worker strikes received nowhere the attention, either from the left or mainstream media, nor public support that the BLM protests did. And you better believe that they received no support, moral or otherwise, from the corporate world. Indeed, had the demand over the summer of 2020 been "General Strike," "Workers Unite," or "Socialism Now," these protests would have been condemned as traitorous by companies and media alike.

As I write these words in December 2020, around 250 million workers and farmers are striking and demonstrating in India, waving red flags with hammers and sickles, in what may very well be the largest strike in human history.[21] Of course, the mainstream media is barely covering this historic event either, not wanting to give anyone in this country any bright ideas.

And why the difference between the corporate support for BLM and its antipathy toward unions and united worker activity? Because the 1 percent in this country want to keep their hold over a disproportionate share of the wealth. Unions and strikes threaten their hold over this wealth, while racial inclusion and diversity in the workplace and even in the ranks of the rich—goals I obviously view as laudable and positive—do not. They want as much wealth as possible; they really do not care how the scraps left over for the rest of us are apportioned.

And indeed, neither the BLM protests nor the pandemic did anything to slow down the profit-making machine of the capitalist class one bit. As *Market Watch* explained, "Economic inequality was already one of the pressing issues of our time long before the coronavirus led to what Brookings describes as 'the most unequal [recession] in modern US history.' Nowadays, with the economy reeling, the old adage that 'rich get richer' has never been more pronounced, data shows, as the most vulnerable among us have taken the brunt of the pandemic."[22] And so, all was as it should be.

One of the few people whom I saw expressing frustration about all this was Boots Riley, famed Black radical activist, film director, and rapper. Thus, in November 2020, in an interview on the show "Bad Faith" with Briahna Joy Gray, Riley explained that he tried to get progressives and leftists interested in these strikes, but to no avail.[23] Riley, relying on statistics from Paydayreport.com and its "strike tracker," explained that there were over 900 wildcat strikes, many involving workers of color, between March and the end of November 2020—one of the largest strike waves in US history. When I checked the "strike tracker" in early December 2020, the figure it gave was over 1,100 such strikes.

One strike, Riley noted, was that of the International Longshore Workers Union (ILWU), a union with a strong left-wing history, which shut down the entire West Coast for a day in support of Black Lives Matter. As Riley notes, the hope of the ILWU was that this strike would trigger a greater and more expansive strike wave throughout the United States. But again, the strike got little traction from the media and from a left, Riley laments, more interested in "taking it to the streets" than in shutting down the economy by withholding labor. As Riley notes with disapproval, the left in fact has not been interested in class struggle since the late 1960s. What could have been—the uniting of the strike waves with the protests throughout the US—never was, and both Riley and Briahna Joy Gray expressed sadness that much of the energy of the BLM demonstrations was thereby squandered.

Still, in all fairness, the "woke" did unite to demand that Trader Joe's, regardless of what it did for or to its workers, change the names of some of their ethnic food items that were deemed to be racist (e.g., Trader José, Trader Ming's, Arabian Joe's, Trader Giotto's, and Trader Joe San).[24] It's always important, after all, to prioritize demands, which really won't help anybody.

Sadly, the self-described "left" who took to the streets day after day had few concrete demands at all, just as the Occupy Movement before it was devoid of demands, and that is a big reason it inevitably failed. As explained by the late leftist journalist Andre Vltchek in an article in which he criticized the 2020 protests as lacking any truly revolutionary potential:

> There are many explanations for this. One of them: regime created society built on extreme individualism, selfishness, and shallow perception of the world. To organize, to commit, actually requires at least some discipline, effort, and definitely great dedicated effort to learn (about the world, a person, or a movement) and to work hard for a better world. It is not easy to become a revolutionary when one is positioned on a couch, or a gym, or while banging for hours every day into a smartphone.
>
> The results are sad. Anarchism, consisting of countless fragmented approaches, is increasingly popular, but it will definitely not change the country.[25]

Vltchek gave the example of the CHOP—a short-lived police-free zone in Seattle that purported to be a zone of revolutionary foment—as emblematic of these shortcomings. As Vltchek wrote, "When leaders of the 'revolutionary commune' in Seattle were approached by sympathetic journalists and asked about their goals, they could not answer. These were, undoubtfully, people with good intentions, outraged by racism, and by the killing of innocent people. But do they have plans, strategy, an organization to overthrow the system which is literally choking billions of lives on all continents? Definitely not!"

Meanwhile, as the working class, left to fend for itself, was condemned for trying to flout the questionable lockdown measures, we witnessed something quite strange—the carving out of one, single exception to this condemnation. Thus, while it was unsafe, we were scolded, for children to go to schools, for adults to go to work, for families to go to church or to the beach, and for people to protest (in relatively small numbers) for the permission to engage in just such activities, it was safe, and indeed in the interest of public health, to engage in massive Black Lives Matter (BLM) protests day after day. Indeed, BLM protesters, including the few who engaged in rioting and looting, received an almost religious dispensation from the lockdown rules that governed everyone else.

While it is true, as I witnessed during my own participation in several of these protests in Pittsburgh, that the vast majority of BLM protestors wore masks, there was absolutely no social distancing, and masks were often pulled down for comfort in the intense summer heat or by people wishing to address the crowd.

Certainly, small funerals, meetings with family and friends, and even conducting most small businesses, at least with masks and social distancing, would be safer than a lot of these giant protests. For example, what is the difference between the BLM protests, which both Governor Cuomo and Mayor DeBlasio publicly sanctioned and praised, and the Orthodox Jewish funerals in Brooklyn, which the police were sent in to break up? Seemingly nothing, as explained by the Jewish paper *Haaretz* on April 30, 2020:

> Two days after New York City's mayor called out "the Jewish community" when vowing to crack down on gatherings, city police intervened in another funeral in a Jewish neighborhood, resulting in a tense scene and at least one arrest. . . .
>
> Dozens of police officers directed a large group of visibly Orthodox Jews away from the area, *many of whom wore masks and stood in the street* [emphasis added]. Some were crowded together behind yellow police tape. . . .
>
> The episode comes two days after a funeral for a Hasidic rabbi in Williamsburg drew at least a thousand people to the streets in violation of social distancing rules imposed to stop the spread of the coronavirus, which has hit the city's Orthodox Jewish population hard.
>
> Despite the New York Police Department's knowledge of the funeral beforehand, the crowd grew unmanageable and ultimately was dispersed by police, who issued 12 summonses in the process.
>
> The event also drew the censure of Mayor Bill de Blasio, who came to the scene to help disperse the crowds and later addressed

"the Jewish community" on Twitter, saying that "the time for warnings has passed."[26]

As the article explains, "[t]he mayor was widely criticized for singling out the Jewish community," and this seems understandable, given the double standards being applied to their gatherings and to the daily BLM protests. In other instances, some Brooklyn Jews, in an obvious attempt to point out this disparate treatment, chanted "Jewish Lives Matter" as police broke up their gatherings.[27]

Ultimately, while the mainstream media pushed the line about the inexplicable safety of BLM protests quite hard, and while there was nearly no questioning later about whether the surge in COVID-19 cases a few weeks after the protests began could be attributed to the protests, there were a couple of stories that admitted that there probably was such a connection.

One such article appeared in the *New York Times*, which otherwise faithfully parroted the party line and was titled "Are Protests Dangerous? What Experts Say May Depend on Who's Protesting What."[28] As this article explained,

> As the pandemic took hold, most epidemiologists have had clear proscriptions in fighting it: No students in classrooms, no in-person religious services, no visits to sick relatives in hospitals, no large public gatherings.
>
> So when conservative anti-lockdown protesters gathered on state capitol steps in places like Columbus, Ohio, and Lansing, Mich., in April and May, epidemiologists scolded them and forecast surging infections. . . .
>
> And then the brutal killing of George Floyd by the police in Minneapolis on May 25 changed everything.
>
> Soon the streets nationwide were full of tens of thousands of people in a mass protest movement that continues to this day, with demonstrations and the toppling of statues. And rather than decrying mass gatherings, more than 1,300 public health officials signed a May 30 letter of support, and many joined the protests.

That reaction, and the contrast with the epidemiologists' earlier fervent support for the lockdown, gave rise to an uncomfortable question: Was public health advice in a pandemic dependent on whether people approved of the mass gathering in question? To many, the answer seemed to be "yes."

The article then went on to quote epidemiologists who sheepishly admitted their hypocrisy and lack of professionalism when it came to giving advice on this subject. Meanwhile, Fox News (for its own, obvious political reasons) printed a story reporting that "Several big-city mayors and top officials are acknowledging that weeks of anti-police protests and riots may have contributed to surging coronavirus rates, weeks after Democrats and even some epidemiologists openly encouraged Black Lives Matter allies to demonstrate in the streets. In public statements and interviews with Fox News this weekend, officials in Los Angeles, Seattle, and Miami-Dade County, Fla., have indicated that some link between protests and new cases was at least possible."[29]

To me, it is quite obvious, especially given the timing of the COVID-19 surge in the summer of 2020, that the BLM protests had to play some role in this surge. But besides the two articles I cite above, one would be hard-pressed to see any indication that this was so. Indeed, my own Google search shows that three weeks into the BLM protests, the media just stopped asking any questions about this possible connection, apparently because the answer was not what they wanted.

Meanwhile, when the "deplorables" gathered en masse in Tulsa (for a Trump rally) and in Sturgis, South Dakota (for a huge motorcycle rally), the mainstream media immediately condemned these people as "super spreaders," and they did somersaults to back up their severe judgment. Thus, when the San Diego State University's Center for Health Economics & Policy Studies published a study showing that there was not indeed a COVID-19 surge after the Tulsa rally, the media simply ignored this.[30] But then, when the same researchers concluded, based upon very shaky grounds, that the Sturgis rally resulted in the significant spread of the virus, causing, they claimed, an increase of over a quarter million new cases, and the resulting billions of dollars in healthcare costs, the media had a field day, licking their lips at the prospect that these mostly white working-class bikers were as dumb and selfish as everyone assumes.

However, the editorial board of the *Wall Street Journal* would later take this study, and the media's reaction to it to, task.[31] As the *WSJ* explained, even if it were true that the Sturgis, SD, rally led to the increase in cases claimed by the study, it did not appear to lead to a significant rise in mortality or hospital visits. As the *WSJ* reported, "South Dakota still has among the lowest per capita death rates in the country (19 per 100,000) and fewer deaths and cases per capita than its neighbors Nebraska and North Dakota. Covid patients currently occupy 3 percent of state hospital beds and 6 percent of intensive-care units. So it seems that attendees at least didn't expose the society's vulnerable to the virus even if they were putting themselves at risk." In other words, even if the researchers were correct in their conclusions, it still appears that the bikers were not as reckless and stupid as they were judged to be.

Moreover, the *WSJ* questions the ultimate conclusions of these researchers:

> Where the study jumps off the rails is linking all of the relative increase in virus cases in counties with attendees compared to those without rally participants. The modelers multiplied the percent increase in cases for counties with attendees by their pre-rally cumulative cases to get a total of 263,708 additional cases—266,796 including South Dakota's increase.
>
> But many "high inflow" counties like Los Angeles, Maricopa (Arizona), Clark (Nevada) and El Paso were experiencing flare-ups before the rally. These counties may have shared other characteristics like higher population density that contributed to their increases. There could be other "endogenous" variables—for instance, counties with more people who attended the motorcycle rally may also have had populations less observant of social distancing.
>
> The study's authors nonetheless assign each of these 266,796 COVID-19 cases a public-health cost of $46,000—ergo $12.2

billion—though the vast majority of all virus cases are mild or moderate. Talk about a case study in statistical overreach—and double standards.

At the same time, as the *WSJ* points out, it has been verboten to even question whether the BLM protests, attended by around 30 million people around the country over several months (as contrasted to the half a million bikers who went to Sturgis for one weekend), might have led to some increase in COVID-19.

Again, I myself participated in some of the BLM protests, so I am not at all saying that they should not have taken place. But what I do find troubling is that, just as we on the left criticize the right for politicizing science and public health issues, the ostensible left is also guilty of this, and it is just as galling when they do it. Indeed, when the liberal establishment compromises its own credibility on issues of science as they have done in this instance, it makes it difficult to impossible to then demand that the right "listen to science," for example in the case of climate change or COVID-19 itself.

Imagine the small shopkeeper who lost his/her business during the pandemic, or the daughter or son who was unable to visit their dying parent or gather for the funeral, or the many children who lost many months of education and socialization being told, in essence, that their sacrifices were pointless; that only those protesting certain issues were entitled to do as they pleased during the pandemic; that possibly these protesters were magically protected because of the rightness of their convictions. Many such people should have been outraged to be told such things, as we all should have been. We should be outraged because these messages were not true, were not fact-based, and were not fair. And I for one do not wish to live in a world in which truth and fairness no longer matter.

What's more, going out of one's way to vilify working-class people as somehow morally and intellectually inferior simply does not help the goal of social change. These are people we should be reaching out to in order to find our common ground in challenging our real enemies—the 1 percent who are taking everything from us and who are destroying our Earth.

These are also the people we could work with in fighting for social benefits that would help everyone in the 99 percent to survive the pandemic without having to risk their lives. Thus, demanding a national program of paid sick leave and vacation, national healthcare (a.k.a., "Medicare for All"), and a universal basic income, especially so that no one would have to make the choice between starving or risking getting COVID-19—a very real dilemma that many front-line workers have had to face[32]—would make much more sense than condemning people who have been judged to make the wrong choice in this regard.

There is actually some historical precedent for the success of linking the struggles of the poor from all backgrounds. Thus, Michael Harrington, one of the founders of Democratic Socialists of America (DSA), successfully advocated for the modern-day welfare programs to lift the poor out of poverty. He famously did so in his book *The Other America*, which was read by John F. Kennedy, who was inspired by this book to begin what came to be known as "The Great Society" and "War on Poverty" programs under his successor, Lyndon Johnson.[33]

As the *New York Times* explained,[34] Harrington woke up US leaders and middle-class America by revealing a world unknown to them at that time—a world that existed in the cities, the farmlands, and Appalachia alike. As the *Times* related:

> Harrington argued that American poverty constituted "a separate culture, another nation, with its own way of life." He elaborated on this idea in *The Other America: Poverty in the United States*, published in the spring of 1962. It was a short work with a simple thesis: poverty was both more extensive and more tenacious than most Americans assumed. An "invisible land" of the poor existed in rural isolation or in crowded slums where middle-class visitors seldom ventured. "That the poor are invisible is one of the most important things about them," Harrington wrote. "They are not simply neglected and forgotten. . . . What is much worse, they are not seen."
>
> Harrington argued that poor Americans were "people who lack education and skill, who have bad health, poor housing, low levels of aspiration and high levels of mental distress. . . . And if

one problem is solved, and the others are left constant, there is little gain." Instead of relying on a rising tide of affluence to lift all
boats, he argued, America needed a broad program of "remedial
action"—a "comprehensive assault on poverty."

Harrington's revelations about US poverty, particularly about poverty
among white people in Appalachia—a poverty few realized existed
then and that many have now forgotten still exists—shocked the con-
science of the country.

While the "War on Poverty" unleashed by President Johnson,
in part inspired by Harrington's exposé, was quite successful, it was
short-lived—in part because of the Vietnam War that sucked both
resources and enthusiasm out of the project, and because the American
political elite would shortly turn against the antipoverty program. It
was Republican and Democrat alike who dismantled this program,
beginning with Ronald Reagan and continuing into the Clinton
Administration, which lived up to its vow to "end welfare as we know
it."

As a result, the poor still live among us in the millions, and their
number grows as the pandemic has spread and as the resulting economic crisis has deepened. And yet, there was very little activism
around such issues in the summer of 2020, just when it was sorely
needed. To the contrary, the demand for social goods for the poor and
working class was largely derailed during this time.

An excellent opinion piece on this subject appeared in the *New
York Times* under the title "The Second Defeat of Bernie Sanders." In
that piece, Ross Douthat writes,[35]

> Throughout his career, Sanders has stood for the proposition that
> left-wing politics lost its way after the 1970s by letting what should
> be its central purpose—the class struggle, the rectification of eco-
> nomic inequality, the war against the "millionaires and billion-
> aires"—be obscured by cultural battles and displaced by a pro-busi-
> ness, pro-Wall Street economic program . . .

Sanders himself has been a victim of such "cultural battles," and oftentimes unfairly. Thus, the establishment Democratic leaders, such as Hillary Clinton and Elizabeth Warren, attacked Bernie for allegedly failing to rein in what came to be known as the "Bernie Bros"—a group of mostly white men on social media who, we were told, were aggressively trolling female candidates. However, as an article on *Salon* explains, there is hard evidence

> reaped from studying hundreds of thousands of interactions online—that reveals the Bernie Bro myth as, well, a myth. Jeff Winchell, a computational social scientist and graduate student at Harvard University, crunched the numbers on tweet data and found that Sanders' supporters online behave the same as everyone else. Winchell used what is called a sentiment analysis, a technique used both in the digital humanities and in e-commerce, to gauge emotional intent from social media data.[36]

As the article continues, "'Bernie followers act pretty much the same on Twitter as any other follower,'" Winchell says of his results. "'There is one key difference that Twitter users and media don't seem to be aware of . . . Bernie has a lot more Twitter followers than Twitter followers of other Democrat›s campaigns,' he added, noting that this may be partly what helps perpetuate the myth."

According to Fairness and Accuracy in Reporting (FAIR), during the 2020 campaign, an often-utilized "line of attack [was] the revival of the 'Bernie Bro' as a means to discredit the Sanders campaign. A central trope of the 2016 campaign, based on anecdotal evidence and repeated endlessly by Clinton supporters and journalists, the idea that Sanders supporters are predominantly white, male, and viciously offensive on social media lingers on—despite its utter lack of basis in reality." As FAIR notes, "[i]n fact, a March 2016 study found that, among voters, Sanders supporters were perceived as much less 'aggressive and/or threatening online' (16 percent) than were Clinton supporters (30 percent), who in turn were perceived as much less so than Trump supporters (57 percent)."[37]

Still, the result of such attacks was to effectively cancel the most progressive Democratic Presidential hopeful in many years and may, ironically, have been the nail in the coffin for his progressive agenda. As Ross Douthat in the *New York Times* explains:

> Under these strange coronavirus conditions, we're watching a different sort of insurgency challenge or change liberalism, one founded on an intersectional vision of left-wing politics that never came naturally to Sanders. Rather than Medicare for All and taxing plutocrats, the rallying cry is racial justice and defunding the police. Instead of finding its nemeses in corporate suites, the intersectional revolution finds them on antique pedestals and atop the cultural establishment.[38]

As Douthat notes, "[t]he fact that corporations are 'outdistancing' even politicians, as [intersectionality theorist Kimberlé] Crenshaw puts it, in paying fealty to anti-racism is perhaps the tell. It's not that corporate America is suddenly deeply committed to racial equality; even for woke capital, the capitalism comes first. Rather, it's that anti-racism as a cultural curriculum, a rhetoric of re-education, is relatively easy to fold into the mechanisms of managerialism, under the tutelage of the human resources department. The idea that you need to retrain your employees so that they can work together without microaggressing isn't Marxism, cultural or otherwise; it's just a novel form of Fordism, with white-fragility gurus in place of efficiency experts."

Ajamu Baraka, of the Black Alliance for Peace, also expressed disappointment over the fact that the protests over the summer did not address, and indeed seemed to push aside, the most pressing problems facing all Americans, but especially African Americans, right now. For his part, Baraka attributed this to what he believed to be the cooptation of this protest movement by corporate America, including the corporate media, which was able to couch these protests in purely racial and intersectional terms.

As Baraka explained in an article in Black Agenda Report:

Throughout the first few months of COVID-19 pandemic in April and into May, stories started to surface that revealed how environmental racism, neoliberal privatization that devastated the public health system, poverty, Black and Brown workers concentrated in the lowest rungs of the employment ladder—the "essential" workers—had created the conditions that made the virus a plague for us.

But those stories just about disappeared for several months, beginning at the end of May. And what happened? George Floyd.

The streets were filled with righteous indignation demanding "justice" for Floyd and correctly linking the other cases of police violence such as the execution of Breonna Taylor. Yet, while the marches demanded that we say the names of Floyd and Taylor and remember Tamir Rice and Sandra Bland—out of sight in run-down nursing homes, overcrowded hospitals, and alone in apartments, our folks were dying in silence. The movement would not claim them; would not say their names or, it seemed—fight for them.

And even as the lines for food extended for miles, the unemployment check stopped coming and people were driven into the streets by landlords released from moratoriums against evictions. Somehow these crimes of capital did not fit the definition of an assault on our people. It was as if this was neither a "racial justice" issue nor a crime of racialized capitalism.[39]

Many of us saw with frustration exactly what Ajamu Baraka describes above, including local BLM chapters who are now calling for accountability, both political and fiduciary, from the national organization—an organization flush with tens of millions of dollars in donations that never made it to the local branches.

As Baraka opines, "It is clear to me that the chapters raising questions about BLM from the frontlines are doing so not out of a desire to destroy but to strengthen the movement by generating this discussion. Will it be a tough conversation? Yes. Because partially obscured by the liberal appropriation of intersectionality is the issue of class that the largely petit bourgeois classed-based leadership of the movement will not even acknowledge, let alone struggle with." That is to say, Baraka believes that there are many questions that need to be asked about the

BLM movement, and that they should be asked and answered. That is how a movement is able to progress, after all.

Meanwhile, over the summer of 2020 and in the face of massive street demonstrations that sadly abandoned all questions of economic justice, the DNC voted overwhelmingly to exclude Medicare for All from its platform, despite its popularity with the electorate who favors this program by huge numbers. Thus, according to surveys taken in the spring of 2020, 69 percent of voters support such a program.[40] The Democrats, along with their Republican counterparts, also failed to pass a second COVID-19 stimulus package in the summer and fall, even as the elections were nearing, apparently not feeling much if any pressure to do so.

Imagine a movement that tapped into the well of support and the well of desperate need for social programs as opposed to focusing on the hugely unpopular demand to "defund the police." I certainly have no problem with arguing that we should take money from policing, and from the military as well, to fund social programs. Indeed, I am all for this. But sadly, there was very poor articulation of this redistributive goal in the protests. It is almost as if those demanding first and foremost to "defund the police," while telling everyone curious about what exactly this meant to figure it out for themselves, wanted to fail. And in a big way, they did, at least in terms of the political goal of the protests that seemed linked to the fate of the Democratic Party in the elections. Judging from the Democratic Party Convention, which openly and often embraced the BLM protests, the Party certainly believed that its goals were somehow linked with those of BLM, at least symbolically.

But it would seem that the BLM protests, as narrowly focused as they were on one, poorly drafted slogan, helped Trump and the Republicans do as well as they did in the 2020 election—an election that many believed would produce a "Blue wave" for the Democrats, but that ultimately did not. Moreover, these protests have also failed, apparently, to push Biden toward the left, as many hoped would happen, as demonstrated by his cabinet picks, which have been drawn from the old neoliberal trough and which include no one from the progressive wing of the Democratic Party.

A Democratic pollster, Danny Barefoot, found just that through focused exit polling. As he explains, "[o]ne of the major takeaways from my discussion with these voters was their distaste for the slogan 'defund the police'. While 80 percent agreed racism exists in the criminal justice system and 60 percent had a favorable view of Black Lives Matter, only one participant agreed we should 'defund the police'. Another participant was exasperated, 'That is crazier than anything Trump has ever said.'" And Barefoot found that trying to explain this slogan was to no avail:

> We tried to explain the actual policies behind the slogan "defund the police". We noted that many activists who use this phrase simply want to reduce police funding and reallocate some of it to social services. One woman interrupted us to say "that is not what defund the police means, I'm sorry. It means they want to defund the police." "I didn't like being lied to about this over and over again," added another woman. "Don't try and tell me words don't mean what they say," she continued. The rest of the group nodded their heads in agreement. . . .
>
> We followed up by asking if participants supported reducing police funding and reallocating it to social services and other agencies to reduce police presence in community conflict. Seventy per cent said they would support that proposal.
>
> It is almost beyond parody that progressive activists would build popular consensus on police reform only to slap on a slogan that is deeply unpopular with voters and doesn't accurately communicate our policy goals. We don't want to abolish the police. We don't want to zero out funding for law enforcement. So we should forcefully reject slogans that imply we do. We should instead run on the broadly popular policies behind the slogan. It's policy that changes lives. Unpopular framing that makes reform harder does favors to no one but those who want to protect the status quo.[41]

Despite what is very clear—that the "defund the police" slogan was a horrible error that turned off huge swaths of the American electorate and derailed other, more pressing and popular calls for reform—I still see many people on social media and elsewhere defending this slogan to the hilt and attempting to cancel those who are questioning it. In this latter-day religion, apparently, such religious incantations are sacred and must never be questioned, even as they lead us down the road to perdition.

Another insightful article appeared in *The Guardian* newspaper and was titled "Democrats fail to persuade swaths of rural America's heartlands." As this article explains,

> America's rural heartland stuck firmly with Donald Trump on Tuesday, dashing Joe Biden's hope of a decisive victory that would have allowed him to claim he had reunited the country . . .
>
> Results across the Midwest showed the US still firmly divided as Trump again won a solid victory in Iowa, a state that twice voted for Barack Obama, and the Republicans held on to crucial Senate seats targeted by the Democrats.[42]

Given that Iowa twice voted for Barack Obama, it is hard to argue that the Iowa electorate's pivot toward Trump was motivated by racism, though many might be tempted to claim that. And indeed, there were other reasons for this move. First, as per usual, "the Democrats failed to persuade swaths of rural America that the party had much to offer them or was even paying attention to their communities and concerns."[43] Again, the Democrats have simply decided to shun the huge swath of the US known as "middle America," while Trump at least paid lip service to their concerns and actually took some affirmative steps intended to help rural farmers through trade policies with China and farm subsidies. In addition, as the *Guardian* also explained, the rural Midwest also believed "that Trump got it right when he opposed [pandemic] lockdowns as too economically damaging."

The *Guardian* noted that even in states that went to Biden, like Minnesota, the rural areas largely went to Trump. And again, this was because the electorate there felt that the Democratic Party had abandoned workers and farmers, once the backbone of the Democrats.

In an accompanying piece, the *Guardian* quoted one Minnesota mayor, Larry Cuffe:

> Cuffe, who twice voted for Barack Obama, is one of six mayors
> from a stretch of Minnesota mining country, known as the Iron
> Range, who turned their back on the Democratic party and signed
> a joint letter endorsing Trump even as the state is swinging behind
> the president's opponent, Joe Biden.
>
> The mayors said that after decades of voting for Democrats,
> they no longer regarded the party as advocating for workers.
>
> "Lifelong politicians like Joe Biden are out of touch with the
> working class, out of touch with what the country needs, and out of
> touch with those of us here on the Iron Range and in small towns
> like ours across our nation," they said.[44]

Again, it would be unfair to portray someone like Cuffe, who voted
twice for Obama, as a racist or reactionary.

And indeed, I happen to know quite a bit about the Minnesota Iron
Range that produced the Cuffes of the world. This is because the iron
miners in this region are all represented by the United Steelworkers
union that inherited them in the 1950s after merging with the Mine
Mill & Smelter Workers union (MMSW)—the union that represented these workers at the time of the merger. The MMSW, in turn,
was a radical union led by Communists. This union was famous not
only for its labor militancy, but also for its successes in integrating
the mines and battling racism. The struggles of the MMSW and its
mostly Latino members in the Southwest became the subject of one of
the most famous labor films of all time—*Salt of the Earth.*

The culture that developed in the Iron Range as a consequence
of the efforts of the MMSW was a radical and progressive one, and
one that would give rise to the "voice of a generation" (the 60s protest
generation) in the person of Robert Zimmerman—the favorite son of
Hibbing, Minnesota, who would come to be known as Bob Dylan.
The area around Hibbing gave rise to gay icon Judy Garland.

That the Democratic Party and its liberal base would turn their
back on these people says much about their lack of proper focus and
priorities and, frankly, their sheer ignorance. It also points to why,
I believe, they will keep failing. And, while the old adage says that

"there is no success like failure," Hibbing native Bob Dylan quite rightly added, "and failure is no success at all."

In the end, many living in the Iron Range voted for Trump, not because they are racist, but because they believed, and for good reason, that Trump helped save the mining industry in the region, at least temporarily through steel tariffs and the lifting of some environmental regulations,[45] something that the Democrats made no pretense of doing.

The other thing that apparently, and not surprisingly, impacted the way that those in "middle America" voted in the 2020 elections was the summer of protests and, in particular, the violence associated with them. As the *Guardian* explained,

> Democratic support for the Black Lives Matter protests following the police killing of George Floyd in Minneapolis in May also complicated Biden's campaign.
> Opinion polls showed two-thirds of voters supported BLM in the early weeks but that fell sharply as demonstrations, and at times rioting and looting, spread across the country and the movement led calls to "defund the police", widely if wrongly interpreted as a call to shut down police departments. The Trump campaign's attempts to paint Democrats as anti-police and the party of rioters played well in parts of the Midwest.[46]

As for Mayor Cuffe in the Iron Range, "he watched the protests and destruction in Minneapolis following the death of George Floyd, and what he regards as the Democrats complicity in it, with despair. He scoffs at the calls to defund the police. He's shocked that Minneapolis council passed an ordinance to dismantle the city's force."[47] Cuffe, while supporting police reform, believes that our violent nation needs police to keep order. Cuffe was also turned off by some of the tactics of the protesters, saying that "we are gravitating toward the actually erasing our entire history of the United States by pulling down these monuments."

Again, while people may disagree with the Cuffes of the world, those who want meaningful social change may want to at least listen to what they have to say and to try to find common ground with them—a common ground that I believe is there to find.

Another revelatory piece that every Democrat should read appeared in *Politico* in December 2020. In that piece, titled "Why Democrats Keep Losing Rural Counties Like Mine,"[48] Bill Hogseth, chair of the Dunn County Democratic Party in Wisconsin, explains why the persistent organizing he and his fellow Democrats did in the swing county of Dunn came to naught in the 2020 elections. As he relates, "after conversations with dozens of voters, neighbors, friends and family members in Dunn County, I've come to believe it is because the national Democratic Party has not offered rural voters a clear vision that speaks to their lived experiences. The pain and struggle in my community is real, yet rural people do not feel it is taken seriously by the Democratic Party."

As Hogseth explains, complete with photos:

> The signs of desperation are everywhere in communities like mine. A landscape of collapsed barns and crumbling roads. Main Streets with empty storefronts. The distant stare of depression in your neighbor's eyes. If you live here, it is impossible to ignore the depletion.
>
> Rural people want to share in America's prosperity, but the economic divide between rural and urban America has widened. Small-business growth has slowed in rural communities since the Great Recession, and it has only worsened with COVID-19. As capital overwhelmingly flows to metro areas, the small-town economy increasingly is dominated by large corporations: low-wage retailers like Dollar General or agribusiness firms that have no connection to the community.

For all of the feel-good liberal slogans in the cities about "farm-to-table" food and restaurant dining—a slogan that inevitably means you're going to be overcharged for your meal—this country has turned its back on the small farmers who create this food. As Hogesth explains, "[t]he source of our wealth is in the things we grow. But today, those things get shipped off into a vast global supply chain, where profits are siphoned off and little remains for us to save or invest. Farmers' share of every retail food dollar has fallen from about 50 percent in 1952 to 15 percent today."

The Democrats have offered absolutely nothing to reverse this situation, and most of the liberal/left in this country do not care. Ironically, while some of the protesters over the summer donned t-shirts and flew flags with the Communist hammer-and-sickle emblem, they simply do not care about the people who wield either the hammer or the sickle. Instead, they go home at night and watch *Hillbilly Elegy* on Netflix and wallow in the satisfaction that they are not like those people on the screen. They marvel at how those people, with all of their "white privilege," could be doing so poorly. And they wonder why those people don't see the world as they see it, and why they don't vote the way they should, and they hate them for it.

Meanwhile, *quelle surprise*, those few candidates who openly ran on a platform that included Medicare for All and other like social programs did very well in the 2020 elections. As the left-wing *In These Times* points out,

> While many had hoped that Election Day would result in a sweeping rebuke of Trump and Trumpism, neither a pandemic nor an economic recession were enough to deliver an overwhelming rejection. And although it's looking likely that Biden will eke out a victory, the 2020 election was in many ways a bust for the Democratic Party, which lost seats in the House and most likely did not win a majority in the Senate.
>
> But democratic socialism, popularized by near-presidential nominee Bernie Sanders (IVt.), had a much better night. The Democratic Socialists of America (DSA), an organization that boasts nearly 80,000 members nationwide, endorsed 29 candidates and 11 ballot initiatives, winning 20 and 8 respectively. There are now democratic socialist caucuses in 15 statehouses, including Montana [which ultimately went to Trump].[49]

And, as this article explains, all of the democratic socialists who won ran on platforms that included the very popular Medicare for All and a Green New Deal—that is, they actually offered people concrete benefits that could change their lives in positive ways. Again, there may be some very real lessons to learn from this.

The elections in my hometown of Pittsburgh were quite illuminating on this subject. One quite interesting election result was that involving progressive Democrat Sara Innamorato—a candidate endorsed by Bernie Sanders and one who supports policies like Medicare for All and affordable housing—who ran for a state office in some areas overlapping with that of the more conservative Democrat, Connor Lamb, who ran for a seat in the US House of Representatives.

As a local opinion piece pointed out, Innamorato outperformed "Lamb in the portion of their districts that overlap. This includes overwhelmingly white and suburban areas north of the Allegheny River—Aspinwall, Etna, Millvale, O'Hara, Reserve, Ross, Shaler, and Sharpsburg. Out of nearly 25,000 votes in the overlapping district, Innamorato received 321 more votes than Lamb and 358 more votes than the president-elect."[50] What this at least potentially shows is that people we may expect to be conservative will vote for a candidate who is actually offering them programs, even those associated with more liberal politicians, that they value. But instead of being willing to listen and converse with such voters, they are often simply written off as irredeemable.

One example of this cancellation of a huge swath of the American electorate can be found in the liberal *Atlantic* magazine. In his article titled "A Large Portion of the Electorate Chose the Sociopath," author Tom Nichols wrote, "[s]adly, the voters who said in 2016 that they chose Trump because they thought he was 'just like them' turned out to be right. Now, by picking him again, those voters are showing that they *are* just like him: angry, spoiled, racially resentful, aggrieved, and willing to die rather than ever admit that they were wrong."[51]

First, I must note that we as the American electorate are never given anything but the choice between sociopaths for President. For example, when you look at the destruction that Barack Obama wrought throughout the world, with Joe Biden at his side as Vice-President—e.g., his utter destruction of Libya, his massive drone bombing throughout the Middle East, his deportation of three million immigrants, and his aiding and abetting of Saudi Arabia in its geno-cidal war in Yemen—one would have to conclude that Obama is as much a sociopath as Trump. Really, it is just a matter of choosing which style of sociopath you might like—like being given the choice between the handsome and dapper Teddy Bundy on the one hand, or John Wayne Gacy, the "Clown Killer," on the other. Take your pick!

In addition, there is much that can be said against this vilification of the 75 million people who voted for Trump—a population greater than that of all of France. Probably a lot of these people are "angry" and "aggrieved," just as many who voted for Biden are angry and aggrieved, and rightfully so. We are living through tumultuous times in which the rich have gotten richer during a pandemic while the poor and working people have gotten poorer, and not by accident. Even as the election drew near, moreover, Congress could not even get it together to give another much-needed stimulus that was months overdue and that could have saved millions from eviction and hunger. If this is not enough to justify anger by all but the wealthiest among us, I don't know what is. But "spoiled"? "Spoiled" by whom? Again, all of us who actually work for a living have seen our living standards decline as a few have gotten superrich. And meanwhile, our government at all levels failed to pro-tect us from the coronavirus. Indeed, it did a worse job than any other government on Earth. Who indeed has been "spoiled" in this scenario?

And, of course, Nichols levels the claim against these millions that they are "willing to die" to justify their original decision to vote for Trump. I assume he is referring here to what appears to be many Trump voters' dismissal of the dangers of the pandemic and concom-itant refusal to take the necessary social distancing steps to prevent its spread. There may be some legitimate criticism here, but again, this criticism is quite selective.

Not only were we told that we did not have to socially distance if we engaged in BLM protests, but once Biden was declared the winner, liberals took to the streets in droves to celebrate, body to body, with wine and song. I did not hear or see any criticism of these people by the media pundits who so disdain the millions of Trump voters. To the contrary, the press seemed to revel in the Biden victory celebrations.

For example, Gia Kourlas, writing in our paper of record, the *New York Times*, related:

> In celebration of the victory of Joseph R. Biden Jr., New York City—and so many other cities across the country—found its groove. From that shimmering, unseasonably warm morning until well after dark, cars became boomboxes. Line dances sprouted up from nowhere. There were duets between strangers. Drivers, catching a bystander's eye, turned up the music to encourage a moment of free-spirited improvisation. (It was a window down kind of day.)
>
> The past few years have been exhausting. And when you factor in the past eight months of coronavirus lockdown, protests in the street and the election, many Americans are tightly wound. It felt right that collective stress, sleepless nights, frustration and fear would spill out of bodies and into the streets. And that it was genuine said something, too. This wasn't a performative response, but a gut reaction—a way to express churning emotions, most conspicuously joy, when words alone couldn't do the trick.[52]

This article was complete with photos of people dancing in the streets, many without masks.

I wholeheartedly agree with the positive feelings expressed about this revelry, but it seems hypocritical given how others, usually with the "wrong" political leanings, were condemned as psychopaths for engaging in similar—and in many cases more necessary—activities by the *NYT* and its ilk. Indeed, one New York City councilman complained that, as these celebrations went on unimpeded, NYC's finest were in Queens harassing a pottery store owner—a single Orthodox Jewish mother of five children—for allegedly flaunting lockdown rules by preparing craft kits to sell for the holiday.[53]

As for the claims by pundits like Tom Nichols in the *Atlantic* that all 75 million Trump voters are racist—or "racially resentful," as he put it—there is much evidence pointing to how unfair this characterization is, as well.

First of all, this simply ignores the fact that Trump had a significant share of Latino and African American support in the election.

As the *New York Post* related, "Team Trump and Republicans nation-wide made unprecedented inroads with Black and Hispanic voters. Nationally, preliminary numbers indicated that 26 percent of Trump's voting share came from nonwhite voters—the highest percentage for a GOP presidential candidate since 1960."[54] This means that over 18 million nonwhites voted for Trump. Indeed, the only demographic that Trump did worse with in 2020 than in 2016 was the dreaded white male voter.

And it appears that it was socioeconomic levels that accounted for such voting shifts more than race.

As the *Financial Times* explained, "The expectation that the long-term trend towards a more racially diverse America will play in Democrats' favor looks like it may be oversimplified," with data suggesting that "level of education is becoming a more important divide and is clashing with racial identity as a driver of voting patterns. College-educated non-white voters, who favor Democrats, were broadly unchanged in their voting patterns compared to 2016. But non-college educated minority voters increased their support for Mr. Trump from 20 per cent to 25 per cent."[55] The *FT* also notes that "Mr. Trump's relative success with Latino voters, particularly in Florida and Texas, demonstrates the fallacy of treating broad racial groups as blocs."

In addition, Trump's voters came disproportionately from areas of the country, largely rural, left behind by our economy. As *USA Today* noted,[56] "Trump's losing base of 2,497 counties represents just 29 percent of the economy." Meanwhile, Biden won in areas, largely urban, representing over 70 percent of the nation's gross domestic product, and these areas, in addition to certainly being more diverse, are also "far more . . . educated and white-collar professional."[57]

In other words, it is not all about race and racism, as we are so often told it is, and as it may be tempting to believe.

There were some other quite curious developments in the 2020 elections. For example, California, a liberal-leaning state that went easily for Joe Biden, also approved an antiworker and antiunion referendum (Proposition 22) that was pushed by Uber and Lyft, and that would allow these two companies to continue to treat their drivers as independent contractors, rather than employees.[58] This referendum, which was opposed by the union attempting to organize these very workers, guarantees that these workers will not have the legal right to organize.

This is but another example of the liberal tone deafness, if not outright hostility, to workers and workers' rights. It would seem that as long as better-off Californians can get their cheap rides on Uber and Lyft, and get their food delivered through these same companies as they comfortably nest during the lockdowns, the workers who serve them can just be damned.

Of course, Uber and Lyft made a point early during the George Floyd protests to publicly show their support for these protests and the BLM movement. And indeed, this was part of their strategy to push Proposition 22. As Cherri Murphy, an activist and Lyft driver based in Oakland, California, explained,

> They even spent part of their war chest convincing voters that it was racist to oppose the measure, a particular affront when 78 percent of drivers in San Francisco are people of color and 56 percent are immigrants. Lyft ran ads quoting Maya Angelou's "Lift up your eyes" poem, and Uber bought billboards stating "If you tolerate racism, delete Uber" to capitalize on the Black Lives Matter movement. The Prop 22 campaign touted the support of BLM Sacramento, only to retract it when the group's leader said she personally supported it but the group as a whole did not. All this while trying to strip a majority Black and brown workforce of fundamental labor rights.[59]

While many voters were fooled by this, the drivers themselves were not. As Cherri Murphy, who happens to be a Black woman, explains, the drivers are painfully aware that this Proposition, if left to stand, will not only prevent them from unionizing, but will also condemn them to poverty. As Murphy relates, this Proposition "promises substandard healthcare, a death sentence to many in the middle of a pandemic. We're promised a sub-minimum wage in the middle of a recession that an independent study showed would be as low as

$5.64 an hour—not the eventual $15 state minimum. We're given no family leave, no paid sick days, and no access to state unemployment compensation."

Meanwhile, the Biden-loving Californians voted against rent control, which might help poorer renters and save them from homelessness—a serious epidemic itself in California. As the UN Human Rights Council (HRC) explained with alarm in 2018, there are over 72,000 homeless in Los Angeles and San Francisco alone,[60] and this, of course, was prepandemic. Meanwhile, "[t]he criminalization of homeless individuals in cities that provide almost zero public toilets seems particularly callous. In June 2017, it was reported that the approximately 1,800 homeless individuals on Skid Row in Los Angeles had access to only nine public toilets. Los Angeles failed to meet even the minimum standards the United Nations High Commissioner for Refugees sets for refugee camps in the Syrian Arab Republic and other emergency situations." As the HRC further explained,

> Ever more demanding and intrusive regulations lead to infraction notices for the homeless, which rapidly turn into misdemeanors, leading to warrants, incarceration, unpayable fines and the stigma of a criminal conviction that in turn virtually prevents subsequent employment and access to most housing. Yet the authorities in cities such as Los Angeles and San Francisco often encourage this vicious circle. On Skid Row in Los Angeles, 14,000 homeless persons were arrested in 2016 alone, an increase of 31 percent over 2011, while overall arrests in the city decreased by 15 percent.

One might think that the famously liberal Californians might wish to prevent people from facing such a fate, particularly in the midst of a pandemic, but apparently not enough to vote for a measure that would keep their fellow citizens' rents down.

Similarly, Californians also voted against a measure that would have banned cash bail as a prerequisite to remaining out of jail pending trial—again, a measure that would have benefited poor people, and especially poor people of color.[61] This measure, rejected by Californians, could indeed be truly transformative for poor in California. Again, the HRC has condemned our nation's current system of cash bail, explaining that the system, which

> affects the poor almost exclusively is that of setting large bail bonds for a defendant to seeks to go free pending trial. Some 11 million people are admitted to local jails annually, and on any given day more than 730,000 people are being held, of whom almost two thirds are awaiting trial, and thus presumed to be innocent. Yet judges have increasingly set large bail amounts, which means that wealthy defendants can secure their freedom while poor defendants are likely to stay in jail, with severe consequences such as loss of jobs, disruption of childcare, inability to pay rent and deeper destitution.[62]

The Californians also voted against a measure that would have instituted racial and gender preferences for university students and government jobs[63]—that is, the very type of affirmative action program created by the United Steelworkers in the 1970s.

Again, California may be solid "blue," but its electorate is not willing to support measures that would actually help the less fortunate, including racial minorities.

Then, of course, there is Florida, which went pretty easily to Donald Trump. Despite this fact, Floridians voted to increase the state minimum wage to $15 an hour.[64]

This is all to say that not all those who voted for Trump are terrible, uncaring people, and not all those who voted for Biden are so virtuous. And this means that finding common ground is more within reach than we are told.

CHAPTER FOUR

We Are All Snitches Now

*Any talk about any kind of identity—racial, gender, national,
sexual orientation—if it is not grounded in moral integrity
and universal solidarity that puts poor and working people at
the center of their vision, it's just another form of what brother
Adolph [Reed] has been teaching us for 40 year—class politics.
And so identity politics in that way has to be measured by
something deeper than simply itself, and measured by something
more deeply than what the pundit class presents itself as being on
the progressive cutting edge to make the class hierarchy and the
imperial hierarchy more colorful.[1]*

—Cornel West, November 2020

In the wonderful play from 1945, *An Inspector Calls*, we learn of a
young woman's suicide. While everyone in the house quickly reacts
defensively, telling the inspector that they never heard of this woman,
we quickly find that everyone in the house had something to do with
her demise. In the case of the paterfamilias, we discover that he had
fired the young woman because she had asked for better wages. His
daughter, meanwhile, had gotten her fired later from a dress shop
because she was jealous over how the young woman looked in a dress
she wanted and because the young woman smiled at her in a way
she found offensive. Not surprisingly, these acts left her destitute and

ultimately contributed to her decision to commit suicide. The moral of the story, of course, is that we can have an impact on others in ways of which we are sometimes unaware, and that it therefore serves to be cautious in acting too rashly and harshly against others.

The lessons of such works of literature have sadly been lost today, for now many seem to see it as a badge of honor to effectively get someone else fired, so long as they are fired in the ostensible interest of social justice or antiracism.

Ironically, while it was a badge of honor among leftists during the McCarthy period to risk everything by refusing to name the names of other leftists, and while those who did name names (e.g., the film director Elia Kazan) were shunned, the opposite is true today. Thus, many on the ostensible left view ratting out others to their employers or to the public at large for perceived breaches of ever-shifting "social justice" norms as one of the highest forms of activism. In other words, we are being encouraged to be a bunch of snitches, including in the workplace. This seems to play right into the hands of the employers and the ruling class in general, as other commentators have noted.

Thus, in an article titled "The Great Wall of Wokeness," Haydar Kahn, who describes himself vaguely as "a former mathematics researcher and instructor at a public university in the US South" (most likely for fear of losing his job at said university), writes:

> A telling sign that the neoliberal order is fully capable of withstanding and conquering the protest movement's energy is in the astonishing frenzy of corporate and media discussion about systematic racism. From corporate ads in support of Black Lives Matter to the US Chamber of Commerce pledging to "*develop and advance data-driven business and policy solutions to bridge opportunity gaps and ensure that Black Americans and people of color and have greater opportunities to succeed,*" corporations are tripping over themselves to signal that they care. Why would corporations and the media spend so much discussing such a topic? Out of moral concern? As Professor Cedric Johnson stated in his recent essay, "The Triumph of Black Lives Matter and Neoliberal Redemption," "*Black lives matter to the front office, as long as they don't demand a living wage, personal*

protective equipment and quality health care". If corporations really cared about Black lives or worker lives in general, they would drop all opposition to unions and give labor a place at the bargaining table. No, the reason is that corporations wish to shape the national discussion, redirecting attention away from broader issues of class and corporate greed, issues that have impacted the Black working class and Black poor the most but have also crushed the non-Black working class and poor.[2]

As Kahn further opines, the dogma of "intersectionality" being promoted throughout society "is a divisive way of viewing the world . . . and is a powerful way to inhibit clear communication between people, thus inhibiting the formation of a multiracial working-class political coalition. This concept has thoroughly permeated the lexicon of the American 'Left' and is marching its way through corporate and government HR departments, the media, and the academy. From the viewpoint of the ruling elite, this disruptive ideology, coupled with diversifying the managerial elite of American institutions, should be enough to placate the Black community (critic Cornel West's comment about 'Black faces in high places' comes to mind) and help repel all future disruptors of the "prevailing exploitative economic model."

For his part, the long-time activist, Marxist scholar, and University of Pennsylvania Professor Emeritus Adolph Reed, Jr. (who is himself Black) expressed similar sentiments in an interview with the show, "Useful Idiots."[3] Reed expressed the view that antiracism in the 21st century may end up being used for the same purposes as racism was in the 20th century—to divide the working class in ways that undermine its ability to fight corporate and state power. This, of course, is a controversial, but nonetheless profound, statement. One thing that Reed claimed, and I tend to agree with him on this, is that, in the current discourse, the working class is viewed as synonymous with the white working class, which itself is portrayed as backward, racist, and, in the words of Hillary Clinton, "deplorable."

This view, of course, makes united working-class action and self-defense difficult, to say the least. Interestingly, another commentator has recently expressed the converse of this view—that when Black workers take action, they are rarely seen as engaging in working-class struggle, but rather are only seen as engaging in racial justice action.[4] If Blacks and whites are not even viewed as toiling in the same class, how will they be able to effectively fight for matters of common concern? The corporations spending millions on diversity training in the workplace hope that the answer is that they cannot.

For his part, Martin Luther King recognized the working-class status of the vast majority of African Americans, and he indeed was killed in Memphis just after speaking at a rally in support of the Black garbage workers in that city who were striking for better wages, working conditions, and for dignity. King, who can be seen famously marching arm in arm with United Autoworkers union (UAW) President Walter Reuther and who himself was also an honorary member of the International Longshoremen's Workers Union (ILWU)—a largely white, but integrated union on the West Coast that went on strike to honor King's assassination—believed strongly that the fate of African Americans is tied to the fate of labor and the working class generally, regardless of race.[5]

Indeed, the famous 1963 March on Washington, "The March for Jobs and Freedom," in which Martin Luther King gave his famous "I Have a Dream Speech," began as a march specifically in support of the demands of the Black working class. As Bill Fletcher, an African American who served as a senior staff person at the AFL-CIO, explains, "while Dr. King was a major player, the March on Washington did not begin as a classic civil rights march and was not initiated by him. There is one constituency that can legitimately claim the legacy of the march—one that has been eclipsed in both history as well as in much of the lead-up to the August 2013 commemorations: *Black labor* [emphasis in text]."[6]

Fletcher explains, "[i]nitiated by A. Philip Randolph, president of the Brotherhood of Sleeping Car Porters, the march" was "responding to the fact that the Black worker was largely being ignored in the discussions about civil rights. In addition, the economic situation was becoming complicated terrain for Black workers." Specifically, "the elements of what came to be known as deindustrialization— which was really part of a reorganization of global capitalism—were beginning to have an effect in the United States, even in 1963. As with most other disasters, it started with a particular and stark impact on Black America."

Fletcher laments the fact that "Black workers have been largely abandoned in most discussions about race and civil rights. As National Black Worker Center Project founder Steven Pitts has repeatedly pointed out, with the economic restructuring that has destroyed key centers of the Black working class, such as Detroit and St. Louis, much of the economic development that has emerged has either avoided the Black worker altogether or limited the role of Black workers to the most menial positions. Thus, unemployment for Blacks remains more than double that of whites and hovers around Depression levels in many communities."[7]

In today's discussions about issues of race and of the struggle for Black lives, the entire issue of class—one that could unite workers of all races in common struggle—is conspicuously missing. And, quite incredibly, those who try to discuss this issue do so at their peril. One such individual is Adolph Reed himself, who was cancelled from speaking at an event of the Democratic Socialists of America (DSA) as the result of an article he wrote about the issue of the pandemic disproportionately hurting people of color.

As the *New York Times* explained,

> Adolph Reed is a son of the segregated South, a native of New Orleans who organized poor Black people and antiwar soldiers in the late 1960s and became a leading Socialist scholar at a trio of top universities.
>
> Along the way, he acquired the conviction, controversial today, that the left is too focused on race and not enough on class. Lasting victories were achieved, he believed, when working class and poor people of all races fought shoulder to shoulder for their rights.
>
> In late May, Professor Reed, now 73 . . . was invited to speak to the Democratic Socialists of America's New York City chapter. The match seemed a natural. . . .
>
> His chosen topic was unsparing: He planned to argue that the left's intense focus on the disproportionate impact of the coronavirus

on Black people undermined multiracial organizing, which he sees as key to health and economic justice.[8]

As the *Times* noted, the point intellectuals like Reed are trying to make is that the left should unite the most people they can to fight for social change, and this requires focusing on what we have in common rather than on our differences, racial and otherwise. According to the *Times*, "[w]hile there is a vast wealth gap between Black and white Americans, poor and working-class white people are remarkably similar to poor and working-class Black people when it comes to income and wealth, which is to say they possess very little of either."

Because Reed and his analysis are being largely canceled, and because I happen to agree with his analysis, it is worth quoting Reed at length. In a recent article he cowrote with Professor Walter Benn Michaels, he explains:

> If you look at how white and Black wealth are distributed in the US, you see right away that the very idea of racial wealth is an empty one. The top 10 percent of white people have 75 percent of white wealth; the top 20 percent have virtually all of it. And the same is true for Black wealth. The top 10 percent of Black households hold 75 percent of Black wealth.
>
> That means, as Matt Bruenig of the People's Policy Project recently noted, "the overall racial wealth disparity is driven almost entirely by the disparity between the wealthiest 10 percent of white people and the wealthiest 10 percent of Black people." This is not to say there aren't differences almost all the way down the line: poor Black people are in the main even poorer than poor white people. But it does mean that when you tell the 80 percent of white people who have less than 15 percent of white wealth that the basic inequality in the US is between Black and white, they know you are wrong. More tellingly, if you say the same thing to the 80 percent of Black people in the same position, they also know you're wrong. It's not white people who have white wealth; it's the top ten percent of whites, plus some Blacks and Asians. The wealth gap among all but the wealthiest Blacks and whites is dwarfed by the class gap,

the difference between the wealthiest and everyone else across the board.[9]

And so, Reed argues, the best way to confront this situation, benefitting both Blacks and whites alike, is to decrease the class gap in wealth through progressive wealth redistribution measures, which would include much more progressive income and capital gains taxation; a guaranteed, living wage for all workers; and universal, free healthcare and education through college. And Reed and like-minded advocates argue that, given the universal appeal of such measures, many more people of all colors and ethnic groups will rally together to fight for such change, if only it were in the offing.

However, the very opposite is being done, as we witnessed quite starkly during the pandemic, with billionaires such as Jeff Bezos, Warren Buffett, Bill Gates, and Elon Musk raking in further billions during the crisis while millions were thrown out of work, losing their healthcare in the process, with a paltry stimulus check of $1,200 in the first nine months to tide them over, along with a $600 unemployment compensation supplement. Liberal Democrats enabled all this to happen even while they knelt and wore Kinta cloth in support of Black Lives Matter.

Longtime Black activist and commentator Ajamu Baraka summarized this situation well in October 2020, when it became clear that Congress would not come up with a new stimulus package before the November elections: "Both parties are playing politics with the lives of workers & the poor not providing the desperate relief the people need. That would be different if there was some street heat. But that pivot is being blocked by the bourgeois identity politics supported & financed by liberals."[10]

This is exactly the type of hypocrisy and empty gesturing that Reed finds so offensive. Thus, as the *Times* article explains, "Democratic Party politicians, Professor Reed and his allies say, wield race as a dodge to avoid grappling with big economic issues that cut deeper, such as wealth redistribution, as that would upset their base of rich donors."

Another very glaring, but not so well-known, example of this dodging of bigger economic issues by liberals in favor of spouting platitudes about racial justice can be found in Ben & Jerry's. Thus, while Ben & Jerry's has long held itself out as a crunchy, socially progressive company, and while it was one of the first companies to issue what was viewed as a powerful statement in support of the BLM movement, Ben & Jerry's has not been so progressive in action. Thus, as explained in a 2018 article in the *Guardian*, Ben & Jerry's was successfully taken on by immigrant-rights advocates who accused it of using contractors that abused migrant workers. As the *Guardian* related:

> "Ben & Jerry's is one of the biggest purchasers of milk in Vermont," [migrant worker and advocate] Balcázar announced. "They've made a powerful brand by advertising that their products are fair trade. Milk with Dignity will make sure that this trade is truly fair."
>
> Despite its hippie origins, the famous ice-cream company was sold in 2000 to the multinational food conglomerate Unilever. Executives insisted that the company's corporate responsibility code protected workers well enough. Balcázar disagreed.
>
> Migrant Justice activists protested outside Ben & Jerry's stores in 16 cities. On International Workers' Day 2015, speakers at a rally outside Ben & Jerry's Vermont headquarters described working conditions in the company's supply chain.
>
> One worker, Víctor Díaz, told of injuries he'd received when glass milk bottles exploded and chlorine (used to disinfect milking rooms) sprayed his eyes. Others spoke of sleep deprivation, because of midnight milking. Twelve-to-14-hour shifts, without a day off, are common. And workers have been housed in barns and unheated trailers through long, frigid Vermont winters.[11]

What many "good" liberals have found is that if you say things like "Black Lives Matter," and "Defund the Police," you can get away with treating workers like slaves.

Meanwhile, true to form, instead of preparing to debate Reed on the merits of his rather reasonable arguments, a number of DSA leaders pushed to cancel Reed's appearance as a "provocation" in light of the times, as if being provocative were something bad for a radical political speaker to be.

In the end, Reed's talk was canceled. As the *Times* explains, other Black scholars reacted with shock: "'God have mercy, Adolph is the greatest democratic theorist of his generation,' said Cornel West, a Harvard professor of philosophy and a Socialist. 'He has taken some very unpopular stands on identity politics, but he has a track record of a half-century. If you give up discussion, your movement moves toward narrowness.'" That is indeed the very point Reed has been trying to make—that the current social justice movement is too narrow, and thus doomed to failure. Right or wrong, and I happen to think he is right, he deserves to be heard.

Some concrete proof that the "woke" cancel culture is being used, and indeed intentionally so, to undermine the working class is the Trump labor board decision in the case of *General Motors*, 369 NLRB, No. 127 (December 2019). First, some background on the NLRB under President Trump.

Not too surprisingly, Trump's National Labor Relations Board—the institution created in 1935 to protect workers' rights to organize a union, to engage in union activity, and to collectively bargain—is the most antiunion NLRB this country has ever seen. I can say that as a labor lawyer with 26 years of experience. As the Economic Policy Institute (EPI) explained in a policy paper titled "Unprecedented: The Trump Board's Attack on Workers,"

> Under the Trump administration, the National Labor Relations Board (NLRB) has systematically rolled back workers' rights to form unions and engage in collective bargaining with their employers, to the detriment of workers, their communities, and the economy. The Trump board has issued a series of significant decisions weakening worker protections under the National Labor Relations Act (NLRA/Act). Further, the board has engaged in an unprecedented number of rulemakings aimed at overturning existing worker protections. Finally, the Trump NLRB general counsel (GC) has advanced policies that leave fewer workers protected by

the NLRA and has advocated for changes in the law that roll back workers' rights.

The Trump board and GC have elevated corporate interests above those of working men and women and have routinely betrayed the statute they are responsible for administering and enforcing.[12]

The EPI policy paper, published on October 2019, shortly before the board's *General Motors* decision, gave the following examples of the Trump board's antiworker and antiunion actions: (1) it overruled the *Specialty Healthcare* case (which, by the way, I had worked on), thus making it harder for unions to organize smaller bargaining units as they may choose; (2) it changed rules regarding "management rights clauses," thereby giving "employers more power to make unilateral changes and undermine the collective bargaining process"; (3) it is in the process of weakening rules that streamlined the union representation election procedure; (4) it is in the process of changing rules on collective bargaining to allow employers, even in a union shop, to unilaterally impose "discretionary discipline" without first bargaining with the union; and (5) it is in the process of allowing employers to deny employees the right to use the employer email system and the right to access of employer property for the purpose of communicating amongst themselves about workplace concerns.

It is against this background that we must view the NLRB's decision in *General Motors*. The *General Motors* case involved the discipline of a longtime Black employee and union committeeperson and revisited the long-standing law regarding the use of offensive language by an employee, particularly of a discriminatory nature, in the process of engaging in what is otherwise protected, concerted activity to advance employees' interests in terms of wages and working conditions.

In relevant part, the NLRB described Robinson's conduct as follows:

On April 25, 2017, Robinson attended a meeting on subcontracting paint-shop work with two other union committeepersons and a dozen managers. Robinson became very loud and pointed his finger while speaking. When Manager Anthony Stevens told Robinson he was speaking too loudly, Robinson lowered his voice and mockingly acted a caricature of a slave. Referring to Stevens, Robinson said, "Yes, Master, Your Master Anthony," "Yes, sir, Master Anthony," "Is that what you want me to do, Master Anthony?" and also stated that Stevens wanted him "to be a good Black man." The Respondent suspended him for 2 weeks.

On October 6, 2017, Robinson attended a manpower meeting with another union committeeperson and four managers, including Stevens. At the meeting, Robinson kept repeating the same questions. When Stevens said they were going to move on, Robinson said he would "mess [Stevens] up." Stevens asked if that was a threat, and Robinson replied Stevens could take it how he wanted. Later in the meeting, Robinson began playing loud music from his phone that contained profane, racially charged, and sexually offensive lyrics. The music went on for 10 to 30 minutes. When Stevens left the room once or twice, Robinson turned off the music, only to turn it back on when Stevens returned. The Respondent suspended him for 30 days.

The NLRB, overturning decades of prior law, decided that Robinson's language was not privileged because he was engaging in union activity at the time. It therefore overruled the Administrative Law Judge who had invalidated Robinson's discipline based upon the long-standing law, and the Trump-appointed NLRB took the occasion to announce a new rule making it much easier for employers to discipline and discharge employees in such circumstances. While the Board had, prior to this decision, privileged such language, though possibly offensive, made in the course of union conduct, so long as it could not be objectively construed as amounting to a physical threat, the NLRB now shifted the balance of this inquiry in the employer's favor, allowing the employer to subjectively decide if the language was offensive enough to justify discipline or discharge.

Incredibly, both General Motors, as well as the NLRB chair, a right-wing lawyer appointed by Trump, trumpeted this decision as a victory against racism and sexism. As a *Bloomberg* opinion piece titled "It is Now Easier to Fire US Workers for What They Say" related, both GM and the NLRB chair couched their language in the "woke" parlance of the time:

> "GM stands against harassment and discrimination," the company said in an emailed statement. "This NLRB decision is a step towards more inclusive workplaces."
>
> The NLRB said its ruling will stop the agency from providing cover for inappropriate behavior. "This is a long-overdue change in the NLRB's approach to profanity-laced tirades and other abusive conduct in the workplace," the agency's chairman, John Ring, said in an emailed statement. "For too long, the NLRB has protected employees who engage in obscene, racist, and sexually harassing speech not tolerated in almost any workplace today."[3]

However, such claims should obviously not be taken at face value given the sources, and many proworker groups are certainly not. As the *Bloomberg* piece continues:

> Worker advocates say the new guidance will have the opposite effect, making it easier for companies to punish those who criticize or organize against bigotry at work just as the pandemic and killing of George Floyd have spurred a new wave of employee activism.
>
> "Employees who are fighting back against racism will be fired if an employer thinks a word is not genteel enough," said American Federation of Teachers union president Randi Weingarten. "It's a way of thwarting speech, and it's a way of thwarting activism."
>
> Mark Gaston Pearce, who served as NLRB chair under President Obama, said, "The employer's ability to establish a defense will be a hundred times easier."

I must note here that when I worked for the USW, I saw videos of striking, white Steelworkers hurling racial epithets at Black strike breakers, and I was very upset by this. I complained to my superiors about this. I argued that this was wrong and also counterproductive, as it would naturally discredit the Union's cause. But my advice was for the Union to educate its members about these issues and take a very hard line against such conduct in order to prevent it in the future. And, in worst-case scenarios, I argued, the Union could discipline its members. However, what neither I, nor any union person, would ever advocate is to go to the employer to have strikers fired.

Still, many amongst the "woke," far from opposing the firing of employees for speaking in ways less than genteel on issues of race and gender, may even push for such employees to be fired. This, after all, is seen as activism in certain circles.

This type of "wokeness," I believe, is nothing more or less than a form of elitism in which the better educated look down on the less educated—lesser education many times a proxy for working class. Ultimately, this amounts to dismissing a huge swath of the American people, and the swath, firmly in the 99 percent, with whom we could be working to change our society for the good.

However, as political philosopher Michael J. Sandel recently wrote in the *New York Times*, this type of elitism is socially acceptable in our society—even in that part of society that prides itself on supporting equality and social justice. As Sandel explains, we now have a society and political system built upon the requirement of a college education, even though such an education is becoming increasingly out of reach for most Americans. The result, he explains, is devastating:

> Building a politics around the idea that a college degree is a pre-condition for dignified work and social esteem has a corrosive effect on democratic life. It devalues the contributions of those without a diploma, fuels prejudice against less-educated members of society, effectively excludes most working people from elective government and provokes political backlash. . . .
>
> It is important to remember that most Americans—nearly two-thirds—do not have a four-year college degree. By telling workers that their inadequate education is the reason for their troubles, meritocrats moralize success and failure and unwittingly promote credentialism—an insidious prejudice against those who do not have college degrees.
>
> The credentialist prejudice is a symptom of meritocratic hubris. By 2016, many working people chafed at the sense that well-schooled

elites looked down on them with condescension. This complaint
was not without warrant. Survey research bears out what many
working-class voters intuit: At a time when racism and sexism are
out of favor (discredited though not eliminated), credentialism is
the last acceptable prejudice.[14]

And again, I would argue, this type of "credentialism" often takes
the form of berating working-class people for failing to know the latest, and ever-changing, permutations of race and gender politics and
language requirements. This ultimately becomes anti-working class as
those who work with their hands, and not just their heads, for a living
are vilified as "deplorables."

In short, the victory of the "woke," at least "woke" intellectuals,
beyond the walls of the academy and into the corporate boardrooms
and the National Labor Relations Board may ultimately be a defeat
for workers—both Black and white. But again, it is fairly certain that
these intellectuals are not fighting for workers' rights, but for something altogether different.

The strange place that all of this is leading us was recently man-
ifested by the union, the National Writers' Guild, representing journalists at the *New York Times*. As Glenn Greenwald explains,[15] the
Guild publicly condemned a colleague, Bret Stephens, for writing
a piece expressing numerous criticisms of the Pulitzer-Prize winning "1619 Project"—a project that argues that the birth of the US
was not 1776, but, rather, 1619, when the first slaves were brought to
our shores. As Greenwald relates, the "denunciation was marred by
humiliating typos and even more so by creepy and authoritarian censorship demands and petulant appeals to management for enforcement of company 'rules' against other journalists. To say that this is
bizarre behavior from a union *of journalists*, of all people, is to woe-
fully understate the case." Greenwald continues:

> Then there is the tattletale petulance embedded in the Union's com-
> plaint. In demanding enforcement of workplace "rules" by manage-
> ment against a fellow journalist—they do not specify which sacred
> "rule" Stephens allegedly violated—these union members sound

more like Human Resources Assistant Managers or workplace informants than they do intrepid journalists. Since when do unions of any kind, but especially unions of journalists, unite to complain that corporate managers and their editorial bosses have been *too lax* in the enforcement of rules governing what their underlings can and cannot say?

In short, as this case illustrates, worker solidarity is breaking down in favor of a "cancel culture" in which workers are uniting with management to punish fellow workers for perceived breaches of "woke" norms. The result is a weakening of the class struggle as well as, particularly in this instance, freedom of expression and the free flow of ideas. How this is seen as somehow progressive is beyond my comprehension.

CHAPTER FIVE

Intersectional War and Imperialism

You're a sexist if you criticize the defense contractor lobbyists Biden seeks to appoint, a racist if you oppose tech and bank lobbyists Dems are bringing to power. That's the point of identity pol—a weapon to silence dissent and rebrand the ruling class as untouchable.

—Journalist Lee Fang

One of my favorite memes that I have seen lately contains a picture of two military planes dropping bombs. One is labelled "Republicans" and the other "Democrats." The two planes and the bombs they are dropping are identical in every way with the following exception: the "Democrats" plane contains three symbols that the other plane lacks—a BLM logo, the LBGTQ+ rainbow flag, and a sign reading, "Yes We Can." To me, this says much about the reality of our two-party system. The two parties are nearly identical, and certainly so in respect to their commitment to war and destruction. The Democrats just purport to be more diverse and intersectional in carrying out the destruction, and sadly, this seems good enough for way too many liberals.

In the end, the "cancellation" of Molly Rush not only destroyed the reputation of a lifelong peace and justice activist, but it greatly undermined what was left of the peace movement in Pittsburgh—represented by Molly and the Thomas Merton Center for nearly 50 years—with her. Whether that was the intention or not, I do not know, but many of us suspected as much. In any case, the destruction was done quite knowingly.

I say that "what was left of the peace movement" was severely undermined because, in truth, there hasn't been much of this movement since the run-up to the US invasion in Iraq in 2003, when this country and the world witnessed some of the largest such demonstrations ever. But since that time, the peace movement has gone quiet.

There are many reasons for this, I am sure, including the fact that people were greatly disheartened about not being able to prevent the 2003 invasion. There was surely a sense of futility that folks felt after the failure to stop the war. I'm sure many antiwar protesters felt, "Why bother?" Indeed, I suspect that a significant reason why many people have largely stopped fighting for real change—peace, healthcare for all, a better standard of living for workers—and instead have limited themselves to the symbolic battles of fighting over the use of language and which statutes should be allowed to stand is that they feel they have a much better chance of winning the purely symbolic battles. Of course, this is undoubtedly true, but, as with most things in life, it is the harder battles—the ones of real consequence—that are far more worth fighting.

Another reason for the decline of the peace movement, however, was the election of Barack Obama in 2008. I vividly remember the election campaign of Obama. Like many, I was so excited at the prospect of our nation's first Black president that I saw in him what I wanted to see, including that, somehow, he was going to be a peace president. I guess I was not the only one who thought this given that Obama was awarded the Nobel Peace Prize barely nine months into his presidency, and for no discernable reason.

In the end, Obama proved to be anything but a peace president. Indeed, some of us on the left dubbed him "Bomber Obama" in light of the eagerness he showed for using drones to bomb people throughout the world. As an article by the Bureau of Investigative Journalism explains:

There were ten times more air strikes in the covert war on terror during President Barack Obama's presidency than under his predecessor, George W. Bush.

Obama embraced the US drone program, overseeing more strikes in his first year than Bush carried out during his entire presidency. A total of 563 strikes, largely by drones, targeted Pakistan, Somalia and Yemen during Obama's two terms, compared to 57 strikes under Bush. Between 384 and 807 civilians were killed in those countries, according to reports logged by the Bureau. . . .

That figure does not include deaths in active battlefields including Afghanistan—where US air attacks have shot up since Obama withdrew the majority of his troops at the end of 2014. The country has since come under frequent US bombardment, in an unreported war that saw 1,337 weapons dropped last year alone—a 40 percent rise on 2015. . . .

Obama also began an air campaign targeting Yemen. His first strike was a catastrophe: commanders thought they were targeting al Qaeda but instead hit a tribe with cluster munitions, killing 55 people. Twenty-one were children—10 of them under five. Twelve were women, five of them pregnant.[1]

As Media Benjamin, longtime director of the peace organization Code Pink, further explained, "in 2016 alone, the Obama administration dropped at least 26,171 bombs. This means that every day last year, the US military blasted combatants or civilians overseas with 72 bombs; that's three bombs every hour, 24 hours a day. . . . One bombing technique that President Obama championed is drone strikes. As drone-warrior-in-chief, he spread the use of drones outside the declared battlefields of Afghanistan and Iraq, mainly to Pakistan and Yemen. Obama . . . automatically painted all males of military age in these regions as combatants, making them fair game for remote controlled killing."[2] Such targeting of civilians, simply because they were male and of a certain age, is a war crime and may even be considered genocidal. Sadly, few, including on the left, have seemed to care.

Few also seemed to care that Obama helped launch the eight-month bombing campaign against Libya that converted that once-prosperous country into a failed state where, for the first time in living memory, Blacks are now being sold as slaves in public markets.[3] Similarly, few seem to be concerned about the Saudi onslaught upon Yemen, which Obama backed to the hilt beginning in 2015 and which has created the greatest humanitarian crisis in the world.[4]

The undeniable fact of these horrible crimes, for which Obama could have been tried and severely punished in a Nuremberg-style tribunal, has not prevented Obama from becoming a liberal icon with near-saint status. The reasons for this are multifold, but I believe that a big reason is that the liberal-left mindset is so focused on identity politics to the near exclusion of all else that Obama—our first African American president, and a president who certainly knew how to talk the talk about racial and gender inclusivity—gets a pass for things other presidents would have been taken to task for. And so, you have the bizarre situation in which the same people who would enthusiastically "cancel" others for using the wrong pronoun or the wrong language in reference to race lionize a mass murderer like Obama who destroyed tens of thousands of lives, and mostly Black and brown lives at that. This is downright pathological.

By the way, the role of Obama in selling war to America and the world, and especially to the liberal citizens thereof, was well understood by the CIA, which, as detailed in an internal memo described by intrepid reporter Glenn Greenwald, saw Obama as the only real asset they had to guarantee that the US's endless wars would keep going.[5] He was the salesman that George W. Bush, the Texas rube, could never be and the salesman that Trump, who at least publicly decried these wars, did not want to be. The other thing the CIA recognized is that they could sell the continuation of the war in Afghanistan, in particular, to the same audience by focusing on the plight of women and claiming that the US was the only thing protecting them there.

Glenn Greenwald also recently made the point that the left in the US is strangely more ready to condemn people for thought and speech than they are people, like Obama, for murderous actions. Greenwald made this point in reference to the attempt of liberals to cancel popular podcaster Joe Rogan because, for example, he believes that transgender women should not be allowed to play women's sports because of the competitive advantage that their male anatomy undoubtedly gives them. As Greenwald points out, Bernie Sanders was attacked by liberals for accepting and touting the endorsement of Joe Rogan, who has never done physical harm to anyone else, while the same liberals applauded the endorsement of Biden by people who have done real harm to people of color, such as former Michigan Governor Rick Synder, who was responsible for poisoning the water supply of the largely Black city of Flint, and Michael Bloomberg, who, as New York City mayor, oversaw the repressive and racist "stop-and-frisk" campaign in that city.[6]

Similarly, liberals were excited when our first Black secretary of state, Colin Powell, endorsed Joe Biden despite his long track record of war crimes—from helping cover up the brutal My Lai massacre in Vietnam, to quarterbacking the mass murder of retreating Iraqi soldiers at the end of the first Gulf War, to providing the key "yellow cake" lie that helped pave the way for the second Gulf War.

Meanwhile, the turning away from issues of war and peace did not stop with Obama. Rather, in order to be consistent—consistency being the "hobgoblin of little minds," as Ralph Waldo Emerson explained—many liberals, having overlooked Obama's war crimes, have felt compelled to overlook the war crimes of other presidents, like George W. Bush, who was once reviled for his disastrous invasion of Iraq, but who has now been publicly rehabilitated. Bush is now a beloved grandfather figure, in part because he gets along with the Obamas so well. But notice that Donald Trump has also been given a pass for war crimes. Indeed, this is the only thing that he does get a pass for from liberals and the more liberal-leaning media.

Sadly, the acceptance of war crimes by liberals is not merely the product of their trying to deal with the cognitive dissonance that their worship of Obama creates for them. There seems to be something even deeper here. Thus, many liberals have gone beyond merely accepting such crimes to applauding and even demanding them. For example, liberal pundits applauded Trump for bombing Syria after an alleged chemical attack there, with such pundits as CNN news host Fareed Zakaria stating that this bombing represented the first time that Trump showed himself to be "presidential."[7] Moreover, liberal pundits such as Scott Simon of NPR have been critical of Trump's decision to end the wars in Afghanistan and Iraq.[8] And NPR host Michel Martin was happy to have war monger John Bolton on her show to talk about how Trump was allegedly failing to keep the US safe by having refused Bolton's foreign policy advice—advice that included trying to push Trump to militarily attack such countries as Iran and Venezuela.[9]

While some of this can be attributed to liberals simply showing (a quite unprincipled) contrariness to Trump—e.g., if he wants out of Afghanistan, then they will want to stay in—this does not fully account for the liberal drift toward supporting war. Indeed, military intervention and war are now being sold as a means to advance diversity and intersectional goals in other countries.

A great example of this is the conflict in Afghanistan that liberals are pushing to continue, even after 20 years of combat there, in the name of women's rights—just as the CIA hoped liberals would do. I must note that, as I am writing this, *The Intercept* just broke the story of the CIA's running death squads in Afghanistan. As *The Intercept* explains,[10] "[b]eginning in December 2018 and continuing for at least a year, Afghan operatives believed to belong to an elite CIA-trained paramilitary unit known as 01, in partnership with US special operations forces and air power, unleashed a campaign of terror against civilians. This unit carried out night raids in which they killed civilians, including children. In one night raid alone, targeting a religious school known as a madrassa, 12 children, as young as nine years old, were killed." This received little coverage in the mainstream press, which seemed unmoved by this story.

As just one example of the liberal media's support for the continuation of the Afghan war, NPR ran a story about a women's soccer team in Afghanistan, claiming that such a team would not exist in the absence of the US invasion of 2001 that overthrew the Taliban and may not continue into the future if Trump gets his way in withdrawing the troops from there.[11] Indeed, this line—that US boots on the ground are necessary to protect women's rights in Afghanistan—has been pushed quite aggressively by liberals for some time.

This message came through loud and clear from Democratic law-makers who recently grilled the Trump Administration about its peace efforts in Afghanistan and its decision to withdraw all US troops by May 2021. As NBC News put it, "President Donald Trump's envoy to Afghanistan faced tough questioning . . . by Democratic lawmakers who accused the administration of jeopardizing the rights of Afghan women in pursuit of a peace deal."[12]

The assumption being successfully pushed by the Democrats and many liberals is that the US has somehow advanced the cause of women in Afghanistan since the US began intervening in that country in 1979. For example, in a recent opinion piece, Ved Nanda, University Professor and director of the Ved Nanda Center for International Law at the University of Denver Sturm College of Law, also urged the US to tread carefully in withdrawing from Afghanistan because, in his words, "Afghanistan is at a crossroads—people there are thirsting for peace and stability, of which they have dreamt for 40 years. It wants to keep the progress it has made on human and minority rights, media freedom, and building democratic institutions. The future remains uncertain, but the US must not abandon the country once again, which it did after helping the Mujahadeen to repel the Russians from its territory." Nanda's assumption is that progress, including in women's rights, is advanced by US intervention in Afghanistan and is somehow threatened by its withdrawal.[13]

Such assumptions ignore key facts about the history of US inter-vention in Afghanistan, and about the nature of the US military in general. First of all, the US did not, as Nanda claims, support the mujahideen in order to repel the Russians from Afghanistan. Rather, as later admitted by the architect of the US's intervention in Afghanistan at that time, Zbigniew Brzezinski—the National Security Adviser for Democratic President Jimmy Carter, the self-described "human rights president"—the US began supporting the mujahideen in Afghanistan *six months before* the Soviet Union invaded that country, and the US did so, moreover, in order to draw the USSR *into* a protracted war there.[14] Brzezinski's explicit goal was to give the USSR its own Vietnam War so as to undermine the Soviet Union.

The fate of the Afghanis in that conflict, and of women in particular, was of little concern; indeed, they were nothing but collateral damage in Brzezinski's cynical "chess game" with the Soviet Union. And damaged they were. At the time the US began supporting the radical, misogynist jihadists in Afghanistan (one of whose leaders was Osama bin Laden), Afghanistan was being led by the secular Taraki government, which had been doing much to advance women's rights.

The US intervention destroyed that progress for decades to come; it did not advance it. As history scholar Michael Parenti explains,[15] "[t]he government . . . continued a campaign begun by the king to emancipate women from their age-old tribal bondage. It provided public education for girls and for the children of various tribes. A report in the *San Francisco Chronicle* (17 November 2001) noted that under the Taraki regime Kabul had been 'a cosmopolitan city. Artists and hippies flocked to the capital. Women studied agriculture, engineering and business at the city's university. Afghan women held government jobs—in the 1980s, there were seven female members of parliament. Women drove cars, traveled and went on dates. Fifty percent of university students were women.'"

All of this was shattered with the rise and conquest of the US-backed mujahideen. Thus, as Parenti explains, when the US's jihadist friends eventually came to power, "[t]hey ravaged the cities, terrorized civilian populations, looted, staged mass executions, closed schools, raped thousands of women and girls, and reduced half of Kabul to rubble. In 2001 Amnesty International reported that the mujahideen used sexual assault as 'a method of intimidating vanquished populations and rewarding soldiers.'" So much for advancing women's rights!

And, what has been the consequence of the US invasion of Afghanistan in 2001 and its subsequent, nearly two-decade occupation? More suffering for the Afghani population: men, women, and children alike. First, we must start from the fact that, after the US's long occupation of Afghanistan, that country is ranked at the very bottom of all countries in the world for women's rights—this, according to a piece in *Time* magazine, citing a report from Amnesty International and lamenting how this possibly could be given that the

US "war was billed, in part, as 'a fight for the rights and dignity of women.'"[16]

Of course, the assertion that the US military would ever fight for the rights of women simply misapprehends the goals and nature of that military. Thus, the US military does not even protect its own female soldiers from their male comrades. The incidence of sexual harassment and sexual assault within the US military is high and climbing, with 13,000 female soldiers in fiscal year 2018 (the last year for which complete data are available) reporting that they were sexually assaulted or raped.[17] A whopping 38 percent of female veterans and active military personnel have been treated for "Military Sexual Trauma"; nearly a quarter of all female military personnel have reported being sexually harassed, and one-fifth of these report being raped thereafter.[18]

These terrible statistics were highlighted by the 2020 murder of Army Spc. Vanessa Guillen, a female soldier at Fort Hood in Texas.[19] She was brutally killed and dismembered by a fellow, male soldier after she privately reported being sexually harassed by him. One-third of the female soldiers at this base have officially reported being sexually harassed by soldiers.

US forces are guilty of abusing, harassing, and sexually assaulting women in virtually every country it has a presence. In the US war on Vietnam, for example, soldiers reported that the rape of Vietnamese women and girls was "standard operating procedure" for US infantrymen.[20] And the Vietnam War was not unique in this regard, with a *Duke Law Review* article explaining that rape and sexual violence has been perpetrated on a significant scale by the US military in every conflict it has been engaged in since at least WWII, and including during WWII.[21] What's more, this is not just during wartime, but also during peacetime at nearly all of the US's 800 global military bases, where US troops are serviced by prostitutes and trafficked persons with a limited degree of consent.[22] As feminist commentator Elizabeth Mesok explains, "US imperialism [is] dependent on sexual torture."[23]

Indeed, all imperial intervention is dependent upon the abuse of women. This is why the main legal instrument purporting to advance women's rights, the Convention on the Elimination of all Forms of Discrimination Against Women (CEDAW), makes it clear in the preamble "that the eradication of . . . colonialism, neo-colonialism, aggression, foreign occupation and domination and interference in the internal affairs of States is essential to the full enjoyment of the rights of men and women."[24] That is, the very idea that US intervention in other nations will advance women's rights is anathema to the main international treaty created to protect such rights. It is no surprise then that the US is one of only a handful of nations that has refused to ratify this Convention—but another reason to doubt the US's bona fides in claiming to protect women's rights abroad.

Instead of focusing on the reality of the sexual violence endemic to the US military and its foreign adventures, the liberal establishment has been adept at focusing the attention of the public, in an incredible sleight of hand, on issues of inclusion in the ranks of the military and its leadership. There seems to be a belief that, somehow, even the worst actions are somehow better and more virtuous because a woman or person of color is leading the effort. One example of this is the case of the first female secretary of state, Madeleine Albright, who is a beloved liberal and feminist icon, despite the fact that she oversaw a brutal sanctions regime against Iraq that killed at least 500,000 children. When asked about this later, Albright would say that this death toll was "worth it."[25] Instead of being held accountable for such a massive crime in any way, Albright travels around the world showing off her button collection.[26]

Another great example of this phenomenon is the disastrous destruction of Libya that was apparently spearheaded by the troika of Hillary Clinton, Samantha Power, and Susan Rice[27]—three self-described warriors for human and women's rights.

Journalist Maureen Dowd, a liberal and feminist, absolutely cooed over this troika's push for this war. As Dowd wrote at the time, "[t]hey are called the Amazon Warriors, the Lady Hawks, the Valkyries, the Durgas."[28] Of course, quite appropriately, these terms of endearment place all emphasis on these individuals' war-like qualities rather than their desire to protect human rights. And this excited Maureen Dowd, for she lauded all of this as a breakthrough for feminism. As she wrote,

> There is something positively mythological about a group of strong women swooping down to shake the president out of his delicate sensibilities and show him the way to war. And there is something positively predictable about guys in the White House pushing back against that story line for fear it makes the president look henpecked.
>
> It is not yet clear if the Valkyries will get the credit or the blame on Libya. But everyone is fascinated with the gender flip: the reluctant men—the generals, the secretary of defense, top male White House national security advisers—outmuscled by the fierce women around President Obama urging him to man up against the crazy Qaddafi.

When Hillary Clinton heard that Qaddafi had ultimately been killed in the process of this operation, she famously channeled Julius Caesar by exclaiming with glee, "We came, we saw, he died."[29] Again, while many would otherwise be appalled at such a response to a brutal murder, many liberals celebrated this as evidence that women were really moving up in the world.

Sadly, the results of the intervention, which hurt women and men alike in Libya, and especially women and men with Black skin who were the victims of a genocide as a result of the intervention,[30] cannot be seen as some victory for feminism. Indeed, war never can be. Yet, there seems to be little honest reflection about this.

A person who has engaged in such reflection is antiwar feminist (a term now becoming an oxymoron) Elizabeth Mesok. In a journal article, Mesok critiques liberal feminists, including luminaries such as Gloria Steinem who advocate for integration of women into the ranks of the military while failing to criticize, and indeed while at least implicitly accepting, the US imperial project.[31] As Mesok relates, this is a sea change from the past in which there existed a forceful feminist critique of militarism and war—a critique that has largely disappeared. In Mesok's view, "this strategy of advocating for women's incorporation into the military institution while eliding any critique of US militarism, or even acknowledging the global victims of US sexual and imperial violence, perpetuates the myth of the military as an institution capable of justice, both for its US enlistees and the civilians it 'helps' across the globe."

There is a huge irony that while there has been increased focus in the US by liberals and leftists on racial and gender oppression, as well as on the dangers of "toxic masculinity," the oppression of women and people of color by the US military—one of the most toxic masculine entities on Earth—has been all but forgotten. As Mesok complains, "[e]ntirely erased" from the current feminist movement "is the global violence of the US military, both sexual and imperial."

Caitlin Johnstone, writing about the fawning of liberals about the possibility of Biden appointing a woman, Michele Flournoy, to the position of secretary of defense, is more pointed about this phenomenon:

> Let's clear this up before the girl-power parade starts: the first woman to head the US war machine will not be a groundbreaking pioneer of feminist achievement. She will be a mass murderer who wears Spanx. Her appointment will not be an advancement for women, it will be imperialism in pumps.
>
> Modern mainstream feminism has abandoned women's interests so thoroughly and completely in almost all spheres of importance that it has largely become only superficially distinct from the patriarchy it purports to oppose. The plight of mothers, elderly women, young girls, caregivers and wives have been almost entirely shuffled out of popular discourse, with focus instead shifted onto discussions about whether women are being adequately rewarded for their service to the God of Capitalism, or how they're just as qualified as men to murder thousands of people at a time.[32]

The more sophisticated position, of course, is one that argues that the fight should be focused on not simply diversity in the ranks of government as the end game, but on getting women and women of color who are committed to the feminist values of peace and nonaggression in positions of power. This was well articulated recently by three antiwar feminist authors—Christine Ahn, Yifat Susskin, and

Cindy Wiesner—in an opinion piece in *Newsweek*.[33] In this piece, these authors argue, I believe quite correctly, that:

> We need to question the drivers behind US foreign policy, specifically the patriarchal assumptions that underlie militarist logic and the gendered notion that proliferating violence makes a nation more secure. These notions of "security" coincide with the control of others through violence at home and abroad, and they are used to justify unnecessarily massive military budgets for weapons of mass destruction and the perpetuation of endless wars.
>
> As a result, US foreign policy has harmed communities worldwide for generations with zero mechanisms for accountability. In the past 20 years, the US has launched wars and fomented violence in Afghanistan, Iraq, Libya, Pakistan, the Philippines, Somalia, Syria, Yemen and beyond; and the so-called "war on terror" has killed some 801,000 people and displaced at least 37 million globally.

As these authors explain, "[t]he brunt of US militarism is deeply misogynistic. In the US, Navajo women and their children have high levels of uranium in their bloodstreams as a result of nuclear weapons testing from decades ago. And in Fallujah, Iraq, women are still dealing with the legacy of US bombings that took place nearly 20 years earlier, giving birth to babies with congenital disabilities who often cannot survive. For too many global communities impacted by US wars, women often bear the responsibility to ensure their families' survival." They specifically argue that we must push for Black women, Arab women, and indigenous women who understand this reality, and who wish to radically transform US foreign policy, to take positions of leadership in our government. In other words, they advocate for having women in power, not for its own sake, but to pursue values commensurate with feminism and social justice.

Commentators, such as Marxist scholar Adam Lehrer, see the failure of most of the left to advocate for such measures, and instead to be satisfied with diversity alone, as a broader problem in US society that has developed quite recently. As Lehrer explains, "[t]he cultural hegemony has shifted in the last 30 years" as many people have become "intellectually trapped in the banal culture wars of the '90s and attracted to the intersectional aesthetics of [a] liberal elite (the [Democratic Party] and its backers in the surveillance state, Silicon Valley, and Wall Street), [that] willfully overlook[s] or latently support[s] the neoliberal and imperial politics of the elite."[34]

The question is, how did we get here? I believe there are several answers to this.

One place is to start with people like Gloria Steinem herself. Steinem, critiqued above, is an interesting figure, and a quite relevant one to the current discussion. This is so because she, while an icon of the liberal feminist movement, was also a proud asset of the Central Intelligence Agency. As the *Chicago Tribune* explains, "Steinem spoke openly about her relationship to 'The Agency' in the 1950s and '60s after a magazine revealed her employment by a CIA front organization, the Independent Research Service. While popularly pilloried because of her paymaster, Steinem defended the CIA relationship, saying: 'In my experience The Agency was completely different from its image; it was liberal, nonviolent and honorable.'"[35]

Of course, Steinem's whitewashing of the CIA's operations while she was in its employ is absolutely stunning and demonstrates the level of her delusions—delusions that she helped promulgate internationally for "The Agency." Thus, far from being "liberal, nonviolent and honorable," the CIA during the 1950s and 60s engaged in numerous nefarious deeds, including: the overthrow of the progressive and democratically elected governments of Mohammed Mossadegh in Iran in 1953, and of Jacobo Arbenz in Guatemala in 1954; the assassination of Congo's first democratically elected prime minister, Patrice Lumumba in 1960—this would come to be known as "the most important assassination of the 20th century"; the arrest of Nelson Mandela in South Africa in 1962; and the overthrow of Brazil's progressive government in 1964, just to name a few of the CIA's biggest hits during this time.

Still, as the *Chicago Tribune* emphasizes, "[s]trange as it may seem, Steinem's personal views and CIA political goals aligned. Her brand of social revolution, promoted by American tax dollars, was meant to counter Soviet-sponsored revolutionary messaging." And what was the "Soviet-sponsored revolutionary messaging" that was being countered?

At heart, this messaging was of an anticolonial nature; it was a message, backed with great material support from the USSR, for people of the Global South to throw off the chains of Western (that is, British, Spanish, Portuguese, Dutch, French, German, Belgian, and US) colonialism and domination. As Belgian intellectual Jean Bricmont notes in his book *Humanitarian Imperialism*,[36] "the main lasting effect of the Russian Revolution is probably the Soviet Union's not insignificant support to the decolonization process. The process freed hundreds of millions of people from one of the most brutal forms of oppression. It is major progress in the history of mankind, similar to the abolition of slavery in the 18th and 19th centuries."

While this Soviet messaging would seem to be a quite "woke" one, it has indeed been effectively countered and smothered, including in the minds of many liberals and left-leaning Americans, who tend to believe that the US is somehow liberating people throughout the world instead of simply killing and repressing them and who tend to be skeptical, if not downright hostile, to independence movements such as the Chavista movement in Venezuela, the Sandinista movement in Nicaragua, and the MAS movement in Bolivia. In the case of Nicaragua, for example, liberals in the US have been attacking the Sandinista government there for years on ostensible feminist grounds even though Nicaragua, under the Sandinista leadership, was just ranked 5th in the entire world (much higher than the US, for example) in gender equality for the third straight year.[37] I myself was canceled by a faculty group in Edinburgh, Scotland, who initially agreed to host my presentation of a documentary film I had made about Nicaragua. A few professors, raising undefined concerns about human and women's rights in Nicaragua, successfully pushed for my event to be canceled on the very eve of the event and after plane tickets had been bought. It was not clear that any of those complaining had even seen my recently made film, but the fact that I was known to be pro-Sandinista was enough to have my event canceled as opposed to allowing for people to voluntarily see the film and to comment and ask questions about it. The hosts of the event did not even bother telling us of its cancellation; rather, they simply put a post on Twitter saying it was being canceled, and that was it—no proper notice and surely no opportunity for making our case for why we should be allowed to go forward. This is the level of closed-mindedness that is now passing for "wokeness" in the academies of the West.

The marriage of the CIA, and the military-industrial complex as well, with portions of the liberal and left movements, as well as with "woke" culture, is quite profound and has greatly distorted what passes for "progressive" in this country.

Take what is considered one of the most "woke" major-release movies in recent years—*Black Panther*. Understandably, this became a beloved movie, especially for African Americans who have been craving to see someone who looks like them as a blockbuster Superhero. What made this film groundbreaking was that, while nearly every protagonist was Black, it was marketed to and received by a wide and diverse audience. In addition, the movie centered on a fictional African country—Wakanda—that was ahead of the rest of the world in terms of technology and civilization. And it was so because it had isolated itself from the intervention and exploitation of the rest of the continent by white invaders. Wakanda and Black Panther are often referenced, in particular by African Americans, as symbols of Black strength, heroism, and innovation. All good so far.

But then, there is something in the movie that is not at all progressive. Thus, the only white protagonist in the film—a protagonist who helps Wakanda—is a CIA agent. But the truth is that the CIA has never been a friend to Africa as portrayed in "Black Panther." Rather, the CIA has been Africa's mortal enemy, having assisted in the arrest of Nelson Mandela in 1962; the assassination of African independence leaders such as Congo's Patrice Lumumba (a leader that greatly resembles the heroic Black Panther character in his desire to use Africa's resources for Africa); and its substantial support to counterrevolutionaries in Angola in the 1970s and 1980s.[38]

The strange appearance of the CIA hero in *Black Panther* may not have been a mere accident of the screenwriters. Rather, as Lynn Stuart Parramore writes, the CIA has a long history of meddling in Hollywood in attempts to make US enemies look bad and the US and the CIA in particular look good. She believes that this dynamic may have played out here. As she explains,[39]

By the end of the Cold War, the agency needed an image makeover. So it hired Chase Brandon, a veteran secret operative, to help it get cozy with filmmakers, actors, and producers. CIA agents in the movies soon became heroes working for a highly moral organization desperately needed in the world.

The 1990s saw the birth of the Tom Clancy film franchise, with Alec Baldwin, Harrison Ford, and Ben Affleck portraying intrepid CIA agent Jack Ryan. Since 9/11, the CIA has worked directly on programs like "24" and "Homeland." Jennifer Garner, who played agent Sydney Bristow in the TV show "Alias," even did a CIA recruitment commercial. The moviemakers behind "Zero Dark Thirty," a film about hunting down Osama bin Laden, worked closely with the agency.

Indeed since 9/11, as author Nicholas Schou laid out in his article, "How the CIA Hoodwinked Hollywood," the agency has been working overtime with moviemakers to bolster its image. Langley regularly grants special access and favors to movie people at its headquarters—access often denied to journalists.

As for the Jack Ryan franchise, John Krasinski, who played the affable Jim in *The Office*, is the latest actor to star in this series. And, in the most recent season, his task is to overthrow the Chavez-like leader of Venezuela. Talk about getting the public primed for yet another CIA-backed coup in Latin America.

A glaring example of the marriage of Hollywood with government intelligence agencies is the recent interview that liberal Hollywood luminary Angelina Jolie had with the British intelligence service known as MI6. This was noted by Alan Macleod in the alternative news source, *MintPress*, in an article titled "Angelina Jolie's MI6 Interview Shows Just How Connected Hollywood Is To the Deep State."[40] As Macleod related, "with election fever still gripping the US, talk of rigging or interference in the democratic process is reaching new levels, high enough that even Hollywood legend Angelina Jolie is talking about it. In an extraordinary interview in *Time* magazine, the star of *Wanted, Maleficent,* and *Lara Croft: Tomb Raider* sat down with the former head of the UK's MI6 spy network, Sir Alex Younger, to ask how worrying the threat from Russia or China really is."

Macleod also relates that Jolie worked with the CIA during the making of the pro-CIA, anti-Russian movie *Salt* and penned an op-ed with former Senator John McCain calling for US intervention in Syria and Myanmar. As for *Salt*, which debuted in 2010, Macleod points out that this movie "marked the beginning of hardening American relations with Moscow, ending up at the point where some have declared the beginning of a new Cold War." Macleod quotes investigative journalist Tom Secker for the proposition that this movie "was the first big cultural product reflecting this geopolitical change, for most of the 2000s Hollywood had no interest in evil Russians."

It should be noted, especially for those truly concerned about issues of bigotry and ethnic discrimination, that the promotion of the idea of "evil Russians" in recent years has resulted in a massive increase in anti-Russian discrimination in the United States. As *RT News* relates, "more than 44 per cent of US-based Russians surveyed had faced discrimination on the basis of their nationality. Around one in four reported having felt they had to hide their background. The way Russia is portrayed in the media appeared to be a cause of this, with almost 64 per cent of those responding saying coverage was *'unfair.'*"[41]

Angela Jolie is not alone in working with and promoting the military-industrial-intelligence complex. As Macleod explains,

> The level of state involvement in *Salt* is far from abnormal. In fact, Alford and Secker's book *National Security Cinema* details how, since 2005, documents they obtained showed that the Department of Defense alone had closely collaborated in the production of over 1,000 movies or TV shows. This includes many of the largest film franchises, such as *Iron Man*, *Transformers*, *James Bond*, and *Mission: Impossible*, and hit TV shows like *The Biggest Loser*, *Grey's Anatomy*, *Master Chef*, and *The Price is Right*.
>
> In general, the military or the CIA will offer free services to productions, such as the use of prohibitively expensive military equipment, or technical direction, in exchange for editorial control over scripts. This allows the agencies to make sure the power,

> prestige, and integrity of these organizations are not challenged.
> Sometimes entire movies are radically rewritten.

As *Dissident Voice* further notes, "two films that won Oscars for best picture (*Argo* and *Hurt Locker*) were essentially pure CIA and Pentagon propaganda."

And the resulting prointelligence services propaganda has worked wonders. As Macleod explains: "Democrat-aligned voters' opinion of the FBI has been steadily rising over the last decade, to the point that 77 percent hold a favorable view of the institution (and almost two-thirds of the country supports the CIA)."

In other words, some of the proimperialist sentiments among liberals and ostensible leftists have been actively and intentionally cultivated by sectors of the US intelligence services themselves, and this has borne very strange fruit indeed.

A very concrete example of this was the Russiagate scandal that followed the 2016 election of Donald Trump and that continued for a solid four years. And, in this fairytale, it was the CIA and FBI that, quite incredibly, became the heroes of liberals because it was these intelligence agencies that actively promoted the Russian interference narrative, as weak and transparently phony as it was. In short, these agencies turned a very modest number of social media posts by entities claimed to be of Russian origin, as well as an alleged hack of DNC emails—which very well may not have been a hack after all, and which very well may not have been done by the Russians in any case[42]—into a giant scandal that captivated liberals for years and won over their hearts and minds to the idea that the CIA and FBI were the defenders of democracy and liberty in our country.

This irony has not been lost on everyone, thankfully. As David Maciotra explained in a piece in *Salon* titled "Resistance' liberals love the FBI and CIA. History says they don't love you back," [43] there is a "lamentable blind spot in the mainstream, Democratic revolt against the disastrous leadership of Donald Trump. Democrats in Congress, along with pundits on MSNBC, and columnists for the *New York Times*, [who] have made former CIA officers and directors, and veterans of the FBI—most notably the pitiful Robert Mueller—into the

face of the opposition." And, they have done so, Masciotra rightly points out, despite the fact that the CIA and FBI have a long track record of spying on progressive dissidents within the US and are "two organizations with endless résumés of human rights violations, political persecution of dissidents, and overseas coups directed at democratic governments."

CHAPTER SIX

Russia-baiting of Bernie Sanders and Tulsi Gabbard and The New McCarthyism

This was probably one of the greatest propaganda feats ever, and it was the gift that kept giving, being used by the Democratic Party to smear people like Tulsi Gabbard and Bernie Sanders as the recipients of Russian support for their upstart primary campaigns. And, of course, this fruit was grown from the same rotten tree that the other Russiagate claims came from.

The first time the Democratic Party leadership started using the Russiagate propaganda against its own candidates was back in 2019. At that time, Hillary Clinton began to insinuate that Tulsi Gabbard, a Democratic congresswoman from Hawaii, was in fact a Russian asset, and that Russia was "grooming" Tulsi to run on a third-party ticket.[1] History would ultimately show how absurd this claim was, with Gabbard not running on any third-party Presidential ticket and not even attempting to defend her congressional seat, which was up in 2020.

But meanwhile, the dirty smear campaign against Tulsi Gabbard continued into 2020 with the media's eager collaboration. As Glenn Greenwald, writing in *The Intercept*, explained,

NBC NEWS PUBLISHED a predictably viral story . . . claiming that "experts who track websites and social media linked to Russia have seen stirrings of a possible campaign of support for Hawaii Democrat Tulsi Gabbard."

But the whole story was a sham: The only "expert" cited by NBC in support of its key claim was the firm New Knowledge, which just got caught by the New York Times fabricating Russian troll accounts on behalf of the Democratic Party in the Alabama Senate race to manufacture false accusations that the Kremlin was interfering in that election.[2]

Gabbard was the target of such smears because she represented a threat as the only principled antiwar candidate in the Democratic primary. Despite being a woman of color who served in the military and has indeed continued to serve in the National Guard, Tulsi was marginalized and vilified because she advocated for an end to US wars abroad. Indeed, on one of the only times she was portrayed on *Saturday Night Live*, she was likened to the Dalmatian-hating Cruella de Vil. Tulsi was effectively "canceled" for her antiwar views, and mostly by liberals.

The other sin Gabbard committed was to call out Kamala Harris for her awful track record as the attorney general of California. Gabbard was willing to talk about what no other Democratic candidate was—that Harris, as the top prosecutor in California, acted just like the cops that would soon be protested on a mass scale. As Gabbard pointed out, "Senator Harris says she's proud of her record as a prosecutor and that she'll be a prosecutor president. But I'm deeply concerned about this record. There are too many examples to cite but she put over 1,500 people in jail for marijuana violations and then laughed about it when she was asked if she ever smoked marijuana. She blocked evidence—she blocked evidence that would have freed an innocent man from death row until the courts forced her to do so. She kept people in prison beyond their sentences to use them as cheap labor for the state of California."[3]

This attack, during a televised debate, proved a death knell to Harris's bid for president. But, of course, Harris soon emerged as The

Phoenix from the ashes to become the aging Joe Biden's running mate and to be poised to be president. Harris is now a liberal icon as the first woman of color to rise to this political level, and her past terrible actions seem to be all but forgiven. An example of this is a cartoon that has gone viral of Harris walking down the street in pumps and with her silhouette appearing as the young Ruby Bridges, who, at six years old, famously broke the color barrier in 1960 by braving a gauntlet of fruit-throwing racists to attend a formerly all-white school in Louisiana.[4]

That these two individuals can be equated in any way does violence to history and to the memory of people like Ruby Bridges, who sacrificed so much to advance the cause of racial equality in this country. Harris, on the other hand, has lived a very privileged life and has used this privilege to gain a career in which she put people, disproportionately Black, in jail. There is simply no equivalency here beyond mere skin color. But this illustrates the problem with today's embracers of shallow identity politics who care little to nothing about history, and who care more about the color of one's skin than the content of their character (to of course borrow a phrase from Martin Luther King that sadly seems to be much reviled). This also shows the banality of rank consumerism, as this cartoon was created to appear on t-shirts to be made (most likely by sweat shop labor) for mass sale.

Another quite interesting thing that Tulsi Gabbard was accused of is appearing too much on Fox news shows, including that of Tucker Carlson.[5] Somehow, her mere association with Fox and such people as Carlson was enough to indict her, at least by people, invariably liberal, who seemed so offended by her antiwar stance. This is a classic tactic of those, having no good arguments on the merits of an argument— such as a defense of the US's endless wars—to foreclose discussion and debate and to cancel someone they wish to muzzle.

For her part, Gabbard, I think quite rightly, defended her appearance on such shows, explaining that "They're giving me a platform to speak to millions of people—one of whom is Donald Trump—to deliver this really important message about making sure that our leaders, specifically, our president is making decisions that actually serve our national security interests, and I think that's critical."[6] She also said that it is "important to share this diversity of views" and "not just shut out a huge segment of the population."[7]

There are a few things that need to be said about this. First of all, as someone who has spent many years writing extensively against US foreign policy aims and against US wars abroad, I can tell you that it is my experience that I get at least as good, if not better, airing on conservative radio and TV shows than I do on more liberal outlets. This is so because (1) there is actually a sizable antiwar sentiment in the conservative community, exemplified by, for example, the *American Conservative* magazine, which may be the most principled antiwar publication in America; and (2) (and this may come as a shock) conservatives tend to me more open-minded, in my experience, than liberals. I am not the only person who has this view. Thus, famous left-wing commentator Noam Chomsky once said that while he was shut out from nearly all mainstream media sources, including the *New York Times*, conservative intellectual William F. Buckley, Jr. was always happy to have him on his show.

Tucker Carlson is one example of an individual, though quite conservative and even right wing on some issues, who is open to having liberal and even left-wing guests on his show. Indeed, my good friends Dakotah Lilly and Anya Parampil have both been on his show numerous times to discuss their opposition to US meddling in Venezuela. There is no other mainstream media personality who would give such people airtime.

But it is not just openness that motivates Carlson to have such guests on his show: he himself appears to be against US wars and meddling abroad. Indeed, there is good reason to believe that Carlson may have personally convinced President Trump not to launch a war against Iran, as his hawkish advisers had been urging him to do.[8] If that is true, then Carlson deserves a Nobel Peace Prize, at least. It would be hard to think of a more concrete, positive, and redeeming act than this. And this demonstrates why it is dangerous and counterproductive to try to pigeonhole and condemn people, like Carlson, who may have different, and even some reprehensible, views.

This is an occasion to say that, in my view, it is more important what you actually do and accomplish in life than what you think or

feel. This seems to be a very radical notion among a left today that
appears to elevate thoughts and feelings above actions and results.

Another quite notable example of someone who exemplifies the importance of deeds over beliefs is John Rebe. John Rebe was a German and member of the Nazi Party living in Nanking, China, during the run-up to the invasion of China by Japan. Nanking, of course, became famous for the brutal attack upon its population by the Japanese, now known as the "Rape of Nanking." Rebe, who had fallen in love with the people of China, could not stop the Japanese invasion, but he would try hard to save as many lives as he could. One of his first acts was to drape a Nazi flag over a bomb shelter so that the Japanese would not bomb it. Ultimately, Rebe was able to convince Adolf Hitler—who of course was allied with Japan at the time—to allow him to set up a safe zone in Nanking for as many Chinese who could be squeezed therein. As a result, Rebe saved around 200,000 residents of Nanking and is known still today as "The Good Man of Nanking." Again, his deeds spoke much more than whichever beliefs he might have held, and there is a lesson there for all of us.

To put a finer point on it, my advice to those who care about social justice and humanity is to forget about mining others and yourselves for "unconscious racism," less-than-noble intentions, or other "impure thoughts" and go out and do something for somebody—make a baby smile, walk someone's dog for them, volunteer on a helpline, etc. Those types of actions mean much more than sitting around striving for some unattainable purity that really does not do anyone any good. And just maybe, if you're lucky, you can do something great like Tucker Carlson and stop the next war.

Tulsi crossed another line in the sand cast by liberals by criticizing the intelligence community the liberals now love for going after Bernie Sanders as well with the Russia smear. As Gabbard wrote in an opinion piece for "The Hill":

> Reckless claims by anonymous intelligence officials that Russia is "helping" Sen. Bernie Sanders (I-Vt.) are deeply irresponsible. . . . Enough is enough. I am calling on all presidential candidates to stop playing these dangerous political games and immediately

condemn any interference in our elections by out-of-control intelligence agencies.

A "news article" published last week in the *Washington Post*, which set off yet another manufactured media firestorm, alleges that the goal of Russia is to trick people into criticizing establishment Democrats. This is a laughably obvious ploy to stifle legitimate criticism and cast aspersions on Americans who are rightly skeptical of the powerful forces exerting control over the primary election process. We are told the aim of Russia is to "sow division," but the aim of corporate media and self-serving politicians pushing this narrative is clearly to sow division of their own—by generating baseless suspicion against the Sanders campaign.[9]

Such attacks against Sanders came fast and furious. For example, "[f]ollowing his resounding defeat in Nevada in the Democratic Party Caucus, Joe Biden blamed the Russians, telling CBS News that the 'Russians don't want me to be the nominee, they like Bernie.'"[10] Of course, no evidence was given of this, but in the Russiagate era, just as in the McCarthy period, the mere allegation is enough to have the intended target canceled. And, just as with the McCarthy period, one of the purposes of such Russia-baiting is to undermine progressive social change—the kind of social change that Bernie Sanders of course represents.

To cancel Bernie's campaign, which was surging in the early primaries, Democrats and Republicans alike mined his past for proof that Bernie was a Communist who was too friendly to countries on the other side of the Cold War divide. As *NBC News* explained, thirty-five years after the young Bernie Sanders's positive words about the achievements of some of these countries,

> Sanders is leading in national polls to become President Donald Trump's Democratic opponent in the 2020 election. Sanders has staked out positions that are clearly to the left of the rest of the field on trade, troop deployments and military action.
>
> Both Republicans and Democrats are already using the c-word to blunt his appeal. In Wednesday night's Democratic debate, Mike

> Bloomberg described Sanders stance on wealth as "communist." Trump, meanwhile, has already called Sanders a Communist.
>
> If Sanders wins the nomination, some Democrats worry that Trump and the Republicans will hammer him on long-buried words in defense of repressive governments in Nicaragua, Cuba and the Soviet Union.[11]

Such attacks against Sanders were rarely accompanied by any discussion about whether he had a point—whether there was anything good to find in these societies from which we could actually learn. And, of course, the answer is yes there was, and one example of this, quite relevant to our current fight against a global pandemic, was how the socialist governments, freed from the demands for profits in the West, showed the way for how to tackle the polio pandemic in the 1950s and '60s.

Columbia University History Professor Louis Proyect details the US government response to the polio epidemic in an instructive article titled "Polio, COVID-19 and Socialism."[12] As he explains, President Franklin Delano Roosevelt, the founder of the New Deal, which Bernie Sanders and other like-minded Democrats hearken back to with their "Green New Deal," "founded the National Foundation for Infantile Paralysis in 1938 and promoted the March of Dimes for polio research. When Harry Truman became president, he committed to a war on polio using language redolent of the 30s New Deal: 'The fight against infantile paralysis cannot be a local war. It must be nationwide. It must be total war in every city, town and village throughout the land. For only with a united front can we ever hope to win any war.'"

As Proyect relates, two doctors, Jonas Salk and Albert Sabin, went on to develop the vaccine that ended up eradicating polio. And, unlike the private pharmaceutical companies of today, they did so without worrying about making money off their efforts. As a result, they forewent billions of dollars in potential profits. Dr. Salk, when asked on national TV by Edward R. Murrow who owned the patent to the vaccine, famously replied, "'Well, the people I would say. There is no patent. Could you patent the sun?"[13] (Had it been patented, it would be worth $7 billion.) As Proyect notes, Salk was under long-term FBI surveillance because of his radical political views, which included sympathies for the Soviet Union.

For his part, Dr. Sabin was actually aided in his efforts to develop a vaccine through his collaboration with Soviet bloc countries, and then later Cuba. As NPR points out, with the assistance of the USSR, Dr. Sabin developed the more efficacious vaccine: "Albert Sabin at Cincinnati Children's Hospital couldn't gain political support in the US for what he viewed as his superior vaccine. So at the height of the Cold War, he tested it in the Soviet Union instead. Both Salk's and Sabin's vaccines are still used today. But Sabin's version, which requires just two drops in a child's mouth, proved much easier to use in mass immunization campaigns. [Dr. John L.] Sever says this oral vaccine was key to wiping out polio in the developing world: 'After all, if you could count to two, you could be an immunizer.'"[14]

As Proyect concludes, citing Bernie Sanders's struggles today:

> Defying Cold War hysteria, Sabin worked closely with Soviet bloc doctors and scientists, thus earning him the reputation of working on a "communist vaccine." In an article titled "Vaccination and the communist state: polio in Eastern Europe," Dora Vargha concludes that the communist states were capable of "doing good things" as Bernie Sanders has said:
>
> > Both East and West shared the perception of what the communist state was and its ideal role in polio prevention. Following the appearance and successful application of live poliovirus vaccines, Eastern European states saw themselves as particularly suited to achieve effectiveness in curbing—and eradicating—polio through their part in vaccine development and its distribution. The West, while not endorsing such political regimes ideologically, agreed. Indeed, Czechoslovakia, Hungary and Poland became pioneers in introducing, testing and applying live poliovirus vaccines on a mass scale, while their Eastern European peers were quick to follow in mass vaccination.[15]

If we were to be honest, we would have to admit that we are learning the same lesson today: that the socialist/communist countries are doing better in fighting the coronavirus at home and abroad than the capitalist West. First of all, in contrast to the profit-driven US, which is just beginning to look for a cure for the novel coronavirus, socialist Cuba already has drugs that appear to be a cure, and it has had them for some time. These drugs, which have been developed in cooperation with the Chinese medical community, are already curing people in China, and other countries are demanding them. As the Venezuelan-based *Orinoco Tribune* explains:

> Cuban medicine could treat thousands of coronavirus patients as production of a "flagship" drug known to combat the disease is set to increase significantly. . . .
>
> President of the BioCubaFarma group Eduardo Martinez explained that the socialist island has developed 22 drugs that are set to be used to contain the outbreak.
>
> So far it is known that one of the drugs manufactured by Cuba, Interferon B, has managed to effectively cure more than 1,500 patients from the coronavirus and is one of 30 drugs chosen by the Chinese National Health Commission to combat respiratory disease.[16]

Tragically, as people die in the US of the virus, they may never know that this cure exists, for the US, in its decades-long quest to destroy the Cuban Revolution, is imposing a near-complete economic blockade against the island—a blockade that will prevent those of us in the US who need these medicines from obtaining them. As *USA Today* reported some time ago, we are also being denied a vaccine for lung cancer that Cuba has developed.[17]

And, in addition to the Interferon drug that it developed and that, in addition to the novel coronavirus, can also be used to treat "Hepatitis B and C, shingles, HIV-AIDS and dengue," Cuba has developed a Meningitis B vaccine that "was awarded a UN Gold Medal for global innovation."[18] What's more, while many might be surprised by this in the US, no one is making a profit off of such medical breakthroughs. Rather, these feats are motivated by humanitarian concerns.

The other incredible thing about these medical miracles is that they have taken place despite years of crippling US sanctions that have devastated Cuba in many ways and have certainly hampered Cuba's medical development efforts. Indeed, it is fair to say that the goal of these sanctions has been to cancel Cuba's "dangerous example" of providing such excellent healthcare to its people with far fewer resources than the US—if Cuba can do this without concern about maximizing profit, the powers-that-be worry, then surely the US can do this for its own people; that is, the US could easily meet the popular demand for such social goods as Medicare for All, and that is not a lesson our government and elites want the American people to understand.

And, while Sanders has also been criticized for speaking favorably about Cuba and its healthcare system, the fact is that Cuba has a highly developed healthcare system, with an incredible nine doctors per one thousand citizens.[19] Cuba is on the cutting edge of medicine, constantly "implementing new development programs such as health informatization, precision medicine, nanomedicine, and robotic medicine."[20] And, with such capacity, Cuba has famously provided medical aid to around 70 poor countries throughout the world. Quite notably, even the *New York Times* itself recognized, Cuba has been at the frontline of the battle against cholera since the 2010 earthquake hit Haiti.[21] As the UN has explained:

> Cuban medical cooperation has saved thousands of lives in Haiti. Present in the country for the last 15 years and with over 700 people working closely with the Ministry of Health, the Cuban Medical Brigades have actively worked to fight cholera. The contingent has worked in 96 health care centers, 65 of which are part of a joint Cuban-Venezuelan program aimed at strengthening the health system in the country.[22]

The US's big contribution to Haiti during the same time, of course, was sending thousands of troops to suppress public unrest, proving the old adage that when you're a hammer, every problem looks like a nail.

Another good example of Cuba's medical solidarity is with Mozambique. Thus, "after the cyclone Idai in Mozambique which killed more than 400 people, Cuba sent a 'field hospital,' with full staff and equipment to the country in March. In the 63 days of stay in that country, the Cuban contingent attended a total of 22,259 patients."[23]

A very recent story of Cuba's human solidarity with the world, including a part of the world that has tried to vanquish it for so long— the UK—has received little notice but is quite instructive. Thus, Cuba accepted a cruise ship of mostly British passengers, some of whom had tested positive for coronavirus, while other countries had refused it. As a press release describing this event explains:

> Dominic Raab, the UK Secretary of State for Foreign and Commonwealth Affairs, thanked the Cuban Government today in parliament for their assistance with the stricken British cruise ship the MS Braemar which had passengers with possible coronavirus infections.
>
> He made the ministerial statement to MPs in parliament today "I spoke to the Cuban Foreign Minister twice over the weekend and we are very grateful to the Cuban government for swiftly enabling this operation and for their close cooperation to make sure it could be successful."
>
> Cuba will allow the British ship MS Braemar to dock in Havana facilitating the mainly British passengers to disembark and fly home. This is after a number of other countries, including the Bahamas and Barbados, refused permission to dock because a number of passengers were infected with coronavirus.
>
> The Cuban Ministry of Foreign Affairs said of its decision: "These are times of solidarity, of understanding health as a human right, of reinforcing international cooperation to face our common challenges, values that are inherent in the humanistic practice of the Revolution and of our people."[24]

It is worth also considering China's international response, which includes providing significant aid to countries like Iran, [25] as well as supplies and personnel to Spain and Italy to fight the coronavirus.[26] Meanwhile, Italy has condemned the EU for abandoning it to its fate.[27] For its part, Serbia, a non-EU country, has also condemned the EU, which has put limits on medical exports to countries like Serbia, with the president of Serbia saying that "European solidarity does not exist. That was a fairytale on paper" and further stating that Serbia's only hope lies with China.[28]

In short, Bernie Sanders had a point about the socialist countries as some force for good in the world that we can learn from. But again, being right does not protect one from being canceled; it only accelerates the cancellation. And sadly, it is not only Bernie Sanders and the chance of progressive social change in this country that have suffered due to this cancellation. Rather, much more has been sacrificed—the very cause of world peace.

After the collapse of the USSR, which, due to the economic collapse that followed, led to the deaths of millions of people in Russia and the former Soviet Republics, some Russians opined that, in the words of dissident Alexander Zinovyev, the West was "aiming at Communism but hit Russia." Similarly, while those who are Russia-baiting people like Bernie Sanders, Tulsi Gabbard, and Donald Trump as well have been aiming at these individuals to derail their political careers, they have also hit Russia, but again. That is, in order to vilify these politicians, they have had to first and foremost vilify Russia itself, painting it as some omnipotent and nefarious force that can alter US elections and manipulate US public opinion. In so doing, we have been brought again to the brink of war with that country.

Thus, drunk on their own Russiagate Kool-Aid, the liberal media are elated by the prospect of a Biden White House being more aggressive in its foreign policy toward Russia. As CNBC explains, for example, "Now there is likely to be a change in the air when it comes to US-Russia relations." At the very least, analysts told CNBC before the result that they expected a Biden win to increase tensions between Washington and Moscow and to raise the probability of new sanctions on Russia. "[E]xperts from risk consultancy Teneo Intelligence said they expected more cooperation between Biden and Europe on global issues such as 'countering China, Russia . . .'"[29]

While one might think that increased tensions with two major nuclear powers would not be a welcome development, years of the false Russiagate narrative have groomed liberals for such tensions. Incredibly, Trump has been portrayed as being soft on Russia, even as he backed out of a major antiproliferation treaty (The Intermediate-Range Nuclear Forces Treaty) that had been signed with the Kremlin back in 1987,[30] and even as he has sent the largest contingent of US troops (20,000) in a quarter of a century to train with European soldiers on the Russian border.[31] I must note here that the converse—Russia's sending tens of thousands of troops to the border with the US—is simply inconceivable and would indeed be seen in Washington as an occasion for war.

I for one am quite alarmed to think of what a Biden policy of "getting tougher" with Russia would look like, and what kind of catastrophe it could bring about.

Meanwhile, Russia has developed a vaccine for COVID-19 known as "Sputnik V," which it claims is almost 92 percent effective.[32] And Russia offered to work with the US on a vaccine—just as it had offered to, and indeed did, help with the US's war on terror—but the US has outright refused this offer.[33] Again, believing our own anti-Russian propaganda, and forgetting the lessons we should have learned with the polio vaccine, the health of American citizens has no doubt been compromised by this refusal.

It simply boggles the mind how the mainstream media and the Democratic Party elite are willing to compromise world peace and public health all in the interest of political gain. In so doing, they have taken "cancel culture" to the very extreme, and they may get us all canceled, permanently, in the process.

CHAPTER SEVEN

Witch Hunt in the Academy

Man Who Agrees With The Media, Universities, Corporations,
And Hollywood Thinks He's Part Of The Resistance.

—Babylon Bee (Satire)

A disturbing and growing phenomenon on college campuses has been the attempt by students and academics to have professors and others censured or even fired because of perceived transgressions, both past and present. Indeed, there are instances in which the would-be cancelers have seemingly gone out of their way to mine a professor's long history of statements and publications to see if there is grist for getting that professor in trouble.

Pulitzer Prize-winning journalist Chris Hedges describes and critiques this phenomenon well in his article "Don't Be Fooled by the Cancel Culture Wars":

> The cancel culture, with its public shaming on social media, is the boutique activism of the liberal elites. It allows faux student radicals to hound and attack those deemed to be racist or transphobic, before these "radicals" graduate to work for corporations such as Goldman Sachs, which last year paid $9 million in fines to settle federal allegations of racial and gender pay bias. Self-styled Marxists in the academy have been pushed out of economic departments and

been reborn as irrelevant cultural and literary critics, employing jargon so obscure as to be unreadable. These "radical" theorists invest their energy in linguistic acrobatics and multiculturalism, with branches such as feminism studies, queer studies and African American studies. The inclusion of voices often left out of the traditional academic canon certainly enriches the university. But multiculturalism, moral absolutism and the public denunciations of apostates, by themselves, too often offer escape routes from critiquing and attacking the class structures and systems of economic oppression that exclude and impoverish the poor and the marginal.[1]

Lest one believe, as apparently many do, that a "cancel culture" targeting professors does not exist, the National Academy of Scholars (NAS) is tracking the numerous examples of this culture in action. As the NAS has concluded, "cancel culture within higher education has reached an extraordinary level. Indeed, many colleges and universities have become progressive seminaries. With every new societal crisis— COVID-19 and racialist protests/riots being two recent examples— comes a fresh wave of academic cancellations."[2]

Here are but a few examples of the 56 cancellations or attempted cancellations documented by the NAS in the year 2020 alone:

- Professor Gordon Klein, a lecturer in accounting at UCLA's Anderson School of Management was suspended, and received death threats, after refusing to accommodate demands to award lenient grades to his African American students in the wake of George Floyd's death. Part of the indictment against him was that he questioned, with tongue in cheek, what he was supposed to do with students of mixed race or with whites from Minneapolis who also might have been traumatized.
- Professor Gregory Patton, USC Professor of Communications, was forced to suspend teaching after being video-taped repeatedly saying the Mandarin word "nei ge" in class, which means "that" in English and sounds somewhat similar to the N-word. He used the expression, in his words, to illustrate "the usage of a

> Chinese filler word for 'that,' comparing it to the usage of 'like,' 'um,' and other American filler words."

- Professor Norman C. Wang, MD, was removed from his position as director of the University of Pittsburgh Medical School's electrophysiology fellowship program after publishing a peer-reviewed article in the *Journal of the American Heart Association* titled "Diversity, Inclusion, and Equity: Evolution of Race and Ethnicity Considerations for the Cardiology Workforce in the United States of America From 1969 to 2019." The article raised questions about the merits and effectiveness of racial preferences in medical school admissions.

- Students demanded the firing of Professor Patricia Simon from her position at Marymount Manhattan College (MMC) for allegedly falling asleep during a Zoom call involving MMC's plan to deal with institutional racism. She claims she was just resting her eyes.

- Dean Neal-Boylan was fired from the University of Massachusetts –Lowell for sending an email to the School of Nursing in which, in response to the recent protests, wrote "BLACK LIVES MATTER, but also, EVERYONE'S LIFE MATTERS." The second half of this sentence was deemed to be racist.

- Students protested for Dr. W. Ajax Paris to be fired from UCLA in response to his reading Martin Luther King's "Letter from a Birmingham Jail" aloud in class, for said letter included the "N-word." He also showed a portion of a documentary which depicted scenes of lynching.

- Provost Mark Richards was reprimanded for sending out a mass email stating that "With 'access and excellence' as our mantra, we are working hard to more effectively link our capital investments to our academic mission and priorities." The use of the word "mantra" was seen as offensive to Buddhists and Hindus.[3]

Another notorious case, which even raised eyebrows at the liberal *Atlantic* magazine, involved Halloween costumes at Yale. In an article titled "The New Intolerance of Student Activism,"[4] *Atlantic* writer Conor Friedersdorf described the bizarre events that surrounded a very innocuous email by Erika Christakis, a professor who resided with her husband Nicholas on campus. As resident faculty, both Erika and Nicholas were tasked to help shape resident life.

In response to concerns raised by some students about the upcoming Halloween festivities and a memo drafted by 13 administrators that purported to give guidelines about proper, culturally sensitive costumes, Erika sent out an email in which she argued, in essence, that students should be able to make up their own minds about which costumes to wear and that she and her husband would not be enforcing any particular guidelines in this regard. As Friedersdorf explained in his article, "[h]er message was a model of relevant, thoughtful, civil engagement." Sadly, that did not save her and her husband from a student mob who took umbrage at being told that students, all adults of course, could do what they wanted for Halloween attire. The risks of someone being offended by such choices were, apparently, too great.

As the article explains, "[f]or her trouble, a faction of students are now trying to get the couple removed from their residential positions, which is to say, censured and ousted from their home on campus. Hundreds of Yale students are attacking them, some with hateful insults, shouted epithets, and a campaign of public shaming. In doing so, they have shown an illiberal streak that flows from flaws in their well-intentioned ideology." This, sadly, is what passes for student activism these days.

Another recent example of this blood sport of academic cancellation involved professor and writer Stephen Pinker, an individual, by the way, with whom I do not agree on many things, including his rosy picture of the alleged progress in the world toward greater prosperity and economic equality—a progress that I believe does not exist in reality. Still, Pinker is an undeniably insightful and intelligent academic who deserves to be heard and to be able to teach.

Matt Taibbi, who has been one of the leading writers against "cancel culture," explains what happened to Pinker:

> [O]ver 500 students and lecturers signed a letter denouncing
> Harvard professor Steven Pinker. Citing five tweets and one line
> from a book, the signatories demanded Pinker be repudiated by

the Linguistics Society of America for a history of "speaking over genuine grievances" at "the exact moment when Black and Brown people are mobilizing against systemic racism."

The charges were beyond obscure. The effort to find traces of racism in Pinker's massive bibliography of public statements recalled the way excited Christians periodically discover the face of Jesus in tree stumps or wall mold.

Pinker for instance is accused of having tweeted "Police kill too many people, black and white" (an "all lives matter" trope, signatories cried!), of using the phrase "urban crime" (a dog whistle!), and of calling it "statistically obtuse" to suggest the incel murderer of six women at UCSB was not acting as part of a sexist pattern.

That last episode particularly enraged signatories, as evidence of "downplaying the actual murder of six women." Unfortunately, none of the accusing lecturers and PhD candidates, who presumably have done research before, noticed the actual spree killing to which Pinker referred involved two women and four *men*, not six women. But who's counting?[5]

In the end, Pinker was not fired or otherwise punished for his alleged crimes because, as Pinker himself recognized, he is a tenured professor. But as Pinker also recognized, many are not so lucky to be tenured and would therefore be much more vulnerable to such an attack. This, I believe, is a very important point that needs more explanation.

Careers in the academy today are not what they once were. While tenure, and therefore job security, used to be the norm, this is not the case anymore. Most who teach at the university level today are contingent labor who can be fired at any time for any reason and who make little money with no benefits.

As the academic chronicle *Inside Higher Ed* explains, "[s]ome 73 percent of all faculty positions are off the tenure track, according to a new analysis of federal data by the American Association of University Professors. 'For the most part, these are insecure, unsupported positions with little job security and few protections for academic freedom,' according to the AAUP.[6] Most of these 'off the tenure track' professors are known as 'adjuncts'—a term itself suggesting how inessential and contingent the universities view these faculty members, in spite of the fact that they do the lion's share of the universities' work. Many of these adjunct professors, as well as some tenured faculty as well, lost their jobs during the pandemic in mass layoffs precipitated by lowering enrollment."[7]

And it should be emphasized that contingent faculty are disproportionately racial minorities. As the American Federation of Teachers points out, "Underrepresented racial and ethnic groups are even more likely to be relegated to contingent positions; only 10.4 percent of all faculty positions are held by underrepresented racial and ethnic groups, and of these, 7.6 percent—or 73 percent of the total minority faculty population—are contingent positions."[8]

I have very intimate knowledge of the conditions of adjunct faculty given that I am an adjunct at the University of Pittsburgh School of Law, having taught International Human Rights there since 2012 as an adjunct. My pay has never changed in this position. I make $3,000 for my 3-credit course, sometimes teaching over 50 students in my class at one time. In turn, these students pay between $36,000 and $46,000 in tuition a year, depending on their state residency. Averaging this out to $40,000 a year of tuition, and assuming students take about 30 credits a year, I figure that for my class of 50, the school brings in a total of $100,000 and gives me $3,000 of that.

In other words, while I make very meager pay, and absolutely no benefits, the Law School is making a hefty profit—a profit that is sucked up by the growing class of administrators and by the few tenured faculty left. Pretty nice for an allegedly nonprofit institution.

Indeed, the academy now looks like the rest of our hypercapitalist economy, with a few at the top making a killing, while those who do the teaching are superexploited and the students drowning in debt. As *Forbes* magazine explains, there is a growing concern with this "administrative bloat" in which a disproportionate share of tuition payments go to administrators who can make hundreds of thousands if not upward of a million dollars a year. And "'[t]he interesting thing about the administrative bloat in higher education is, literally, nobody knows who all these people are or what they're doing,' says Todd Zywicki, a law professor at George Mason University."[9]

It must be noted that there is now a growing group of administrators, well-paid of course, whose job is dedicated solely to diversity
and inclusion. Certainly, it is good that there are people on campus
dedicated to such necessary issues, but there are so many of these
administrators that there is an inevitable pressure on them to find
problems, and problem faculty, where perhaps there are none; that is,
they may feel compelled to go on a witch hunt, and to burn an alleged
witch at the stake once in a while, simply to justify their pay and very
existence.

For example,

> The University of Michigan alone has nearly 100 full-time diver-
> sity-related administrative workers, more than a quarter of whom
> earned in excess of $100,000 in 2018. And at nearby Michigan
> State University, the newly appointed diversity director will earn a
> $315,000 salary. These people aren't getting hired to tell students to
> toughen up and hit the books. Just the opposite: Their livelihoods
> depend on upholding the idea that navigating campus life is a dif-
> ficult struggle, punctuated frequently by invisible forms of bigotry
> whose negative effects can be managed only through the interven-
> tion of a professionalized corps of trained diversity officers.[10]

And as such administrators get rich, there are famous stories of
adjuncts who are living in poverty, sometimes even unable to pay
for a roof over their heads. I actually wrote about one such adjunct,
Margaret Mary Vojtko, who died in penury at age 83 after being let
go (for reasons unrelated to "cancel culture") from her meager-paying
job at Duquesne University of 25 years. As I explained in my article,
"Death of an Adjunct,"[11] which received quite a bit of attention, Ms.
Vojtko used to prepare for her classes at a local diner during the win-
ter because she could not afford to have her furnace fixed. She would
also try to sleep in the University, a Catholic institution, until she was
found out and told to leave. I received numerous emails from around
the country, and even from around the world, from other adjuncts
who saw themselves in Ms. Vojtko and who feared they would end
up like her.

The point here is that while "woke" students may feel that they are really "sticking it to the man" by trying to get someone fired for something they might have said years ago, they are most likely kicking downward on people barely making a living. This would seem the height of cruelty, but in the "cancel culture," anything goes apparently, because the punishment being asked for is, in the view of those demanding it, somehow advancing the cause of social justice. Forget about the fact that what is being done to the one receiving the punishment is hardly just.

One might think that, instead of trying to get those fired who carry out the mission of the university by teaching, students on the ostensible left might wish to challenge this horrible inequality and inequity at the academy. And yet, that inequality and injustice go untouched and unscathed, with students uniting with university administrators—the ruling class of the academy—to drive out teachers—the academy's proletariat.

And sadly, the "woke" witch hunts at the universities do not end at suspect professors. Thus, the "woke," seemingly never wishing to risk anything by fighting those with real power, will kick even farther downward. For example, there is the famous case of Oberlin College, one of the most liberal learning institutions in America, where students, apparently spurred on by administrators, destroyed the business of a 134-year family-run bakery in town.[12]

The students and administrators claimed that Gibson's Bakery was racist because it called police on a student, who happened to be African American, who admittedly shoplifted from the store. As a court later found in a libel case won by the bakery against Oberlin to the tune of $11 million, a number of people had been arrested for shoplifting from the bakery over the years, and the racial background perfectly matched that of the population of the town.[13] Notwithstanding this fact, Oberlin severed its contract of 100 years with the bakery, and students, with support from the administration, protested the Bakery as racist and called for a consumer boycott. While it won the case, Gibson's is still trying to rebuild its business and reputation in the community.

Oberlin was also the site of protests, it should be pointed out, by students who complained, and in some cases protested, that various ethnic dishes being served up by the lunch ladies were not properly prepared according to the traditions of the countries (e.g., Japan, China, and Vietnam) where they originated. As one news article related, "General Tso's chicken was made with steamed chicken instead of fried—which is not authentically Chinese, and simply 'weird,' one student bellyached in the *Oberlin Review*. Others were up in arms over banh mi Vietnamese sandwiches served with coleslaw instead of pickled vegetables, and on ciabatta bread, rather than the traditional French baguette."[14] The claim of the students was not just that this food was not up to snuff, but that it was "insensitive" and "culturally inappropriate."[15] The criticism about the lack of a French baguette for the Vietnamese sandwich is particularly ironic, and hilarious, given that it amounted to a complaint that the dish did not include bread from Vietnam's former colonial master, France.

I must say that the very idea of trying to destroy a small business or to get someone fired is simply alien to me. I was a student activist once, and my energy, and that of my comrades, was directed at things like trying to get the university to disinvest from apartheid South Africa or to stop CIA recruitment on campus. We also marched during this time against Reagan's cruel wars in Central America—wars that included the genocidal slaughter of Mayans in Guatemala. These seemed like issues worth fighting about. It would never have occurred to us to expend energy trying to take someone's livelihood away, especially for the type of minor infractions people are canceled for today.

There are terrible wars being fought today by the US that students could protest, for example, the one in Yemen that threatens to destroy an entire generation of children,[16] but students for the most part are bogged down in battles of little consequence—apart from destroying someone's livelihood, of course. As Marxist Adam Lehrer put it very well, "[c]ulture war is merely the illusion of politics; it's what remains when hope for real change has died."[17] In other words, it is the politics of despair.

Put another way, in the words of William Shakespeare, the story of today's cultural battles "is a tale told by an idiot, full of sound and fury, signifying nothing."

The other thing that stands out about the attempts to cancel people, particularly for something they may have written or said years before, is that this forecloses the very concept of the ability of people to change and grow. This religion of "cancel culture" and "wokeness" is, indeed, unique in that, unlike nearly every other religion, it offers no chance at conversion, forgiveness, or redemption.

In the Christian faith, for example, we are encouraged to honor the Sauls of the world who dramatically change because of a conversion experience on the road to Damascus. Saul the evil tax collector, of course, became St. Paul, servant of God, and we are told to admire him for this change. Indeed, the Gospels teaches us to forgive "7 times 70 times," and Jesus, we are told, would leave 99 members of his flock to bring back the one member who had strayed. He also remonstrated those who were preparing to stone an adulteress, saying that he who has not sinned should throw the first stone. In this religion, as in nearly all others, redemption is offered to us all, even at the last moments of our lives. While I am a fallen-away Catholic, this is one of the aspects of the religion I valued, and that I have tried to take with me; to judge not, lest I be judged.

Today's allegedly progressive culture, on the other hand, is just the opposite of all this. In that religion, St. Paul is always Saul, always doomed to be judged and condemned for his past. Mary Magdalene is forever the prostitute. And all white people are racists who, no matter how hard they try, will always be so even if they never knew it. Redemption is never offered; only the chance to be a tad less racist. Who would be drawn to such a religion? What good does it serve?

There are examples of conversion experiences quite relevant to this discussion. I learned in law school, for example, of the man who would become Supreme Court Justice Hugo Black. Hugo Black had been an active member of the KKK for five years and voted against an antilynching law as US Senator.[18] However, he would ultimately be nominated to the Supreme Court by FDR, and while on the Court, he became a strong advocate for civil liberties and civil rights, voting, for example, against school segregation in the case of *Brown v. Board of Education.* The line I heard about Justice Black's conversion in law school was that "he once wore a white robe and scared Black people; he ended up wearing a black robe and scaring white people." As *History. com* explains, when Justice Black died in 1971, his "legacy reflected not just a changed man—but a changed nation."[19] Senator Robert Byrd of West Virginia had a similar trajectory in his life from KKK member to segregationist senator, and then ultimately to progressive senator who renounced his racist past.

I would think that, as a nation, we would want more stories like those of Hugo Black and Robert Byrd; that we would want to see people evolve like they did and even help encourage this evolution. Canceling people forecloses the possibility of such personal evolution.

The other problem with cancel culture is that it does not allow for people, otherwise good and well-intentioned, to err without being condemned as somehow evil. As explained by Jenny Morrill, a writer who herself was attacked and called a "Nazi" for tweeting a statement that there were most likely some irregularities during the 2020 election, this comes from a "childish good-versus-evil narrative" that now prevails in Western society. [20] As Morrill explains, the problem with the would-be "cancelers" "is that they get the moral prism through which they view the world from Harry Potter, the Marvel movies, and other franchises aimed at children, rather than the nuances of real life. They are infantilized by the corporate blanketing of the 'good v. evil, and by the way we're the good guys, buy our stuff' narrative. Being surrounded on all sides by this simplistic world view inevitably reduces a person's ability to think critically, especially when the punishment for doing so is being ostracized by your peers. It must be difficult being a revolutionary when you're surrounded by every corporation on the planet patting you on the back and charging you for the privilege."

Of course, the other problem with the campus culture war is that, in the words of the National Academy of Scholars, "The threat to academic freedom is obvious: when those within academia are unable to contradict progressive orthodoxy, the disinterested pursuit of truth is lost. Reasoned scholarship is traded in for the cheap, vapid substitute of political activism. And in the long run, higher education itself dies."[21]

The biggest danger to the academy, and to society at large, is that people will simply self-censor rather than discuss issues, though of critical importance, for fear of getting themselves into trouble. George Orwell had some good things to say about this danger. I note here that I am not a huge fan of Orwell the person, as it is well documented that he was an anti-Communist snitch who ratted people out to the CIA.[22] But, notwithstanding this fact, I have not canceled him from my life. I acknowledge that, even though he may have been a fink and a hypocrite, he had many important things to say about society and the human condition. Do you see how that works?

As Orwell wrote in his Introduction to *Animal Farm*, it is not government censorship that is the greatest danger to free thought and free expression, but it is the pressures of societal conformity. As he explains in words that resound today:

> But the chief danger to freedom of thought and speech at this moment is not the direct interference of the MOI [Ministry of Information] or any official body. If publishers and editors exert themselves to keep certain topics out of print, it is not because they are frightened of prosecution but because they are frightened of public opinion. In this country intellectual cowardice is the worst enemy a writer or journalist has to face, and that fact does not seem to me to have had the discussion it deserves. . . .
>
> At any given moment there is an orthodoxy, a body of ideas which it is assumed that all right-thinking people will accept without question. It is not exactly forbidden to say this, that or the other, but it is 'not done' to say it, just as in mid-Victorian times it was 'not done' to mention trousers in the presence of a lady. Anyone who challenges the prevailing orthodoxy finds himself silenced with surprising effectiveness. A genuinely unfashionable opinion is almost never given a fair hearing, either in the popular press or in the highbrow periodicals.

Of course, the very same could be said today when people, frightened about public condemnation, simply will not share comments on the propriety of violence during protests, the necessity and desirability of lockdowns during a pandemic, or that they may like Trump's views on wanting to end US wars abroad and wanting friendlier relations with Russia, etc. And, such things not fully discussed and vetted, society as a whole loses out from the absence of potentially good and constructive ideas.

Understanding the threat to academic freedom posed by such "cancel culture," 150 intellectuals signed an open letter in the summer of 2020 calling for a defense of free speech and an end to the "censoriousness" permeating our society. This letter, titled "A Letter on Justice and Open Debate" and published in *Harper's* magazine, reads in its entirety:

> Our cultural institutions are facing a moment of trial. Powerful protests for racial and social justice are leading to overdue demands for police reform, along with wider calls for greater equality and inclusion across our society, not least in higher education, journalism, philanthropy, and the arts. But this needed reckoning has also intensified a new set of moral attitudes and political commitments that tend to weaken our norms of open debate and toleration of differences in favor of ideological conformity. As we applaud the first development, we also raise our voices against the second. The forces of illiberalism are gaining strength throughout the world and have a powerful ally in Donald Trump, who represents a real threat to democracy. But resistance must not be allowed to harden into its own brand of dogma or coercion—which right-wing demagogues are already exploiting. The democratic inclusion we want can be achieved only if we speak out against the intolerant climate that has set in on all sides.
>
> The free exchange of information and ideas, the lifeblood of a liberal society, is daily becoming more constricted. While we have come to expect this on the radical right, censoriousness is also spreading more widely in our culture: an intolerance of opposing views, a vogue for public shaming and ostracism, and the tendency

to dissolve complex policy issues in a blinding moral certainty. We uphold the value of robust and even caustic counter-speech from all quarters. But it is now all too common to hear calls for swift and severe retribution in response to perceived transgressions of speech and thought. More troubling still, institutional leaders, in a spirit of panicked damage control, are delivering hasty and disproportionate punishments instead of considered reforms. Editors are fired for running controversial pieces; books are withdrawn for alleged inauthenticity; journalists are barred from writing on certain topics; professors are investigated for quoting works of literature in class; a researcher is fired for circulating a peer-reviewed academic study; and the heads of organizations are ousted for what are sometimes just clumsy mistakes. Whatever the arguments around each particular incident, the result has been to steadily narrow the boundaries of what can be said without the threat of reprisal. We are already paying the price in greater risk aversion among writers, artists, and journalists who fear for their livelihoods if they depart from the consensus, or even lack sufficient zeal in agreement.

This stifling atmosphere will ultimately harm the most vital causes of our time. The restriction of debate, whether by a repressive government or an intolerant society, invariably hurts those who lack power and makes everyone less capable of democratic participation. The way to defeat bad ideas is by exposure, argument, and persuasion, not by trying to silence or wish them away. We refuse any false choice between justice and freedom, which cannot exist without each other. As writers we need a culture that leaves us room for experimentation, risk taking, and even mistakes. We need to preserve the possibility of good-faith disagreement without dire professional consequences. If we won't defend the very thing on which our work depends, we shouldn't expect the public or the state to defend it for us.[23]

This letter was signed by a diverse group of individuals that included legendary jazz musician Wynton Marsalis and left-wing intellectual and writer Noam Chomsky.

While this letter, in my view, is a pretty tame and balanced defense of free speech, the backlash against it was fast and furious. Thus, a group of 160 individuals quickly penned a counter letter that questioned the very existence of the "so-called counterculture" and chided the signatories of the first letter for being largely "white, wealthy, and endowed with massive platforms . . ."[24]

As Michel Martin noted on NPR, however, this was not true; in fact, many people of color signed the *Harper's* letter.[25] For his part, Thomas Chatterton Williams, himself an African American who helped spearhead the *Harper's* letter, explained to Michel Martin that the letter had signatures from refugees and some individuals who were jailed for their speech in other countries.[26]

The other point Williams made, however, should be an obvious one—that the substance and argumentation of the letter, as is true with any piece of writing, should stand on their own merits; it is not about the particular individuals who happen to sign on to the letter. A Williams explained, "[t]hese are principles that anyone could sign and that everybody should actually be able to uphold. And I think that part of what the letter is trying to do is trying to argue against the idea that you have to look around and Google every statement that anybody on the list has ever said to know if you feel comfortable signing it. The point is that that's irrelevant."

The hilarious aspect of the counter letter was that 24 of the individuals who signed on to this claim denying the very existence of "cancel culture" did so anonymously—*for fear of being canceled.* As the counter letter explained, "[m]any signatories on our list noted their institutional affiliation but not their name, fearful of professional retaliation. It is a sad fact, and in part why we wrote the letter."[27] According to the counter letter, among those signing on anonymously, three were from the *New York Times*, three from NPR, two from NBC News, and others worked for *The Hill*, *Politico*, and *Condé Nast*.

CHAPTER EIGHT

"Radical Ingratitude" of the "Woke"

In his landmark book, *The Revolt of the Elites*, Christopher Lasch explains how the new intellectual elite exhibit a "radical ingratitude" to the past and to history, believing that they have emerged enlightened in a way never seen before without owing anything to those who came before and who helped to bring about the progress we enjoy today. As Lasch explains:

> The mass man . . . took for granted the benefits conferred by civilization and demanded them "peremptorily, as if they were natural rights." Heir of all the ages, he was blissfully unconscious of his debt to the past. Though he enjoyed advantages brought about by the general "rise in the historic level," he felt no obligation either to his progenitors or to his progeny. He recognized no authority outside himself, conducting himself as if he were "lord of his own existence." His "incredible ignorance of history" made it possible for him to think of the present moment as far superior to the civilizations of the past and to forget, moreover, that contemporary civilization was itself the product of centuries of historical development, not the unique achievement of an age that had discovered the secret of progress by turning its back on the past.[1]

Lasch, who died in 1994, never saw the half of it, with activists, in the name of "wokeness" and "antiracism," attempting to tear down statues, not just of confederate soldiers, which certainly makes some sense, but also of abolitionists, Abraham Lincoln, and Walt Whitman, just to name a few.

As I write this, civil rights legend John Lewis has just died, and ongoing efforts to rename the famous "Edmond Pettus Bridge" in Selma the "John Lewis Bridge" have accelerated. This bridge, of course, was the famous site of voting rights marches in which John Lewis and Martin Luther King participated in 1965, and which was marked by brutal racist violence by Selma, Alabama, police. Lewis himself was a victim of this violence.

However, John Lewis did not want this bridge, named after a racial segregationist and KKK grand dragon, renamed. His reasoning for this position, set forth in an open letter coauthored with Congressman Teri Sewell in 2015, can apply to much of the current arguments about whether historical monuments should continue to stand. As Lewis and Sewell wrote:

> Renaming the Bridge will never erase its history. Instead of hiding our history behind a new name we must embrace it—the good and the bad. The historical context of the Edmund Pettus Bridge makes the events of 1965 even more profound. The irony is that a bridge named after a man who inflamed racial hatred is now known worldwide as a symbol of equality and justice. It is biblical—what was meant for evil, God uses for good.
>
> The landmark Voting Rights Act of 1965 was born from the injustices suffered on the Edmund Pettus Bridge, and the Bridge itself represents the portal to which America marched towards a brighter, more unified future. The name of the Bridge will forever be associated with "Blood Sunday" and the marches from Selma to Montgomery, not the man for whom it was named.
>
> America is not a perfect union. Rather our democracy is constantly evolving as each generation challenges its ideals and values, pushing us forward to greater equality and inclusion. From the fight for racial equality, to the struggle for gender equality and to our

current quest to end discrimination based on sexual orientation—the history of America has been a journey from struggle to redemption. With each new generation, we are given new opportunities to eliminate the divisions that separate us.

We can no more rename the Edmund Pettus Bridge than we can erase this nation's history of racial intolerance and gender bias. Changing the name of the Bridge would compromise the historical integrity of the voting rights movement. . . .

We must resist the temptation to revise history. The Edmund Pettus name represents the truth of the American story. You can change the name but you cannot change the facts of history. As Americans we need to learn the unvarnished truth about what happened in Selma. In the end, it is the lessons learned from our past that will instruct our future. We should never forget that ordinary people can collectively achieve social change through the discipline and philosophy of nonviolence.[2]

One would think that people who truly care about the legacy of John Lewis would honor his wishes about the naming of the bridge, but it does not appear that this will be the case.

It is not just bridges and monuments that are being aimed at by the "woke."

For example, in San Francisco, there has been a movement to either destroy or cover a series of paintings created by a communist, Victor Arnautoff, during the 1930s as part of FDR's public work projects.[3] The objection to these paintings, titled *The Life of Washington*, is that they too graphically depict the subjugation of Native Americans and African slaves by George Washington and his associates. One would think that this would please progressives, who are all about exposing this legacy. However, the concern was that the paintings would be too triggering to the students at the school whose walls they adorn.

This is not a grade school, by the way: this is a high school. And so, in order to "protect" high schoolers from the realities of our nation, the local school board initially voted to destroy these historic paintings. In this way, these students could be shielded during their school day from art and history—what use do they have for such things after all?—so that they could peacefully go on their way in the evening to watch shows like *Game of Thrones* or *Breaking Bad* and to play *Call of Duty* on their game consoles. Of course, this is San Francisco, so, in all fairness, some of these students are probably homeless and are actually being spared from historic art during the day only to stare all evening at the graffiti on the walls of the underpass in which they live.

In the end, as the result of lobbying by calmer and more sensible heads, including actor Danny Glover, the school board reversed itself and voted by a slim margin to simply cover the offending paintings. As one article explains, "[a]fter heated debate, a 4-to-3 board vote ensured that the murals would be covered up with paneling, keeping them intact while hiding them from the eyes of high schoolers."[4] And so, the world was safe, we were told, at least for now.

The "left," we see, which used to defend history and free speech, has now become the censors, and seemingly with no rhyme or reason. And the censoriousness of the "left" has now extended to classic authors and works of literature, as well. And so, we now see the "woke" coming after some of my favorite authors like Charles Dickens and Mark Twain.

Thus, over the summer of 2020, in the midst of the BLM protests, a Green Party official in Britain defaced the Dickens Museum in Kent with the words "Dickens Racist."[5] As one article on this event explains, "[t]he Dickens graffiti followed the wave of statue toppling in the US and the UK, in which 'anti-racist' Black Lives Matter protesters demanded the removal of 'racist' statues. Except some of these statues were of Abraham Lincoln and Ulysses S. Grant—conveniently forgetting their role in the abolition of slavery. Even the Emancipation Memorial—which depicts Lincoln and a slave breaking his chains and was actually paid for by freed slaves—was targeted by BLM." As the same article, written by history student Luke Casey, relates, this is not an isolated incident: "[f]or years, academics and the media have sought to paint Dickens as a racist, misogynist and imperialist—in other words, an evil man." But, as Casey urges, as in soccer, it is important to play the ball (Dickens's works) and not the man, lest we miss the point of the game.

Charles Dickens was born in 1812 and died in 1870, just five years after the Civil War in the US. He lived in poverty as a child and experienced the cruelties of the Victorian England workhouse to which many poor children at the time were committed. While Dickens was undoubtedly a flawed individual, especially by the standards of the 21ˢᵗ century, his writings were ahead of their times in terms of their sensibilities and their eloquent call for empathy and justice for the poorest amongst us—for child laborers, orphans, and those committed to indentured servitude and debtor's prisons.

These are all conditions that still exist today, and indeed in larger numbers than anytime in human history, and we therefore need Dickens now more than ever. Dickens continues to remind of the existence of those less fortunate than ourselves, and to inspire empathy and concern today for them in the minds and hearts of those who read his works and watch them performed on stage and screen. The *Christmas Carol* alone, which most of us watch every year in one form or another, is enough to secure his legacy as a staunch critic of greed and exploitation. But there is also *Oliver Twist, Bleak House,* and Dickens's favorite, *David Copperfield*—a work that is more than semiautobiographical.

In my view, and the view of many, including Luke Casey, Dickens's works must be judged on their own merits, as any piece of literature or work of art. And so judged, they are great works, both artistically and politically, with few equals even today—or maybe especially today. And even if there are those who do not wish to judge such great works in this way, I would urge that they not impede the ability of others, who could benefit greatly from them, to do so for themselves. In other words, if you don't want to read the likes of Dickens, feel free not to. You are entitled to wallow in your ignorance; just don't impose your ignorance on the rest of us—especially in the name of social justice or in the name of trying to protect us. That just adds insult to injury.

Someone else who understood such things was W.E.B. Du Bois, whose lifetime struggles against racism and economic justice were buoyed by the great Western writers like Dickens. As Du Bois himself wrote, "I sit with Shakespeare, and he winces not. Across the color line I move arm and arm with Balzac and Dumas, where smiling men and welcoming women glide in gilded halls. From out of the caves of evening that swing between the strong-limbed Earth and the tracery of stars, I summon Aristotle and Aurelius and what soul I will, and they come all graciously with no scorn nor condescension. So, wed with Truth, I dwell above the veil. Is this the life you grudge us, O knightly America? Is this the life you long to change into the dull red hideousness of Georgia? Are you so afraid lest peering from this high Pisgah, between Philistine and Amalekite, we sight the Promised Land?"[6] Du Bois saw the inherent truth and beauty in the works of such writers, not bothering to worry about whether the writers themselves, some who lived centuries before, lived up to his own, quite enlightened political views in the 20th century.

This brings us to Mark Twain and what is considered his greatest work, *The Adventures of Huckleberry Finn*. *Finn*, as well as Harper Lee's *To Kill a Mockingbird*, have been on the chopping block for some time. These two books have been among of the most banned books in the past 20 years.[7] Recently, school districts in Minnesota banned these books from their curriculum for 9th and 11th grade students, meaning for students who are, on average, at least 14 years old and up to 17 years old—again, not young children. And the reason for the ban is the fact that that racial slurs, and in particular the "N" word, appear multiple times in these books. The concern is that such language could make students feel "humiliated or marginalized."[8]

Of course, while some may be offended by some of the language in these books, both books challenge racial injustice and are quite critical of it, and the use of the "N" word by the characters highlights just how unjust US society has been, particularly during the time these books were written and during the time the books were set. Twain indeed makes it clear in his "Explanatory" note at the outset of *Finn* that he is using the vernacular of the period—pre-Civil War US before the end of slavery—in which the book is set. As he states,

> In this book a number of dialects are used, to wit: the Missouri negro dialect; the extremist form of the backwoods Southwestern dialect; the ordinary "Pike County" dialect; and four modified varieties of this last. The shadings have not been done in a haphazard fashion,

or by guesswork; but painstakingly, and with the trustworthy guid-
ance and support of personal familiarity with these several forms of
speech. I make this explanation for the reason that without it many
readers would suppose that all these characters were trying to talk
alike and not succeeding.

THE AUTHOR

In the book, Huckleberry Finn, the son of a drunken and abusive
father, befriends a runaway slave, Jim, and the two of them travel down
the Mississippi River together in search of freedom. I remember reading this book in junior high, and it made an incredible impression on
me. The wanderlust of these two characters, and their growing friend-
ship, in spite of the racial boundaries between them, is quite moving.
The book, as I could see even back then, is relentlessly antislavery and
critical of racism in American life. And indeed, the book was banned
almost immediately throughout the South because of this. It is ironic
that it is now being banned mostly in the North, and mostly by liberals in the name of antiracism.

Of course, one might say that there are other books that students
could read with less troublesome language, so what is the big deal?
The problem is that *Finn* is considered one of the greatest, if not the
greatest, American novels, with Ernest Hemmingway opining that
"[a]ll modern American literature comes from [this] one book by
Mark Twain." Therefore, something great is lost by not being exposed
to this book.

And of course, there is a strange issue with this all-powerful "N"
word—it appears throughout US culture. It's not like shielding students from this word in school will shield them from it entirely. The
same students are going to go home and watch Quentin Tarantino
films or watch stand-up comedy routines that liberally use the word,
and they are going to listen to popular music, where this word is also
ubiquitous. Indeed, there is an obvious hypocrisy in banning works of
literature that contain a word that everyone is going to encounter in
everyday life anyway.

Why not deal with the word in school, where students can talk
about it in an intelligent way and dissect it rather than pretend that it

doesn't exist? Indeed, *Finn* could be a great vehicle for finding a way to rule this word rather than having this word rule us.

And while they're at it, teachers could instruct their students about Twain's real-life fights against racism and slavery. Thus, Twain became a champion of the cause of Congo, where King Leopold was enslaving and murdering millions of Congolese to harvest rubber and ivory for him. Twain even wrote a satirical piece in 1905, *King Leopold's Soliloquy*, to draw the public's attention to the massive crimes being committed in Congo. Due to the work of people like Twain, King Leopold's brutal reign over Congo was eventually ended. Twain, a leader of the Anti-Imperialist League, was also very critical of the US's genocidal war in the Philippines following the Spanish-American War.

In addition, Twain wrote about the beauty of Black skin in a famous piece called "Complexions"[9]—a piece which sounds like it came out of the "Black is Beautiful" movement of the 1960s. As Twain wrote:

> Nearly all black and brown skins are beautiful, but a beautiful white skin is rare. . . . Where dark complexions are massed, they make the whites look bleached-out, unwholesome, and sometimes frankly ghastly. . . . The splendid black satin skin of the South African Zulus of Durban seemed to me to come very close to perfection. . . .
>
> The white man's complexion makes no concealments. It can't. It seemed to have been designed as a catch-all for everything that can damage it. Ladies have to paint it, and powder it, and cosmetic it, and diet it with arsenic, and enamel it, and be always enticing it, and persuading it, and pestering it, and fussing at it, to make it beautiful; and they do not succeed. But these efforts show what they think of the natural complexion, as distributed. As distributed it needs these helps. The complexion which they try to counterfeit is one which nature restricts to the few–to the very few. To ninety-nine persons she gives a bad complexion, to the hundredth a good one. The hundredth can keep it–how long? Ten years, perhaps.
>
> The advantage is with the Zulu, I think. He starts with a beautiful complexion, and it will last him through. . . . I think there is

no sort of chance for the average white complexion against that rich
and perfect tint.

This is all to say that by banning works by people like Mark Twain,
and by effectively canceling him in the minds of students who will
most likely never find him as adults in this postliterate country, much
will be lost. The dumbing down of our society will only accelerate, and
the ability of our citizenry to grapple with difficult truths in mature,
nuanced ways will die as a result, if it has not died already.

CHAPTER NINE

Cancellation of Palestine

Another manifestation of the "cancel culture" is the attack on professors, students, intellectuals, and politicians who advocate on behalf of the Palestinian people. As Pulitzer Prize-winning writer Christopher Hedges explains:

> The cudgel of racism, as I have experienced, is an effective tool to shut down debate. Students for Justice in Palestine organizations, which almost always include Jewish students, are being banned on college campuses in the name of fighting racism. Activists in these outlawed groups are often barred from holding any student leadership positions on campus. Professors that dare to counter the Zionist narrative, such as the Palestinian American scholar Steven Salaita, have had job offers rescinded, been fired or denied tenure and dismissed. Norman Finkelstein, one of the most important scholars on the Israel-Palestine conflict, has been ruthlessly targeted by the Israel lobby throughout his career, making it impossible for him to get tenure or academic appointments. Never mind, that he is not only Jewish but the son of Holocaust survivors. Jews, in this game, are branded as racists, and actual racists, such as Donald Trump, because they back Israel's refusal to recognize Palestinian rights, are held up as friends of the Jewish people.[1]

As someone who advocates on behalf of the Palestinian people, and who teaches about their plight in my International Human Rights Law class, I am quite concerned about this very real phenomenon of hounding people for speaking out on this issue. Sadly, this "canceling" has done an effective job at suppressing speech and dissent on this matter. It has indeed gotten to the point that one hears too little about Palestine and the terrible conditions on the ground there at a time when such news could not be more critical.

A bit of information on the Palestinian struggle, therefore, is in order to understand what, or really who, is being "canceled." In short, the move to cancel Palestinian advocates is part of the bigger project to cancel the Palestinian people themselves in their entirety. In other words, it is part of the ongoing genocide against the Palestinians, particularly in the Gaza Strip, by Israel and with the support and assistance of the United States.

Betraying Israel's genocidal intent, Israel's defense minister, Avigdor Lieberman, has stated that there are "no innocent people in Gaza," and this intent is being manifest in the collective punishment of all of Gaza. As Amnesty International explains in a recent annual report,

> Gaza [has] remained under an Israeli air, sea and land blockade, in force since June 2007. The continuing restrictions on imports of construction materials under the blockade, and funding shortages, contributed to severe delays in reconstruction of homes and other infrastructure damaged or destroyed in recent armed conflicts. Continuing restrictions on exports crippled the economy and exacerbated widespread impoverishment among Gaza's 1.9 million inhabitants. The Egyptian authorities' almost total closure of the Rafah border crossing with Gaza completed its isolation and compounded the impact of the Israeli blockade.[2]

Conditions have been so bad in Gaza for so long that the UN predicted back in 2012 that it would become "unlivable" by 2020. Sadly, this prediction has come to pass, as the *Washington Post* explained at the beginning of 2020.[3] *WaPo* quotes a Palestinian psychologist, who says that he now fears the once life-giving sea because "[i]t's full of sewage, pumped in because there's not enough electricity and infrastructure to run Gaza's war-ravaged sewage system. Hospitals, schools and homes are similarly running on empty, worn down by the lack of clean water, electricity, infrastructure and jobs or money. Barely anyone has enough clean water to drink. The only local source of drinking water, the coastal aquifer, is full of dirty and salty water. By 2020—basically, now—that damage will be irreversible, water experts have warned." As the same psychologist explains, "We cannot drink water or eat vegetables safely, [as] there is a fear that it will be contaminated."

The West Bank is suffering a similar fate, finding fresh water and food harder and harder to come by. And there have been instances when Israelis have intentionally destroyed food and water supplies in order to force Palestinians from their homes and lands. As one article explains, "Israeli settlers from Shavei Shomron have recently started dumping untreated sewage on the farmland in Sebastiya, a small Palestinian town in the West Bank just north of Nablus. . . . 'We want to farm our land in peace,' Ahmed Kayed, a resident of Sebastiya . . . told me. 'But the settlers are cutting our olive trees, keeping us from our land. Now their sewage is flowing through our land, poisoning it.'"[4]

In a recent interview in the Israeli paper Haaretz titled "Gaza Kids Live in Hell: A Psychologist Tells of Rampant Sexual Abuse, Drugs and Despair," trauma treatment expert Mohammed Mansour relates that the situation in Gaza has taken a drastic turn for the worse even in recent months. Dr. Mansour explains that, in a recent visit, "I encountered a large number of cases of sexual abuse among the children. That's a phenomenon that has always existed, but in this visit, and also in the previous visit, in August, it suddenly reached far larger dimensions. It's become positively huge. More than one-third of the children I saw in the Jabalya [refugee] camp reported being sexually abused. Children from ages 5 to 13."

Dr. Mansour makes it abundantly clear that it is the Israeli blockade and the resulting "de-development" of Gaza that is leading to this dire situation: "Most people don't work, and those who do, earn pennies—the average salary is 1,000 shekels a month [$285]. Mentally and physically, parents are simply not capable of supporting their children. They are immersed in their own depression, their own trauma. . . . I've seen the starvation. I visit meager, empty homes. The refrigerator is off even during the hours when they have electric power, because there's nothing in it. The children tell me that they eat once a day; some eat once every two days." As Dr. Manour concluded, "The trauma does not end and will not end. Adults and children live in terrible pain, they're only looking for how to escape it. We also see growing numbers of addicts."

As the UN Development Program (UNDP) determined in a series of Arab Development Reports, the Israeli occupation of Palestine has "'adversely influenced' human development." Meanwhile, in 2018, President Trump suspended $65 million of aid to the United Nations Relief and Works Agency for Palestine Refugees in the Near East (UNRWA)[5]—a critical lifeline to 5 million Palestinian refugees—and withdrew another $200 million of aid to Gaza that the US had been administering through the USAID.[6]

While you would not know it from the mainstream press, on Christmas Day, 2020, Israel bombed parts of Gaza, including a children's rehabilitation hospital there.[7] It is apparent that there is almost nothing that Israel can do to warrant press coverage, much less condemnation, for its regular assaults against the Palestinian people— even when its assault is on Christmas and in the Holy Land itself.

Not content to merely wipe out the Palestinian people, Israel is also bent on destroying their cultural heritage, even going so far as to claim that the Palestinians have no heritage or history of their own to begin with. Indeed, a book that quickly shot to number one in Amazon's "Middle East History" category, before being pulled from the website, was *A History of the Palestinian People: From Ancient Times to the Modern Era* by Israeli author Assaf Voll.[8] This book, which purported to be "the comprehensive and extensive review of some 3,000 years of Palestinian history," consisted of 120 blank pages—a cruel joke attempting to show that the Palestinians have no history. As the Israeli newspaper *Haaretz* explained, "[t]he author's argument that the Palestinians are not a people because they are void of history isn't new—it's a mainstay of the Israeli right."[9]

Another sign that the eradication of Palestine's very history and memory is the endgame as far as the United States in particular is concerned is the United States' long-time war with UNESCO—the UN agency tasked with preserving world cultural sites—and President Trump's announcement that the United States was backing out of UNESCO entirely and would not pay the $550 million it already owes to that agency.[10] And, not surprisingly, the United States made this decision precisely because UNESCO was doing its job in trying to preserve Palestinian culture from destruction. As the *New York Times* explains, the United States' decision was in response to the fact that "UNESCO declared the ancient and hotly contested core of Hebron, in the Israeli occupied West Bank, as a Palestinian World Heritage site in danger, a decision sharply criticized by Israel and its allies. And in 2015, UNESCO adopted a resolution that criticized Israel for mishandling heritage sites in Jerusalem and condemned 'Israeli aggressions and illegal measures against freedom of worship.'"[11] The destruction of the Palestinian people and culture must go on, as far as the United States and Israel are concerned.

In order to guarantee that this destruction of Palestine, its people, and its heritage continues unquestioned, there is a concerted effort to silence politicians, professors, academics, and even students who speak out on this subject. And this is not mere conspiracy theory. As an article by Murtaza Hussain in *The Intercept* explained, there is a website called "Canary Mission" that keeps a running list of Palestinian advocates, and appearing on this list can lead to job loss and other recriminations.[12] As Hussain relates,

> Though the site's operators remain cloaked in anonymity, previous investigations into Canary Mission have pointed to a network of wealthy backers, including Israeli American real estate investor Adam Milstein. Unlike the version of "cancel culture" presently being debated by US intellectuals, the version supported by Canary Mission is more dangerous for influencing government actions. The site is believed to be employed by Israeli government authorities for intelligence-gathering purposes. Chillingly, for the question of free

speech in America, the blacklist has reportedly also been used by
the FBI to question individuals over their activism.

Hussain explains that "[f]irings and censorship relating to the
Israel-Palestine conflict long ago became common in both academia and politics. Just this month [October 2020], a prominent academic, Valentina Azarova, had a job offer rescinded by the University
of Toronto Faculty of Law after a major donor reportedly 'expressed
concerns in private over Azarova's past work on the issue of Israel's
human rights abuses in Palestine.'"

Hussain also links to a story about Steven Salaita, a Palestinian
and Native American Studies professor, whose academic job offer was
revoked by the University of Illinois because of his criticisms of Israel's
treatment of Palestinians.[13] As one article explained, the University
cited "Salaita's angry tweets about Israel's invasion and bombing of
Gaza. Salaita's qualifications were not questioned, but Chancellor
Wise said his presence would be 'too disruptive of the University.'"[14]

And being Jewish does not save one from such cancellation.
Thus, there is the famous case of Norman Finkelstein, the son of
two Holocaust survivors, with the "remainder of his family dying
in the Nazi death camps."[15] Finkelstein was denied tenure at DePaul
University because of his very critical writings on Israel and its treatment of the Palestinians, despite the fact that the university recognized
him as a "prolific scholar and outstanding teacher." Now successfully
painted as a "Holocaust Denier," despite his family's tragic history,
which he is painfully aware of and acknowledges, no other university
in the US will hire him.

The cases of people getting canceled for advocating on behalf
of Palestine are too numerous to mention. Thus, "[o]ver 250 cases
of discrimination against Palestinian faculty and students were
reported . . . in 2016 alone. Even Archbishop Desmond Tutu was canceled as a speaker at Minnesota's University of St. Thomas after com-
plaints were made that he was anti-Israel." Recall that Archbishop Tutu
won the Nobel Peace Prize for his efforts to end apartheid in South
Africa. The indictment against Tutu has been that he has compared

the Israeli occupation of the Palestinian Territories to apartheid—something he might know something about.

Another example, which deserves honorable mention, involves my good friend Abby Martin, a journalist and filmmaker. A presentation she was to give was canceled by Georgia Southern University because she would not sign a pledge to affirm that she would not boycott Israel over its abuses in the Palestinian territories. As one article noted, the request to Ms. Martin was made pursuant to "[a] Georgia law passed in 2016 that requires some people to sign an oath pledging not to boycott Israel in order to do business with the state of Georgia."[16] She has subsequently sued the state of Georgia for its violation of her free speech rights.

One may argue that such cancellations are different in kind than the others that I have discussed throughout this book, and that is undoubtedly true. But the problem is that once "cancellation" is accepted as a legitimate tool with which to attack people and take away their livelihoods because of ideas and speech people may find to be disagreeable, then the very concepts of freedom of speech and academic freedom are eroded, and everyone becomes vulnerable to attack. That is to say, an injury to one is an injury to all, as many on the left seem to understand for some purposes, but oftentimes not for this one.

Indeed, in his *Intercept* article, Hussain discusses Hammam Farrah, a Palestinian Canadian and a therapist, who was quite excited about the free speech letter—the one I detail above that was signed by the 150 intellectuals and appeared in *Harper's* magazine over the summer of 2020. As Hussain relates, "[t]he letter resonated with him because he has had very intimate experience with what it feels like to have one's free speech stifled: attacks on his student pro-Palestinian activism have dogged Farah into adulthood, leading to recurring problems in his professional life. 'People are against cancel culture, and that's great. I'm also very against it,' Farah said. 'But the most outrageous cases of people getting canceled are Palestinians and those who stand in solidarity with us. When it comes to Palestinians standing up for our own rights, it's very difficult. Our free speech and freedom of expression has been attacked over and over.'"

Palestinian Mohammed El-Kurd explains that, in his view, the path to Palestinian liberation, and indeed survival, begins with the ability to speak openly about the truth, to call what is happening to his people by its proper term—"ethnic cleansing"—without fear. As El-Kurd relates, "[b]eyond racist rhetoric, Israel has demolished tens of thousands of Palestinian homes since its invasive establishment and will demolish many more. As such, there is nothing complex or ambiguous about this so-called 'conflict.' It is clear who the aggressor is—statistically, historically, and materially."[17] And yet, he laments, "[b]e it on social media or university campuses, I can't part my lips to speak about my experience of living in Jerusalem without having my integrity questioned; without being accused of complicity in atrocities I had no hand in. For years, I policed my language into palatability, carefully selecting the words with which I describe my oppressor so that they aren't manipulated or misconstrued as antisemitism." But now, he has realized, he must speak openly and honestly about the truths he knows in order that the terrible reality his people endure may be altered.

As people of good will, we are called, I believe, to stand with people like Mohammed El-Kurd and defend his right to speak the truth to the hilt, even at the risk that we too may be canceled.

Conclusion

"I was never more hated than when I tried to be honest."
—Ralph Ellison

If you are still reading this book, I suspect that you are not quite ready to cancel me, and I am grateful to you for that. I hope that there are at least a few things herein that you may find useful, or at least thought-provoking. I certainly do not think that there are many people who will agree with everything I say in this book, and that is all right. And I am sure that when I go back to look at this book months from now, I will find things in here that I think were overstated or just plain wrong. But I have tried my best to be honest with my feelings and thoughts, probably to a fault.

One of my best teachers, Brother Ruel at St. Viator's, once said what should be pretty obvious—that you can love flawed things and people. Indeed, given that nothing and no one is perfect, I think that is an absolute necessity. The problem with "cancel culture" is that it does not seem to accept this truth. It does not accept that we are all multifaceted beings who live textured lives. Such a culture therefore forecloses relationships with people and with ideas that could be beneficial and enriching, if still not perfect.

In my own life, I have had to learn to get along with parents who do not think like I do. My parents are both right-wing Republicans. My mother has not voted for a Democrat since John F. Kennedy, and my father never has. They have voted for Trump twice, and they listen religiously to the likes of Rush Limbaugh and Fox News. They are also very conservative Catholics who are quite disappointed that I left the Church long ago.

When I was in college and beginning to break away from my parents' orthodoxy, it was difficult for all of us. My dad and I in particular had many emotional arguments that often left me in tears. I was asked not to come home one summer after being arrested for protesting the war in Central America. We came very close to writing each other off.

But we didn't. As I got older, got married, and had children, the things we disagreed about became less important than the things we had in common—my beautiful boys, first and foremost. We then found ways to talk to each other without fighting. This meant usually avoiding the topics of politics and religion altogether, though not entirely. We did agree, for example, that Russiagate was a joke, that Russia was not so bad, that Trump was right to say he wanted to get us out of our endless wars (whether or not he really meant it), and we all found things to like about our new Pope, Pope Francis. I learned to love my parents again, and I am glad, especially as they have reached their 80s and our time together grows short.

I have actually found my parents, who live in Medina, Ohio, to be a microcosm of Trump supporters in America's heartland. Therefore, I can learn a lot about what the MAGA hat wearers are thinking from talking to my parents. Sometimes, I find, it just pays to listen to them and say nothing.

Are my parents racist? Yes, they are racist, especially my dad. But they also would never hurt anyone, regardless of their race, and they have learned over the years to have some sympathy for what racial minorities are going through in this country. My mother made it clear that she was horrified and saddened by the death of George Floyd. She wanted to see the police who were responsible for his death put in jail. I imagine that nearly all Americans felt that way after seeing the awful video of his murder. That type of empathy is at least a start, and it is something to build upon. And I believe that one of the accomplishments of the BLM protests was to help inspire that empathy in people like my parents, and the protests certainly deserve much credit for that.

My dad loves jazz, and I have learned to love jazz from him. Indeed, I have written this book almost entirely while listening to jazz music. Jazz is, of course, the quintessential American art form, and it was created and perfected by Black Americans. My dad especially loved Louis Armstrong, and I do, as well. For me, it is impossible to love jazz and to not love Black people, for they have given this great gift after all.

One of my Law Professors, Charles Black, who is white by the way, was famously converted upon listening to Louis Armstrong live as a young man. It was truly a Biblical conversion, very much like being struck by a bolt of lightning and becoming a radically different person. Professor Black grew up a racist Southerner in Austin, Texas. He would go on to serve on the legal team, headed up by Thurgood Marshall, that successfully argued against school segregation in the case of *Brown v. Board of Education*. It was Louis Armstrong who led him on his way in this incredible life journey. Professor Black talked about this conversion experience in a wonderful law review article titled "My World with Louis Armstrong."[1]

In this article, Professor Black writes:

> He was the first genius I had ever seen. That may be a structurabled part of the process that led me to the *Brown* case. The moment of first being, and knowing oneself to be, in the presence of genius, is a solemn moment; it is perhaps the moment of final and indelible perception of man's utter transcendence of all else created. It is impossible to overstate the significance of a sixteen-year-old Southern boy's seeing genius, for the first time, in a black. We literally never saw a black, then, in any but a servant's capacity. . . .
>
> That October night, I was standing in the crowd with a "good old boy" from Austin High. We listened together for a long time. Then he turned to me, shook his head as if clearing it-as I'm sure he was-of an unacceptable though vague thought, and pronounced the judgment of the time and place: "After all, he's nothing but a God damn n****r!" The good old boy did not await, perhaps fearing, reply. He walked one way and I the other. Through many years now, I have felt that it was just then that I started walking toward

the *Brown* case, where I belonged. I realized what it was that was being denied and rejected in the utterance I have quoted, and I realized, repeatedly and with growingly solid conviction through the next few years, that the rejection was inevitable, if the premises of my childhood world were to be seen as right, and that, for me, this must mean that those premises were wrong, because I could not and would not make the rejection. Every person of decency in the South of those days must have had some doubts about racism, and I had had mine even then-perhaps more than most others. But Louis opened my eyes wide and put to me a choice. Blacks, the saying went, were "all right in their place." What was the "place" of such a man, and of the people from which he sprung?

The story of Charles Black and how the witnessing of Louis Armstrong's greatness led him toward one of the greatest legal achievements one can imagine is an instructive one. It says a lot about the potential of people to grow and to change. And change in this case did not come through scolding or trolling or condemnation, and I doubt that it ever could. It came through the witnessing of beauty in someone else; it came through inspiration. In this I see the way to a better life and a better world.

Notes

Preface

1   See full list at: https://en.wikipedia.org/wiki/List_of_monuments_and
    _memorials_removed_during_the_George_Floyd_protests.

2   Escobar, Natalie. "One Author's Controversial View: 'In Defense of
    Looting'." *NPR*. August 27, 2020 as revised September 1, 2020. https://
    www.npr.org/sections/codeswitch/2020/08/27/906642178/one-authors
    -argument-in-defense-of-looting

3   "Pro-Trump Capitol invader tells Venezuelans to follow his example &
    take back their freedom." *RT News*, January 7, 2021. https://www.rt.com
    /news/511776-maga-viking-venezuela-freedom/.

4   Flores, Leonardo. "Biden's vision for Venezuela is virtually indistinguishable
    from Trump's." *The Grayzone*. July 9, 2020. https://thegrayzone
    .com/2020/07/09/bidens-venezuela-indistinguishable-trumps/.

5   Macleod, Alan. "While Railing Against Trump Coup, Biden Appoints Chief
    Ukraine Coup-Plotter Victoria Nuland." *Mint Press News*. January 8, 2021.
    https://www.mintpressnews.com/railing-trump-coup-biden-appoints-chief
    -ukraine-coup-plotter-victoria-nuland/274096/.

6   Remnick, David. "Democrats Take the Senate, and a Mob Storms the
    Capitol." *The New Yorker Radio Hour*. NPR, January 8, 2020. https://www
    .npr.org/podcasts/458929150/the-new-yorker-radio-hour.

7   Remnick, David. "Making a Case." *The New Yorker*. February 2, 2003.
    https://www.newyorker.com/magazine/2003/02/03/making-a-case.

8   Turner, Giles. "Tech Under Pressure After Parler Goes Dark, Twitter
    Drops." *Bloomberg*. January 11, 2020. https://www.bloomberg.com/news
    /articles/2021-01-11/tech-under-attack-after-parler-goes-dark-twitter
    -shares-drop.

9   Silverman, Craig; Mac, Ryan. "Facebook Cut Traffic To Leading Liberal
    Pages Just Before The Election." *Buzz Feed*. November 3, 2020. https://
    www.buzzfeednews.com/article/craigsilverman/facebook-cut-traffic-liberal
    -pages-before-election.

10 Colarossi, Natalie. "ACLU Counsel Warns of 'Unchecked Power' of Twitter, Facebook After Trump Suspension." *Newsweek*. January 9, 2021. https://www.newsweek.com/aclu-counsel-warns-unchecked-power-twitter -facebook-after-trump-suspension.

Introduction

1 Wyatt, Edie. "My White Privilege Didn't Save Me. But God Did." *Quillette*. December 8, 2020. https://quillette.com/2020/12/07/my-white-privilege -didnt-save-me-but-god-did/.
2 "The Man and the Record." *Pittsburgh Post-Gazette*. November 9, 2020. https://www.post-gazette.com/opinion/editorials/2020/10/31/editorial -donald-trump-joe-biden-mike-pence-kamala-harris-presidential -candidate-endorsement/stories/202010310021.
3 Beckett, Lois. "Anti-Fascists Linked to Zero Murders in the US in 25 Years." The Guardian. Guardian News and Media, July 27, 2020. https:// www.theguardian.com/world/2020/jul/27/us-rightwing-extremists-attacks -deaths-database-leftwing-antifa.
4 Beckett, Lois. "At Least 25 Americans Were Killed during Protests and Political Unrest in 2020." The Guardian. Guardian News and Media, October 31, 2020. https://www.theguardian.com/world/2020/oct/31 /americans-killed-protests-political-unrest-acled.
5 Dreier, Peter. "Martin Luther King's Fight for Workers' Rights." BillMoyers. com. September 5, 2017. https://billmoyers.com/story/martin-luther-kings -fight-workers-rights/.
6 Ibid.
7 Thompson, J. Phillip. "Taking Freedom: Capitalism, Democracy, and W.E.B. Du Bois' Two Proletariats." Pacific Standard. Pacific Standard, April 16, 2018. https://psmag.com/social-justice/taking-freedom-capitalism-democracy -and-du-bois.

Chapter One

1 powell, john a. "Worlds Apart: Reconciling Freedom of Speech and Equality." *Berkeley Law*. January 1, 1996." https://static1.squarespace .com/static/55d8b07be4b07cfd7eb688eb/t/5bac440a0d9297956ff17 -8e0/1538018402569/Worlds_Apart_Reconciling_Freedom_of_Speech _and_Equality.pdf
2 Ibid.
3 Conley, Julia. "Groundbreaking Study Shows 'Deep Listening' Over 100 Times More Effective in Winning Undecided Voters Away From Trump." *Common Dreams*. September 15, 2020. https://www.commondreams.org /news/2020/09/15/groundbreaking-study-shows-deep-listening-over-100 -times-more-effective-winning.

4 Brown, Dwane. "How One Man Convinced 200 Ku Klux Klan Members to Give Up Their Robes." *NPR*. August 20, 2017. https://www.npr.org/2017/08/20/544861933/how-one-man-convinced-200-ku-klux-klan-members-to-give-up-their-robes.

5 Burch, Audra D.S.; Cai, Weiyi; Gianordoli, Gabriel; McCarthy, Morrigan; Patel, Jugal K. "How Black Lives Matter Reached Every Corner of America." *New York Times*. June 13, 2020. https://www.nytimes.com/interactive/2020/06/13/us/george-floyd-protests-cities-photos.html.

6 Katie, Kelley. "Peaceful Protest Draws Hundreds in Support of BLM Movement." *Hazard Herald*. June 11, 2020. https://www.hazard-herald.com/news/peaceful-protest-draws-hundreds-in-support-of-blm-movement/article_1434ba4c-abc3-11ea-8bf6-27cbed235680.html.

7 Bernstein, Brittany. "Ammon Bundy Comes Out in Support of BLM, Calls to Defund the Police." Yahoo! News. Yahoo! July 21, 2020. https://news.yahoo.com/ammon-bundy-comes-support-blm-135517142.html.

8 Stein, Jeff. "The Bernie Voters Who Defected to Trump, Explained by a Political Scientist." *Vox*. August 24, 2017. https://www.vox.com/policy-and-politics/2017/8/24/16194086/bernie-trump-voters-study.

9 Grzeszczak, Jocelyn. "Bernie Sanders Says Democratic Party Has Become a 'Party of Coastal Elites.'" *Newsweek*. October 30, 2020. https://www.newsweek.com/bernie-sanders-says-democratic-party-has-become-party-coastal-elites-1543532?fbclid=IwAR0zJpYM-JbKFS4YKHn91w1mSw26o_Qwz7cnnYkftU66V_gbJB5Wr8k-nIQ.

10 Frank, Thomas. *Listen Liberal.* New York: Picador, 2017.

11 Ibid, 263.

12 Ibid, 265.

Chapter Two

1 See Facebook Posting, https://www.facebook.com/1319552314/posts/10223097551610066/?d=n.

2 Ibid.

3 Ibid.

4 Friedersdorf, Conor. "Anti-Racist Arguments Are Tearing People Apart." *The Atlantic*. Atlantic Media Company, August 20, 2020. https://www.theatlantic.com/ideas/archive/2020/08/meta-arguments-about-anti-racism/615424/.

5 See Facebook Posting, https://www.facebook.com/1479780092/posts/10218645477436335/?d=n.

6 Khalid, Amna. "Diversity Training Doesn't Work That Well—and May Even Reinforce Stereotypes." *MarketWatch*. August 6, 2020. https://www.marketwatch.com/story/diversity-training-doesnt-work-that-well-and-may-even-reinforce-stereotypes-2020-08-06.

7 See Facebook Posting, https://www.facebook.com/154329797930185/posts/3607541505942313/?d=n.

8 See Facebook Posting, https://www.facebook.com/100025837235995
   /posts/612950446242858/?d=n.
9 "24-Year-Old Facing Federal Charges in Pittsburgh Riots Behind Bars on
   New Charges." *CBS Pittsburgh*. July 23, 2020. https://pittsburgh.cbslocal
   .com/2020/07/23/24-year-old-charged-pittsburgh-riots/.
10 Fonrouge, Gabrielle. "Inside the Privileged Lives of Protesters Busted for
   Rioting in Manhattan." *New York Post*. September 10, 2020. https://nypost
   .com/2020/09/09/inside-the-privileged-lives-of-protesters-busted-for
   -manhattan-riots/.
11 Stockman, Farah. "The Truth About Today's Anarchists." *New York
   Times*. September 30, 2020. https://www.nytimes.com/2020/09/30
   /opinion/anarchists-protests-black-lives-matter.html.
12 BBC News. "27 Police Officers Injured during Largely Peaceful Anti-Racism
   Protests in London." https://T.co/vIq1VL1aiT." *Twitter*, June 7, 2020.
   https://twitter.com/BBCNews/status/1269574979680702470?s=20.
13 Lenin, V.I. "Revolutionary Adventurism." (1902). https://www.marxists
   .org/archive/lenin/works/1902/sep/01.htm.
14 Mobilewalla. "New Report Reveals Demographics of Black Lives Matter
   Protesters Shows Vast Majority Are White, Marched Within Their Own
   Cities." *PRNewswire*. June 18, 2020. https://www.prnewswire.com
   /news-releases/new-report-reveals-demographics-of-black-lives-matter
   -protesters-shows-vast-majority-are-white-marched-within-their-own
   -cities-301079234.html.
15 "The Year of Racial Reckoning and the Dead End of Identity w/ Vivek
   Chibber." Jacobin Show. *YouTube*. December 9, 2020. https://www.youtube
   .com/watch?v=3Zxmg5TA6II.
16 Brown, Lee. "Chicago Locals Fight off Protesters and Shut down BLM
   Rally to Prevent Looting." *New York Post*. August 12, 2020. https://nypost
   .com/2020/08/12/chicago-locals-fight-off-protesters-and-shut-down-blm
   -rally/.
17 Stockman, Farah. "The Truth About Today's Anarchists." *New York
   Times*. September 30, 2020. https://www.nytimes.com/2020/09/30
   /opinion/anarchists-protests-black-lives-matter.html.
18 Staff, FOX 12. "NAACP Says Protests 'Have Become Diluted' as
   Demonstrators Gather Again in Portland." *KPTV.com*. July 24, 2020.
   https://www.kptv.com/news/naacp-says-protests-have-become-diluted
   -as-demonstrators-gather-again-in-portland/article_17977120-cd65-11ea
   -a421-cf695c4c6090.html.
19 Ibid.
20 Gordon, Tim. "'This No Longer Has Anything to Do with Black Lives
   Matter': Neighbors, Business Owners Tired of Portland Riots, Violence."
   kgw.com. September 2, 2020. https://www.kgw.com/article/news/local
   /protests/portland-protests-mayor-apartment-riot-damage/283-f6691f5f
   -b9ca-4951-bf53-241a2c4c1892.
21 Ibid.

22 Wire, Nexstar Media. "George Floyd's Children Denounce Violence Following Protests across the Country." *Siouxland Proud.* June 1, 2020. https://www.siouxlandproud.com/news/national-news/george-floyds -children-denounce-violence-following-protests-across-the-country/.

23 Taibbi, Matt. "The American Press Is Destroying Itself." *TK News by Matt Taibbi.* June 12, 2020. https://taibbi.substack.com/p/the-news-media-is -destroying-itself.

24 Ibid.

25 Mesh, Aaron. "Most Oregonians Think Portland Protests Are Violent and Counterproductive." *Willamette Week.* September 10, 2020. https://www .wweek.com/news/state/2020/09/10/most-oregonians-think-portland -protests-are-violent-and-counterproductive/.

26 "Americans Don't Want to #Defund Police, Instead They Agree on Reform." Cato Institute. October 21, 2020. https://www.cato.org/blog/americans -agree-policing-reform.

27 Chait, Jonathan. "An Elite Progressive LISTSERV Melts Down Over a Bogus Racism Charge." *New York* magazine, Intelligencer. June 23, 2020. https://nymag.com/intelligencer/2020/06/white-fragility-racism-racism -progressive-progressphiles-david-shor.html.

28 Robbins, James S. "Rioting Is Beginning to Turn People off to BLM and Protests While Biden Has No Solution." *USA Today.* August 31, 2020. https://www.usatoday.com/story/opinion/2020/08/31/riots-violence -erupting-turning-many-away-blm-and-protests-column/5675343002/.

29 "Pittsburgh Public Safety: 'Embarrassing' Viral Video of Clash Between Protesters, Restaurant Patrons Under Investigation." *CBS Pittsburgh.* September 8, 2020. https://pittsburgh.cbslocal.com/2020/09/08/pittsburgh -public-safety-statement-restaurant-protesters-clash/.

30 Roos, Meghan. "Trump Retweets Video of BLM Protesters Accosting Black Manager at McDonald's." *Newsweek.* September 8, 2020. https:// www.newsweek.com/trump-retweets-video-blm-protesters-accosting-Black -manager-mcdonalds-1530361.

31 McWhorter, John. "Antiracism, Our Flawed New Religion." *The Daily Beast.* July 27, 2015. https://www.thedailybeast.com/antiracism-our-flawed-new -religion.

32 "White Principal Fired for Post about 'Black Lives Matter'." *AP NEWS.* October 19, 2020. https://apnews.com/article/race-and-ethnicity-vermont -media-social-media-school-boards-ddb8251472b5a7bf0817faaa32010614.

33 Alston, Philip. "Report of the Special Rapporteur on extreme poverty and human rights on his mission to the United States of America." UN Human Rights Council. May 4, 2018. http://undocs.org/A/HRC/38/33/ADD.1.

34 Ibid.

35 *See* Tweet at https://twitter.com/HMSPostgradCE/status/132548398460483 1744.

36 "JK Rowling Says She Got 'Death & Rape Threats'... but Doubles down on Transgender Position." *RT International.* July 5, 2020. https://www.rt.com /usa/493878-jk-rowling-transgender-twitter/.

37 Shilling, Jane. "So Are Women Invisible at 51? As a Survey Says Women Feel Men Stop Noticing Them in Their 50s, Two VERY Different Views..." *Daily Mail Online.* March 28, 2014. https://www.dailymail.co.uk/femail /article-2591199/So-women-invisible-51-As-survey-says-women-feel-men -stop-noticing-50s-two-VERY-different-views.html.

38 Levin, Dan. "A Racial Slur, A Viral Video and a Reckoning." *New York Times.* December 26, 2020. https://www.nytimes.com/2020/12/26/us/mimi -groves-jimmy-galligan-racial-slurs.html.

39 Dewey, Philip. "Paul Robeson and the Unbreakable Bond He Formed with the Miners of Wales." *Wales Online,* April 14, 2019. https://www.walesonline .co.uk/news/wales-news/story-paul-robeson-unbreakable-bond-16114516.

40 Ibid.

41 Muir, Hugh. "Cornel West: 'George Floyd's Public Lynching Pulled the Cover off Who We Really Are'." *The Guardian.* October 19, 2020. https:// www.theguardian.com/us-news/2020/oct/19/cornel-west-george-floyds -public-lynching-pulled-the-cover-off-who-we-really-are?ref=hvper.com.

42 Jilani, Zaid. "The Woke Left v. the Alt-Right: A New Study Shows They're More Alike Than Either Side Realizes." *Quillette.* August 7, 2020. https:// quillette.com/2020/08/03/the-woke-left-v-the-alt-right-a-new-study -shows-theyre-more-alike-than-either-side-realizes.

43 Ibid.

44 Owen, Tess. "Far-Right Extremists Are Hoping to Turn the George Floyd Protests into a New Civil War." *VICE.* May 29,2020. https://www.vice .com/en/article/pkyb9b/far-right-extremists-are-hoping-to-turn-the-george -floyd-protests-into-a-new-civil-war.

45 Beckett, Lois. "'Boogaloo Boi' Charged in Fire of Minneapolis Police Precinct during George Floyd Protest." *The Guardian.* October 23, 2020. https://www.theguardian.com/world/2020/oct/23/texas-boogaloo-boi -minneapolis-police-building-george-floyd.

46 Tracey, Michael. "Riots, Radicals, Race and Political Reverberations." *New York Daily News.* September 5, 2020. https://www.nydailynews.com /opinion/ny-oped-riots-revolution-and-political-reverberations-20200902 -od4avt6yh5hq3dqh7lfjbpu72u-story.html.

47 Speri, Alice. "The FBI's Long History of Treating Political Dissent as Terrorism." *The Intercept.* October 22, 2019. https://theintercept .com/2019/10/22/terrorism-fbi-political-dissent/.

48 Ibid.

49 Rosen, David. "Protests & Provocateurs: Infiltrators Are Disrupting BLM Protests." *CounterPunch.* October 7, 2020. https://www.counterpunch .org/2020/10/08/protests-provocateurs-infiltrators-are-disrupting-blm -protests/.

50 Muhammad, Latifah. "Former Black Panther Party Chairwoman Says Black
    Lives Matter Has A 'Plantation Mentality.'" *Vibe*. October 24, 2016. https://
    www.vibe.com/2016/10/elaine-brown-Black-lives-matter-plantation
    -mentality.

Chapter Three

1 Page, River. "Why Liberals Hate Poor White Trash." *Twink Revolution*.
   August 26, 2020. https://twinkrev.com/2020/08/why-liberals-hate-poor
   -white-trash/.
2 Frank, Thomas. "America, the Panic Room." *Le Monde Diplomatique*.
   October 1, 2020. https://mondediplo.com/2020/10/04usa.
3 Waugh, Rob. "People with Psychopathic Traits 'Are More Likely to Ignore
   Lockdown Restrictions'." *Yahoo!* December 18, 2020. https://money.yahoo
   .com/psychopaths-ignore-lockdown-173702699.html.
4 Rihl, Juliette. "Is Staying Home during the Pandemic a Luxury? Here's What
   Pittsburgh-Area Data Shows." *PublicSource: News for a Better Pittsburgh*.
   May 8, 2020. https://www.publicsource.org/is-staying-home-during-the
   -pandemic-a-luxury-heres-what-pittsburgh-area-data-shows/.
5 See Bernie Sanders Tweet at: https://twitter.com/SenSanders/status
   /1329459827928666121.
6 See Facebook Post at https://www.facebook.com/100001406250683/posts
   /3700588896664616/?d=n.
7 "Covid-related Hunger could Kill More People than the Virus." UN
   Global Compact. https://unglobalcompact.org/take-action/20th-anniversary-
   campaign/covid-related%20hunger-could-kill-more-people-than-the-virus.
8 "Mental Health, Substance Use, and Suicidal Ideation During the
   COVID-19 Pandemic—United States, June 24–30, 2020." Centers for
   Disease Control & Prevention. https://www.cdc.gov/mmwr/volumes/69
   /wr/mm6932a1.htm.
9 Jauhar, Sandeep. "The Hidden Toll of Untreated Illnesses." *Wall Street
   Journal*. April 17, 2020. https://www.wsj.com/articles/the-hidden-toll-of
   -untreated-illnesses-11587128385.
10 "30-40 Million People in America Could Be Evicted from Their Homes by
   the End of 2020." National Low Income Housing Coalition. August 7, 2020.
   https://nlihc.org/news/30-40-million-people-america-could-be-evicted
   -their-homes-end-2020.
11 Steppling, John. "Fascist Kabuki." *Dissident Voice: a radical newsletter in
   the struggle for peace and social justice*. Nov. 23, 2020. https://dissidentvoice
   .org/2020/11/fascist-kabuki/.
12 Doyle, Michael. "Has the WHO Backflipped on Its Own Lockdown Advice?"
   ABC News. October 12, 2020. https://www.abc.net.au/news/2020-10-12
   /world-health-organization-coronavirus-lockdown-advice/12753688.
13 Paavola, Alia. "266 Hospitals Furloughing Workers in Response to
   COVID-19: Many U.S. Hospitals and Health Systems Have Suspended
   Elective Procedures to Save Capacity, Supplies and Staff to Treat

COVID-19 Patients." *Becker's Hospital Review*. April 31, 2020. https://www
.beckershospitalreview.com/finance/49-hospitals-furloughing-workers-in
-response-to-covid-19.html.

14 Ip, Greg. "New Thinking on Covid Lockdowns: They're Overly Blunt
and Costly." *Wall Street Journal*. Dow Jones & Company, August 24,
2020. https://www.wsj.com/articles/covid-lockdowns-economy-pandemic
-recession-business-shutdown-sweden-coronavirus-11598281419.

15 "Coronavirus: Health Experts Join Global Anti-Lockdown Movement." BBC
News. October 7, 2020. https://www.bbc.com/news/health-54442386.

16 Taub, Amanda. "Pandemic Will 'Take Our Women 10 Years Back' in
the Workplace." *New York Times*. September 26, 2020. https://www
.nytimes.com/2020/09/26/world/covid-women-childcare-equality.html.

17 Eban, Katherine. "How Jared Kushner's Secret Testing Plan 'Went Poof
Into Thin Air.'" *Vanity Fair*. July 30, 2020. https://www.vanityfair.com
/news/2020/07/how-jared-kushners-secret-testing-plan-went-poof-into
-thin-air.

18 Jones, Charisse. "GE Workers Demand to Save Jobs, Make Ventilators to
Fight Coronavirus Pandemic." *USA Today*. April 9, 2020. https://www
.usatoday.com/story/money/2020/04/08/covid-19-ge-workers-stage
-protests-demanding-make-ventilators/2973582001/.

19 Graham, Jefferson. "Workers to Protest Conditions at Amazon, Instacart and
Other Retailers Friday." *USA Today*. April 30, 2020. https://www.usatoday
.com/story/money/2020/04/29/amazon-instacart-workers-plan-may-day
-protest-over-covid-conditions/3049180001/.

20 Levitz, Eric. "Corporate America Loves Increasing Racial Inequality."
New York magazine, *Intelligencer*. June 16, 2020. https://nymag.com
/intelligencer/2020/06/corporations-black-lives-matter-amazon-apple-nike
.html.

21 Crowley, Thomas; Marcetic, Brankop; Sunkara, Bhaskar; Karp, Matt;
Featherstone, Liza; Asif Bukhari, Asif; Patel, Raj; Goodman, Jim. "This Is
a Revolution, Sir.'" *Jacobin*. January 12, 2020. https://www.jacobinmag
.com/2020/12/general-strike-india-modi-bjp-cpm-bihar.

22 Langlois, Shawn. "Rich Get Richer? Here's the Math." *MarketWatch*.
November 30, 2020. https://www.marketwatch.com/story/rich-get-richer
-heres-the-math-1160675582.

23 "Boots Riley on Why the Left Abandoned Class Struggle." *YouTube*.
November 30, 2020. https://youtu.be/OSQ18mmL538.

24 Waller, Allyson. "Trader Joe's Defends Product Labels Criticized as Racist."
New York Times. August 1, 2020. https://www.nytimes.com/2020/08/01
/us/trader-joes-jose-ming-joe-san.html.

25 Vltchek, Andre. "Why Is This Ongoing American 'Revolution' Bound to
Fail?" *Popular Resistance*. June 27, 2020. https://popularresistance.org/why
-is-this-ongoing-american-revolution-bound-to-fail/.

26 JTA and Shira Hanau. "New York City Police Break up Another Orthodox
Funeral as Crowds Gather." *Haaretz*. May 1, 2020. https://www.haaretz

.com/us-news/new-york-city-police-break-up-another-orthodox-funeral-as
-crowds-gather-1.8812451.

27 Lewis, Sophie. "Protesters Burn Masks in Brooklyn Coronavirus Hotspot
over Cuomo's Crackdown on Religious Gatherings." *CBS News*. October 7,
2020. https://www.cbsnews.com/news/orthodox-jewish-protesters-borough
-park-brooklyn-coronavirus-cuomo-lockdown/.

28 Powell, Michael. "Are Protests Dangerous? What Experts Say May Depend
on Who's Protesting What." *New York Times*. July 6, 2020. https://www
.nytimes.com/2020/07/06/us/Epidemiologists-coronavirus-protests
-quarantine.html.

29 Re, Gregg. "Anti-Police Demonstrations May Have Sparked New
Coronavirus Cases, Some Cities Now Acknowledge." *Fox News*. July 6,
2020.   https://www.foxnews.com/politics/cities-protests-coronavirus-cases
-black-lives-matter.

30 The Editorial Board. "Opinion | The Sturgis Statistical Misfire." *Wall Street
Journal*. Dow Jones & Company, September 9, 2020. https://www.wsj.com
/articles/the-sturgis-statistical-misfire-11599694411?mod=searchresults.

31 Ibid.

32 Lowrey, Annie. "America Chose Sickness and Lost the Economy." *The Atlantic*.
November 2, 2020. https://www.theatlantic.com/ideas/archive/2020/11
/the-economy-cant-recover-with-sick-workers/616947/.

33 Isserman, Maurice. "Michael Harrington: Warrior on Poverty." *New York
Times*. June 19, 2009. https://www.nytimes.com/2009/06/21/books/review
/Isserman-t.html.

34 Ibid.

35 Douthat, Ross. "The Second Defeat of Bernie Sanders." *New York Times*. June
23, 2020. https://www.nytimes.com/2020/06/23/opinion/bernie-sanders
-protesters-democrats.html.

36 Spencer, Keith A. "There Is Quantitative Evidence Disproving the 'Bernie
Bro' Myth." *Salon*. March 12, 2020. https://www.salon.com/2020/03/09
/there-is-hard-data-that-shows-bernie-bros-are-a-myth/.

37 Hollar, Julie, et al. "Corporate Media Are the Real 'Sanders Attack Machine'."
FAIR. February 13, 2020. https://fair.org/home/corporate-media-are-the
-real-sanders-attack-machine/.

38 Douthat, Ross. "The Second Defeat of Bernie Sanders." *New York Times*.
June   23,   2020.   https://www.nytimes.com/2020/06/23/opinion/bernie
-sanders-protesters-democrats.html.

39 Baraka, Ajamu. "Will This Be the Radicalization of Black Lives Matter?"
Black Agenda Report. December 2, 2020. https://blackagendareport.com
/will-be-radicalization-black-lives-matter.

40 Schulte, Gabriela. "Poll: 69 Percent of Voters Support Medicare for
All." The Hill. April 24, 2020. https://thehill.com/hilltv/what-americas
-thinking/494602-poll-69-percent-of-voters-support-medicare-for-all.

41 Barefoot, Danny. "Here's What Interviewing Voters Taught Me about
the Slogan 'Defund the Police.'" *The Guardian*. November 20, 2020.

https://www.theguardian.com/commentisfree/2020/nov/20/heres-what
-interviewing-voters-taught-me-about-the-slogan-defund-the-police.

42 McGreal, Chris. "Democrats Fail to Persuade Swaths of Rural America's
Heartlands." *The Guardian*. November 4, 2020. https://www.theguardian
.com/us-news/2020/nov/04/democrats-fail-persuade-rural-america
-heartlands-us-election-2020-trump.

43 Ibid.

44 McGreal, Chris. "'The Democratic Party Left Us': How Rural Minnesota Is
Making the Switch to Trump." *The Guardian*. October 16, 2020. https://
www.theguardian.com/us-news/2020/oct/16/minnesota-democrat-switch
-trump-election.

45 Ibid.

46 Ibid.

47 Ibid.

48 Hogseth, Bill. "Opinion: Why Democrats Keep Losing Rural Counties
Like Mine." *Politico*. December 1, 2020. https://www.politico.com/news
/magazine/2020/12/01/democrats-rural-vote-wisconsin-441458.

49 Isser, Mindy. "What Democrats Should Learn from the Spate of Socialist
Wins on Election Day." *In These Times*. November 5, 2020. https://
inthesetimes.com/article/dsa-election-2020-democrats-socialism.

50 Taylor, Will. "Commentary: What Votes for a Progressive and Moderate
Democrat Say about Pittsburgh's Suburbs." *Public Source*. November 18, 2020.
https://www.publicsource.org/can-suburbs-embrace-progressives-democrats
-innamorato-lamb-2020-election-pittsburgh/.

51 Nichols, Tom. "A Large Portion of the Electorate Chose the Sociopath."
The Atlantic. Atlantic Media Company, November 6, 2020. https://www
.theatlantic.com/ideas/archive/2020/11/large-portion-electorate-chose
-sociopath/616994/.

52 Kourlas, Gia. "The Election Brings Dance to the Streets for a Collective
Roar." *New York Times*. November 10, 2020. https://www.nytimes
.com/2020/11/10/arts/dance/biden-election-victory-dancing.html.

53 See Nov. 8, 2020 Tweet at https://twitter.com/chaimdeutsch/status
/1325485832418025473?s=21.

54 Hammer, Josh. "Despite 'Racist' Charges, Trump Did Better with Minorities
than Any GOP Candidate in 60 Years." *New York Post*. November 5, 2020.
https://nypost.com/2020/11/04/despite-racist-charges-trump-did-better
-with-minorities-than-any-gop-candidate-in-60-years/.

55 Zhang, Christine. "By Numbers: How the US Voted in 2020." *Financial
Times*. November 7, 2020. https://www.ft.com/content/69f3206f-37a7
-4561-bebf-5929e7df850d.

56 Fearnow, Benjamin. "Trump Counties Make up Just 29 Percent of U.S.
Economic Output, 2020 Election Study Shows." *Newsweek*. November 12,
2020.   https://www.newsweek.com/trump-counties-make-just-29-percent
-us-economic-output-2020-election-study-shows-1546951.

57 Ibid.

58 Hawkins, Andrew J. "Uber Takes a Victory Lap on Prop 22 and Talks about Taking It National." *The Verge.* November 5, 2020. https://www.theverge .com/2020/11/5/21551136/uber-prop-22-victory-national-q3-2020 -earnings.

59 Murphy, Cherri. "Uber Bought Itself a Law. Here's Why That's Dangerous for Struggling Drivers like Me." *The Guardian.* November 12, 2020. https:// www.theguardian.com/commentisfree/2020/nov/12/uber-prop-22-law -drivers-ab5-gig-workers.

60 Alston, Phillip. "Report of the Special Rapporteur on extreme poverty and human rights on his mission to the United States of America." UN Human Rights Council. May 4, 2018. file:///C:/Users/Owner/Downloads/A _HRC_38_33_Add-1-EN.pdf.

61 Myers, John. "California Voters Embrace Special Rules for App-Based Drivers, Reject Rent Control Plan." *Los Angeles Times.* November 4, 2020.   https://www.latimes.com/california/story/2020-11-04/california -november-2020-statewide-propositions-election-results.

62 Alston, "Report."

63 Ibid.

64 Mower, Lawrence; DiNatale, Sara; Frías, Carlos. "Florida Voters Approved $15 Minimum Wage. So Now What Happens?" *Miami Herald.* Accessed November 4, 2020. https://www.miamiherald.com/news/business /article246971632.html.

Chapter Four

1 "Post-Election Discussion and the Future of Leftist Politics with Cornel West and Adolph Reed." *YouTube.* November 6, 2020. https://youtu.be /RPxiNiVYLZs.

2 Khan, Haydar. "The Great Wall of Wokeness." *CounterPunch.org.* June 29, 2020. https://www.counterpunch.org/2020/07/02/the-great-wall-of -wokeness/.

3 "White Fragility, Plus Adolph Reed on Identity Politics | Useful Idiots." *Rolling Stone. YouTube.* July 3, 2020. https://www.youtube.com /watch?v=0kFTtR34cek.

4 Zombor, Chance. "Why Is It Never 'Class Struggle' When Black Workers Fight Back?" *organizing work.* July 6, 2020. https://organizing.work/2020/07 /why-is-it-never-class-struggle-when-Black-workers-fight-back/.

5 Cole, Peter. "Martin Luther King Jr. Was a Union Man." *In These Times.* January, 21, 2020. https://inthesetimes.com/article/martin-luther-king-jr -union-labor-racism-socialism.

6 Fletcher, Jr., Bill. "Claiming and Teaching the 1963 March on Washington." *Zinn Education Project.* August 20, 2013. https://www.zinnedproject.org /if-we-knew-our-history/the-1963-march-on-washington/.

7 Ibid.

[8] Powell, Michael. "A Black Marxist Scholar Wanted to Talk About Race. It Ignited a Fury." *New York Times.* August 14, 2020. https://www.nytimes.com/2020/08/14/us/adolph-reed-controversy.html.

[9] Reed Jr., Adolph; Michaels, Walter Benn. "The Trouble with Disparity." *Common Dreams.* August 15, 2020. https://www.commondreams.org/views/2020/08/15/trouble-disparity.

[10] See Ajamu Baraka Tweet at https://twitter.com/ajamubaraka/status/1315276345346269185?s=21.

[11] Orleck, Annelise. "How Migrant Workers Took on Ben & Jerry's – and Won a Historic Agreement." *The Guardian.* February 25, 2018. https://www.theguardian.com/us-news/2018/feb/25/ben-jerrys-migrant-workers-dairy-farms.

[12] McNicholas, Celine, et al. "Unprecedented: The Trump NLRB's Attack on Workers' Rights." *Economic Policy Institute.* October 16, 2019. https://www.epi.org/publication/unprecedented-the-trump-nlrbs-attack-on-workers-rights/.

[13] Eidelson, Josh; Kanu, Hassan. "It's Now Even Easier to Fire U.S. Workers for What They Say." *Bloomberg.* July 30, 2020. https://www.bloomberg.com/news/articles/2020-07-30/it-s-now-even-easier-to-fire-u-s-workers-for-what-they-say.

[14] Sandel, Michael J. "Disdain for the Less Educated Is the Last Acceptable Prejudice." *New York Times.* September 2, 2020. https://www.nytimes.com/2020/09/02/opinion/education-prejudice.html.

[15] Greenwald, Glenn. "The New York Times Guild Once Again Demands Censorship of Colleagues." *The Intercept.* October 11, 2020. https://theintercept.com/2020/10/11/the-new-york-times-guild-once-again-demands-censorship-for-colleagues/.

Chapter Five

[1] Purkiss, Jessica; Serle, Jack. "Obama's Covert Drone War in Numbers: Ten Times More Strikes than Bush." *The Bureau of Investigative Journalism.* October 29, 2018. https://www.thebureauinvestigates.com/stories/2017-01-17/obamas-covert-drone-war-in-numbers-ten-times-more-strikes-than-bush.

[2] Benjamin, Medea. "America Dropped 26,171 Bombs in 2016. What a Bloody End to Obama's Reign." *The Guardian.* January 9, 2017. https://www.theguardian.com/commentisfree/2017/jan/09/america-dropped-26171-bombs-2016-obama-legacy.

[3] Norton, Ben. "Media Erase NATO Role in Bringing Slave Markets to Libya." *FAIR.* December 1, 2017. https://fair.org/home/media-nato-regime-change-war-libya-slave-markets/.

[4] "Humanitarian Crisis in Yemen Remains the Worst in the World, Warns UN."| *UN News.* February 14, 2019. https://news.un.org/en/story/2019/02/1032811.

[5] Greenwald, Glenn. "A Long-Forgotten CIA Document from WikiLeaks Sheds Critical Light on Today's U.S. Politics and Wars." *Glenn Greenwald.*

November 23, 2020. https://greenwald.substack.com/p/a-long-forgotten
-cia-document-from.

6   "What Explains Elite Contempt for Joe Rogan? System Update with Glenn
    Greenwald." *YouTube*. September 22, 2020. https://www.youtube.com
    /watch?v=S0tFgPG26vA.

7   Seipel, Brooke. "Dan Rather Hits Journalists Who Called Trump 'Presidential'
    after Syria Missile Strike." *The Hill*, April 8, 201. https://thehill.com/blogs
    /in-the-know/in-the-know/327929-dan-rather-hits-journalists-who-called
    -trump-presidential-after.

8   Simon, Scott. "Opinion: As U.S. Seeks To Withdraw Troops, What
    About Afghanistan's Women?" *NPR*. February 2, 2019. https://www.npr
    .org/2019/02/02/690857773/opinion-as-u-s-seeks-to-withdraw-troops
    -what-about-afghanistans-women.

9   Silva, Christianna; Martin, Michel. "John Bolton Says U.S. Is 'Not Safer'
    Today Than It Was Before Trump Presidency." *NPR*. October 18, 2020.
    https://www.npr.org/2020/10/17/924969450/john-bolton-says-u-s-is-not
    -safer-today-than-it-was-before-trump-presidency.

10 Quilty, Andrew. "The CIA's Afghan Death Squads." *The Intercept*. December
    18, 2020. https://theintercept.com/2020/12/18/afghanistan-cia-militia-01
    -strike-force/.

11 Hadid, Diaa. "Will Afghanistan Force Female Soccer Players From The
    Field For Peace With Taliban?" *NPR*. November 12, 2020. https://www.npr
    .org/2020/11/12/934266508/will-afghanistan-force-female-soccer-players
    -from-the-field-for-peace-with-talib.

12 De Luce, Dan; Williams, Abigail. "Trump's Envoy Grilled by Lawmakers
    over Women's Rights in Afghanistan." *NBCNews.com*. September 22,
    2020. https://www.nbcnews.com/politics/congress/trump-s-envoy-grilled
    -lawmakers-over-women-s-rights-afghanistan-n1240769.

13 Nanda, Ved. "Nanda: Talk of Peace Is Slow in Afghanistan, but the U.S.
    Must Not Abandon Them Now." *The Denver Post*. September 29, 2020.
    https://www.denverpost.com/2020/09/29/afghanistan-peace-talks-slow-us
    -must-not-abandon-them-ved-nanda/.

14 "The Muslim Terrorist Apparatus Was Created by US Intelligence as a
    Geopolitical Weapon." *Emperor's Clothes Interviews*. January 15, 1998.
    http://emperors-clothes.com/interviews/brz.htm.

15 Parenti, Michael. "Afghanistan, Another Untold Story." *Common Dreams*.
    December 2, 2008. https://www.commondreams.org/views/2008/12/02
    /afghanistan-another-untold-stor.

16 Bohn, Lauren. "Why Afghanistan Is Still the Worst Place to Be a Woman."
    Time. December 8, 2018. https://time.com/5472411/afghanistan-women
    -justice-war/.

17 "Facts on United States Military Sexual Assault." *Protect Our Defenders*.
    August, 2020. https://www.protectourdefenders.com/wp-content/uploads
    /2020/08/MSA-Fact-Sheet-2020_FINAL-2.pdf.

18 Ibid.

19 Rempfer, Kyle. "Murder, Sexual Harassment Rates at Fort Hood among Highest in the Service, Army Secretary Says." *Army Times.* August 6, 2020. https://www.armytimes.com/news/your-army/2020/08/06/murder-sexual-harassment-rates-at-fort-hood-among-highest-in-the-service-army-secretary-says/.

20 Barsocchini, Robert J. "American Rape of Vietnamese Women Was Considered 'Standard Operating Procedure.'" *CounterPunch.org.* October 2, 2017. https://www.counterpunch.org/2017/10/03/american-rape-of-vietnamese-women-was-considered-standard-operating-procedure/.

21 Morris, Madeline. "By Force of Arms: Rape, War & Military Culture." *Duke Law Review,* Volume 45, Number 4. February, 1996. https://scholarship.law.duke.edu/cgi/viewcontent.cgi?article=3304&context=dlj.

22 Vine, David; Winchester, Simon. *Base Nation: How U.S. Military Bases Abroad Harm America and the World.* New York: Skyhorse Publishing, 2017.

23 Mesok, Elizabeth. "Sexual Violence and the US Military: Feminism, US Empire, and the Failure of Liberal Equality." *Feminist Studies, Inc.* Vol. 42, No. 1, Everyday Militarism (2016). https://www.jstor.org/stable/10.15767/feministstudies.42.1.41?seq=1.

24 "Convention on the Elimination of All Forms of Discrimination Against Women." United Nations. https://www.un.org/womenwatch/daw/cedaw/cedaw.htm.

25 Mahajan, Rahul, et al. "'We Think the Price Is Worth It.'" FAIR. February 8, 2016. https://fair.org/extra/we-think-the-price-is-worth-it/.

26 Rapaport, Wes. "Pins of Diplomacy: Madeleine Albright Shares Stories behind Legendary Collection." KXAN Austin. October 26, 2017. https://www.kxan.com/news/pins-of-diplomacy-madeleine-albright-shares-stories-behind-legendary-collection/.

27 Dowd, Maureen. "Fight of the Valkyries." *New York Times.* March 23, 2011. https://www.nytimes.com/2011/03/23/opinion/23dowd.html.

28 Ibid.

29 Daly, Corbett. "Clinton on Qaddafi: 'We Came, We Saw, He Died.'" *CBS News.* October 21, 2011. https://www.cbsnews.com/news/clinton-on-qaddafi-we-came-we-saw-he-died/.

30 Samboma, Julia Lahai. "Eighth Anniversary of African Genocide in Libya." *Pambazuka News.* Feb 27, 2019. https://www.pambazuka.org/human-security/eighth-anniversary-african-genocide-libya.

31 Mesok, "Sexual Violence."

32 Barnard, Corinna. "Imperialism in Pumps." Consortium News. November 17, 2020. https://consortiumnews.com/2020/11/17/imperialism-in-pumps/.

33 Ahn, Christine; Susskind, Yifat; Wiesner, Cindy. "Women of Color Should Be the Ones Remaking U.S. Foreign Policy." *Newsweek.* November 17, 2020. https://www.newsweek.com/women-color-should-ones-remaking-us-foreign-policy-opinion-1548013.

[34] Kay, Jonathan. "Workers vs. Wokeness at Smith College: Campus Social Justice as a Luxury Good." Quillette. November 28, 2020. https://quillette.com/2020/11/17/workers-vs-wokeness-recognizing-campus-social-justice-as-a-luxury-good/.

[35] Kounalakis, Markos. "The Feminist Was a Spook." Chicago Tribune. May 11, 2019. https://www.chicagotribune.com/opinion/commentary/ct-gloria-steinem-cia-20151025-story.html.

[36] Bricmont, Jean. Humanitarian Imperialism. New York: Monthly Review Press, 2007, p. 12.

[37] "Global Gender Gap Report 2020." World Economic Forum. http://www3.weforum.org/docs/WEF_GGGR_2020.pdf.

[38] "Four More Ways the CIA Has Meddled in Africa." BBC News. May 16, 2016. https://www.bbc.com/news/world-africa-3630332.

[39] Parramore, Lynn Stuart. "Why Does a White CIA Agent Play the Hero to Killmonger's Villain in 'Black Panther'?" NBCNews.com. March 11, 2018. https://www.nbcnews.com/think/opinion/why-does-white-cia-agent-play-hero-killmonger-s-villain-ncna855401.

[40] Macleod, Alan. "Angelina Jolie's MI6 Interview Shows Just How Connected Hollywood Is to the Deep State." MintPress News. November 20, 2020. https://www.mintpressnews.com/angelina-jolie-mi6-hollywood-connected-cia-national-security/272835/.

[41] "Almost Half of Russians in US Have Experienced Discrimination alongside 'Unfair' Portrayal of Country in Media—Survey." RT International. Nov. 7, 2020. https://www.rt.com/russia/506028-discrimination-russophobia-presidential-election/.

[42] Barnard, Corinna. "PATRICK LAWRENCE: The 'See-No-Evil' Phase of Russiagate." Consortium News. May 12, 2020. https://consortiumnews.com/2020/05/11/patrick-lawrence-the-see-no-evil-phase-of-russiagate/.

[43] Masciotra, David. "'Resistance' Liberals Love the FBI and CIA. History Says They Don't Love You Back." Salon. September 22, 2019. https://www.salon.com/2019/09/21/resistance-liberals-love-the-fbi-and-cia-history-says-they-dont-love-you-back/.

Chapter Six

[1] Merica, Dan. "Hillary Clinton Suggests Russians Are 'Grooming' Tulsi Gabbard for Third-Party Run." CNN. October 21, 2019. https://www.cnn.com/2019/10/18/politics/hillary-clinton-tulsi-gabbard/index.html.

[2] Greenwald, Glenn. "NBC News, to Claim Russia Supports Tulsi Gabbard, Relies on Firm Just Caught Fabricating Russia Data for the Democratic Party." The Intercept. February 3, 2019. https://theintercept.com/2019/02/03/nbc-news-to-claim-russia-supports-tulsi-gabbard-relies-on-firm-just-caught-fabricating-russia-data-for-the-democratic-party/.

[3] Cillizza, Chris. "How You Know Tulsi Gabbard Really Got under Kamala Harris' Skin." CNN. August 1, 2019. https://www.cnn.com/2019/08/01/politics/tulsi-gabbard-kamala-harris-debate/index.html.

4   Cooper, Gael Fashingbauer. "The Artist behind That Inspiring Viral Image
    of Kamala Harris and Ruby Bridges Shares Its Backstory." CNET. November
    11, 2020. https://www.cnet.com/news/the-story-behind-that-viral-image
    -of-kamala-harris-and-ruby-bridges/.
5   Lemon, Jason. "Tulsi Gabbard Confronts The View Hosts Saying, 'You
    Continue to Spread These Innuendos That Have Nothing to Do with Who
    I Am.'" *Newsweek*. November 6, 2019. https://www.newsweek.com/tulsi
    -gabbard-view-behar-interview-1470231.
6   Bonn, Tess. "Gabbard: Appearing on Fox News Allows Me to Speak
    to Trump." *The Hill*. January 10, 2020. https://thehill.com/hilltv/rising
    /477713-gabbard-appearing-fox-news-allows-me-address-trump.
7   Ibid.
8   Tani, Maxwell; Swan, Betsy. "Tucker Carlson Tells Trump in Private: No
    War With Iran." *The Daily Beast*. June 19, 2019. https://www.thedailybeast
    .com/fox-news-tucker-carlson-privately-advises-trump-against-iran-war.
9   Tulsi Gabbard. "Tulsi Gabbard: Presidential Candidates Must Also Condemn
    Election Interference by US Intelligence Agencies." *The Hill*. February
    29, 2020. https://thehill.com/blogs/congress-blog/politics/485051-tulsi
    -gabbard-presidential-candidates-must-also-condemn-election.
10 Kuzmarov, Jeremy. "Anti-Russian Xenophobia Reaches Ridiculous Levels."
    CounterPunch.org. February 24, 2020. https://www.counterpunch.org/2020
    /02/26/anti-russian-xenophobia-reaches-ridiculous-levels/.
11 Dilanian, Ken; De Luce, Dan. "Will Bernie Sanders' Long-Ago Praise of
    Socialist Regimes Hurt Democrats in November?" *NBC News*. February 21,
    2020. https://www.nbcnews.com/politics/2020-election/will-sanders-long
    -ago-praise-socialist-regimes-hurt-democrats-november-n1139811.
12 Proyect, Louis. "Polio, COVID-19, and Socialism." *Louis Proyect: The
    Unrepentant Marxist*. March 14, 2020. https://louisproyect.org/2020/03/14
    /polio-covid-19-and-socialism/.
13 Ibid.
14 Beaubien, Jason. "Wiping Out Polio: How The U.S. Snuffed Out A
    Killer." NPR. October 15, 2012. https://www.npr.org/sections/health
    -shots/2012/10/16/162670836/wiping-out-polio-how-the-u-s-snuffed-out
    -a-killer?utm_campaign=storyshare.
15 Proyect, "Polio."
16 "Cuban Drug Could Save Thousands of Lives in Coronavirus Pandemic."
    Orinoco Tribune. March 17, 2020. https://orinocotribune.com/cuban-drug
    -could-save-thousands-of-lives-in-coronavirus-pandemic/.
17 Jacobs, Sally. "Cuba Has a Lung Cancer Vaccine. Many U.S. Patients Can't
    Get It without Breaking the Law." *USA Today*. January 10, 2018. https://
    www.usatoday.com/story/news/world/2018/01/09/cuba-has-lung-cancer
    -vaccine-many-u-s-patients-cant-get-without-breaking-law/1019093001/.
18 Yaffe, Helen. "Cuba's Contribution to Combatting COVID-19."
    CounterPunch.org. March 17, 2020. https://www.counterpunch.org/2020
    /03/17/cubas-contribution-to-combatting-covid-19/.

19 "Cuba Has 9 Doctors Per 1000 Citizens, Highest in Its History." *teleSUR.* July 23, 2019. https://www.telesurenglish.net/news/cuba-cuban-doctors -highest-number-in-history-20190723-0009.html.

20 Ibid.

21 Archibold, Randal C. "In Haiti's Cholera Fight, Cuba Takes Lead Role." *New York Times.* November 07, 2011. https://www.nytimes.com /2011/11/08/world/americas/in-haitis-cholera-fight-cuba-takes-lead -role.html.

22 "Cholera in Haiti, An End in Sight." United Nations. http://www.un.org /News/dh/infocus/haiti/CholeraHaitiAnEndInSight.pdf.

23 "Cuba Has 9 Doctors."

24 "PRESS RELEASE: Dominic Raab Thanks Cuba for Coronavirus Assistance." *Cuba Solidarity Campaign, Great Britain.* March 17, 2020. https://cuba-solidarity.org.uk/news/article/3957/press-release-dominic -raab-thanks-cuba-for-coronavirus-assistance.

25 "Chinese People, Firms Send New Anti-Corona Aid to Iran." *Tehran Times.* March 13, 2020. https://www.tehrantimes.com/news/446066/Chinese -people-firms-send-new-anti-corona-aid-to-Iran.

26 Sweeney, Steve. "China Sends Medical Experts to Support Italy and Spain's Fight against Coronavirus." *Morning Star.* March 13, 2020. https:// morningstaronline.co.uk/article/w/china-sends-medical-experts-to-support -italy-and-spain-fight-against-coronavirus.

27 Ibid.

28 Evans, Zachary. "Serbian President Labels European Solidarity 'Fairy Tale', Says Only China Can Assist in Coronavirus Response." *National Review.* March 16, 2020. https://www.nationalreview.com/news/coronavirus-outbreak -serbian-president-aleksandar-vucic-labels-european-solidarity-fairy-tale-says -only-china-can-assist-in-coronavirus-response/.

29 Ellyatt, Holly. "As Putin Fails to Congratulate Biden, Experts Predict What the Result Means for US-Russia Relations." CNBC. November 9, 2020. https://www.cnbc.com/2020/11/09/what-does-bidens-victory-mean-for -us-russia-relations.html.

30 "INF Nuclear Treaty: US Pulls out of Cold War-Era Pact with Russia." BBC News. August 2, 2019. https://www.bbc.com/news/world-us-canada -49198565.

31 Murray, Trent. "Trump Sending 20,000 Troops to Train with Europeans on Russian Border." *euronews.* February 4, 2020. https://www.euronews .com/2020/02/04/trump-sending-20-000-troops-to-train-with-europeans -on-russian-border.

32 Kantchev, Georgi. "Russia Says Its Coronavirus Vaccine Sputnik V Shows Over 90% Efficacy." *Wall Street Journal.* Dow Jones & Company. November 11, 2020. https://www.wsj.com/articles/russia-says-its-coronavirus -vaccine-sputnik-v-shows-over-90-efficacy-11605095822.

33 Chance, Matthew; Ullah, Zahra; Salama, Vivian. "Russia Offers to Help US
     with Covid-19 Vaccine; US Says No." CNN. August 13, 2020. https://www
     .cnn.com/2020/08/13/europe/russia-us-coronavirus-vaccine/index.html.

Chapter Seven

1 Editor. "Chris Hedges: Don't Be Fooled by the Cancel Culture Wars."
    scheerpost.com. July 22, 2020. https://scheerpost.com/2020/07/13/chris
    -hedges-dont-be-fooled-by-the-cancel-culture-wars/.
2 David, John. "Tracking 'Cancel Culture' in Higher Education." National
    Association of Scholars. December 9, 2020. https://www.nas.org/blogs
    /article/tracking-cancel-culture-in-higher-education.
3 Ibid.
4 Friedersdorf, Conor. "The New Intolerance of Student Activism." *The
    Atlantic*. November 14, 2015. https://www.theatlantic.com/politics/archive
    /2015/11/the-new-intolerance-of-student-activism-at-yale/414810/.
5 Taibbi, Matt. "If It's Not 'Cancel Culture,' What Kind of Culture Is It?"
    TK News by Matt Taibbi. July 10, 2020. https://taibbi.substack.com/p/if-its
    -not-cancel-culture-what-kind.
6 Flaherty, Colleen. "A Non-Tenure-Track Profession?" *Inside Higher Ed*.
    October 12, 2018. https://www.insidehighered.com/news/2018/10/12
    /about-three-quarters-all-faculty-positions-are-tenure-track-according-new
    -aaup.
7 Sainato, Michael. "Outrage as Coronavirus Prompts US Universities and
    Colleges to Shed Staff." *The Guardian*. August 12, 2020. https://www
    .theguardian.com/us-news/2020/aug/12/us-universities-colleges-job-losses
    -coronavirus.
8 "Facts about Adjuncts." *New Faculty Majority*. Accessed December 20, 2020.
    https://www.newfacultymajority.info/facts-about-adjuncts/.
9 Simon, Caroline. "Bureaucrats And Buildings: The Case For Why College
    Is So Expensive." *Forbes*. September 5, 2017. https://www.forbes.com/sites
    /carolinesimon/2017/09/05/bureaucrats-and-buildings-the-case-for-why
    -college-is-so-expensive/?sh=2d230895456a.
10 Kay, Jonathan. "Workers vs. Wokeness at Smith College: Campus Social
    Justice as a Luxury Good." *Quillette*. November 28, 2020. https://quillette
    .com/2020/11/17/workers-vs-wokeness-recognizing-campus-social-justice
    -as-a-luxury-good/.
11 Kovalik, Daniel. "Death of an Adjunct." *Pittsburgh Post-Gazette*. September
    18, 2013. https://www.post-gazette.com/opinion/Op-Ed/2013/09/18/Death
    -of-an-adjunct/stories/201309180224.
12 Gibson, David. "Oberlin Bakery Owner: Gibson's Bakery Paid a High
    Cost for an Unfairly Damaged Reputation." *USA Today*. Gannett
    Satellite Information Network, June 23, 2019. https://www.usatoday.com
    /story/opinion/voices/2019/06/21/oberlin-college-gibson-bakery-lawsuit
    -column/1523525001/.

13 Dickson, E. J. "How a Small-Town Bakery in Ohio Became a Lightning Rod in the Culture Wars." *Rolling Stone*. July 18, 2019. https://www.rollingstone .com/culture/culture-features/oberlin-gibson-bakery-protest-defamation -suit-controversy-culture-war-850404/.

14 Licea, Melkorka; Italiano, Laura. "Students at Lena Dunham's College Offended by Lack of Fried Chicken." *New York Post*. December 19, 2015. https://nypost.com/2015/12/18/pc-students-at-lena-dunhams-college -offended-by-lack-of-fried-chicken/.

15 Ibid.

16 Ahmed, Kaamil. "Yemen on Brink of Losing Entire Generation of Children to Hunger, UN Warns." *The Guardian*. Guardian News and Media, October 28, 2020. https://www.theguardian.com/global-development/2020/oct/28 /yemen-on-brink-of-losing-entire-generation-of-children-to-hunger-un -warns.

17 Lehrer, Adam. "Art's Moral Fetish." *Caesura*. October 28, 2020. https:// caesuramag.org/essays/arts-moral-fetish.

18 Morgan, Thad. "How an Ex-KKK Member Made His Way Onto the U.S. Supreme Court." *History.com*. A&E Television Networks, October 10, 2018. https://www.history.com/news/kkk-supreme-court-hugo-black-fdr.

19 Ibid.

20 Morrill, Jenny. "Cancel Culture Stems from Good-v-Evil Disney Populism – I Voiced Doubt and Now I'm the Villain." *RT International*. November 16, 2020. https://www.rt.com/op-ed/506869-cancel-culture-disney-populism/.

21 David, John. "Tracking 'Cancel Culture' in Higher Education." National Association of Scholars. December 9, 2020. https://www.nas.org/blogs /article/tracking-cancel-culture-in-higher-education/.

22 Norton, Ben. "Snitch George Orwell's List of Leftists for the British Government." *Ben Norton*. July 8, 2020. https://bennorton.com/george -orwell-list-leftists-snitch-british-government/.

23 "A Letter on Justice and Open Debate." *Harper's Magazine*. August 21, 2020. https://harpers.org/a-letter-on-justice-and-open-debate/.

24 Wulfsohn, Joseph. "Letter Dismissing 'Cancel Culture' Concerns Mocked for Anonymous Signers Apparently 'Fearful of Retaliation.'" *Fox News*. July 10, 2020. https://www.foxnews.com/media/counter-letter-dismissing -cancel-culture-anonymous-signers-fearful-of-retaliation.

25 Silva, Christianna. "Thomas Chatterton Williams On Debate, Criticism And The Letter In 'Harper's Magazine.'" NPR. July 11, 2020. https://www .npr.org/2020/07/11/890052755/thomas-chatterton-williams-on-debate -criticism-and-the-letter-in-harper-s-magazi?ft=nprml.

26 Ibid.

27 Wulfsohn, "Letter Dismissing."

Chapter Eight

1 Lasch, Christopher. *Revolt of the Elites*. New York: W.W. Norton & Co., 1996, p. 40.
2 "Editorial: John Lewis, Terri Sewell Defend Keeping Selma Bridge Named after Edmund Pettus." Congresswoman Terri Sewell, June 18, 2015. https://sewell.house.gov/media-center/in-the-news/alcom-john-lewis-terri-sewell-defend-keeping-selma-bridge-named-after.
3 Dafoe, Taylor. "In a Reversal, the San Francisco School Board Has Voted to Cover, Not Destroy, a Series of Controversial High School Murals." *artnet News*. August 14, 2019. https://news.artnet.com/art-world/san-francisco-mural-controversy-vote-1625311.
4 Ibid.
5 Casey, Luke. "Can Charles Dickens Survive the Woke Purge?" *spiked*. July 24, 2020. https://www.spiked-online.com/2020/07/24/can-charles-dickens-survive-the-woke-purge/.
6 Dubois, W.E.B. *The Souls of Black Folk*. New York: G&D Media, 2019.
7 Simpson, George. "To Kill A Mockingbird and Huckleberry Finn Books BANNED from Minnesota School Syllabuses." *Express.co.uk*. June 29, 2020. https://www.express.co.uk/entertainment/books/1298539/To-Kill-A-Mockingbird-Harper-Lee-Huckleberry-Finn-Mark-Twain-banned-books.
8 Ibid.
9 Mark Twain quotations:"Complexions." Accessed December 20, 2020. http://www.twainquotes.com/Complexions.html.

Chapter Nine

1 Editor. "Chris Hedges: Don't Be Fooled by the Cancel Culture Wars." *scheerpost.com*, July 22, 2020. https://scheerpost.com/2020/07/13/chris-hedges-dont-be-fooled-by-the-cancel-culture-wars/.
2 United Nations High Commissioner for Refugees. "Amnesty International Report 2016/17—Palestine (State of)." *Refworld*. Accessed December 20, 2020. https://www.refworld.org/docid/58b033c5a.html.
3 Balousha, Hazem; Berger, Miriam. "The U.N. Once Predicted Gaza Would Be 'Uninhabitable' by 2020. Two Million People Still Live There." *Washington Post*. January 11, 2020. https://www.washingtonpost.com/world/2020/01/01/un-predicted-gaza-would-be-uninhabitable-by-heres-what-that-actually-means/.
4 Miller, Anna Lekas. "Settlers Dump Sewage On Palestinian Land." *The Daily Beast*. March 8, 2013. https://www.thedailybeast.com/settlers-dump-sewage-on-palestinian-land.
5 Mohammed, Arshad. "U.S. Withholds $65 Million in Palestinian Aid after Trump Threat." *Reuters*. Thomson Reuters, January 16, 2018. https://www.reuters.com/article/us-israel-palestinians-usa/u-s-withholds-65-million-in-palestinian-aid-after-trump-threat-idUSKBN1F52GA.

6   Agence France-Presse. "Donald Trump Cuts More than $200m in Aid to Palestinians." *The Guardian*. August 25, 2018. https://www.theguardian .com/us-news/2018/aug/25/donald-trump-cuts-more-than-200m-in-aid-to -palestinians.

7   Fors, Otto. "Israel Bombs Gaza on Christmas Day." *Left Voice*. December 26, 2020. https://www.leftvoice.org/israel-bombs-gaza-strip-on-christmas -day.

8   "Empty Book on Palestinian History Becomes Instant Best-Seller on Amazon." *Haaretz.com*. April 24, 2018. https://www.haaretz.com/middle -east-news/palestinians/empty-book-on-palestinian-history-is-amazon-best -seller-1.5487473.

9   Ibid.

10 Harris, Gardiner; Erlanger, Steve. "U.S. Will Withdraw from UNESCO, Citing Its 'Anti-Israel Bias.'" *New York Times*. October 12, 2017. https:// www.nytimes.com/2017/10/12/us/politics/trump-unesco-withdrawal.html.

11 Ibid.

12 Hussain, Murtaza. "The Real Cancel Culture: Pro-Israel Blacklists." *The Intercept*. October 4, 2020. https://theintercept.com/2020/10/04/israel -palestine-blacklists-canary-mission/.

13 Hussain, Murtaza. "Professor Hopes To Return After Being Fired for 'Disrespectful' Tweets Against Israel." *The Intercept*. October 20, 2015. https://theintercept.com/2015/10/20/professor-hopes-to-return-after -being-fired-for-disrespectful-tweets-against-israel/.

14 Ibid.

15 Martin, Jeff. "Filmmaker Who Wouldn't Sign Georgia's Israel Oath Sues State." *AP NEWS*. Associated Press, February 12, 2020. https://apnews .com/article/796ae3c36b7f58594207308855b7bfde.

16 Ibid.

17 El-Kurd, Mohammed. "Why Are Palestinians Being Forced to Prove Their Humanity?" *+972 Magazine*. December 6, 2020. https://www.972mag .com/palestinian-humanization-sheikh-jarrah/.

Conclusion

1   Black, Charles. "My World with Louis Armstrong." 69 *Yale Law Review* 145 (1979). https://digitalcommons.law.yale.edu/cgi/viewcontent.cgi?article =3527&context=fss_papers.